HQ
1412
.W48
Cop. 1   Westin, Jeane

                  Making do

DATE DUE

MAKING DO

MAKING

DO How Women Survived the '30s

BY JEANE WESTIN

FOLLETT PUBLISHING COMPANY
CHICAGO

Library of Congress Catalog Card Number: 75–170
ISBN: 0–695–80593–2

First Printing

To Blanche who came before,
and Cara who comes after.

CONTENTS

FOREWORD

THE DEPRESSION BEGAN with the stock market crash and ended more than a decade later with the advent of a second global war. In between, an entire generation of women learned to survive by "making do."

To make do is an old-fashioned way of saying "do the best with what you have." You still hear it today from older people—especially women. During the 1930s, making do became more than a way of stretching food or clothes; it became a philosophy, a state of being, an art.

The Great Depression has been chronicled in movies and books in terms of males: how men leaped to the pavements of Wall Street, how they sold apples, stood in soup lines, and bonus-marched. And the tragic plight of migrants heading for the fool's-gold promise of California was dramatically portrayed in John Steinbeck's *Grapes of Wrath* while the migration was still on.

But average 1930s women—the women who learned to make do or do without—have been literally and historically invisible. What strengths can they share with the women in the 1970s, facing a similarly uncertain future?

Their story covers the scope of human experience. By 1932 over a million wives (and their children) had been deserted by out-of-work men. Millions of other wives were hard at work bolstering their faithful but unemployed husbands—men who felt the Depression was their personal failure.

When women worked, their already low salaries fell even lower.

Thousands of young women—some still in their teens—were adrift
thumbing down the pike from one meal to the next, selling themselves on the street for a dime.

In middle-class homes across the country wives planted vegetable gardens instead of flowers; quilted with neighbors; begged
feed and flour sacks for dress material; and learned to stretch a
husband's salary that was cut 40 percent in 1932, not to be fully
restored in many cases until 1939.

This is a book about the way it was. Written in four parts, *Making
Do* covers women at home, young women growing up, women at
work, and women who helped shape their time. Each part has a
prologue which sets the mood. The stories that follow spotlight the
struggles and triumphs of a generation of American women.

For a few of them—black, Indian, Chicana, Chinese, and Japanese Americans—the conditions they describe in such human
terms existed long before the Depression and, unfortunately, long
after. These women not only surmounted the economic trauma of
the 1930s but the open prejudice of the time as well.

You'll catch only brief glimpses of some of the 160 women
interviewed for this book; others you will get to know as well as they
know themselves. But all of them will add to your knowledge of
those times and, perhaps, a little about who and what *you* are.

Their ages ranged from forty-seven to ninety-one, although most
were in their sixties and seventies. They didn't always recall dates or
places or names. But they all recalled the emotional essence of the
time, and what it was like to be a woman in the shadow of the
Depression. Despite the national misery they lived through, they
remembered a time almost alien to post-Vietnam, post-Watergate
America—a time of fundamental virtues, fellowship, faith, hope,
and thrift.

Why is it important to record their history? At the very least,
today's women will feel a certain pride at being their daughters; at
most, their insights will form a survival handbook for tomorrow.

Many people helped during the writing of this book. Some who
deserve special recognition are Phyllis Evans and Millie Humphries
who transcribed hundreds of hours of taped conversations into
thousands of typed pages; Phoebe German, director of the East

Yolo (California) Senior Citizens Center; and Ann Cousineau, reference librarian at the Sacramento City-County Library.

A writer never lacks critics, but I was fortunate to have two good ones—Helen Sparks and my husband Gene.

Use it up,
Wear it out,
Make it do,
Or do without.
　　　　　—AN OLD SAYING

PART ONE
THE LADY OF THE HOUSE

DURING THE THIRTIES when a door-to-door salesman asked, "Is the lady of the house in?" she 'most always was. The washboard, flatiron, and steam canner consumed a large part of the housewife's day. Although time-saving appliances were on the market, many families couldn't afford them.

Fewer than 3 percent owned their own home. There was little striving to "keep up with the Joneses," since the Joneses, the Smiths, the Brokowskis, and the Genettis were all in the same financial boat. But there was always the dream that someday a family could climb into the upper class and be one of barely 2 percent making 5,000 "smackers" a year.

According to U.S. Department of Labor figures, the average middle-class family in 1935 had an annual income of $1,348 of which it spent 35 percent on food, 33 percent on housing, but only 0.4 percent on taxes. When Mrs. Thirties Homemaker went to the corner grocery, she could feed her family a week with a five dollar bill—buying milk at ten cents a quart, bread at seven cents a loaf, butter at twenty-three cents a pound, and eggs at twenty cents a dozen.

During the Great Depression decade, interest in recipe collecting and cooking reached the boiling point. The desire of the American homemaker to give her family high nutrition at a low cost helped her create ingenious new recipes which were often passed from one woman to another.

Radio was quick to capitalize on the need. Over a million listeners to the "Betty Crocker" radio program registered with the mythical General Mills cooking expert. Aunt Sammy, the "wife of Uncle Sam," appeared on 150 stations dispensing government recipes; Ed and Polly East broadcast cooking advice on their "Kitchen Quiz," as did Eleanor Howe in her "Homemaker's Exchange." In addition to these network programs, each station had its own "Aunt" somebody, who enlightened women in thirties kitchens.

If a woman's allowance permitted—and especially if she lived in the city—the grocery stores of the era were stocked with an increasing variety of convenience foods. Campbell's Soup had twenty-one kinds to choose from, although a few—like mulligatawny, mutton, and printanier—proved to be of less than enduring popularity. Jell-O came in six delicious flavors and was already advertised as "your old friend." Chase and Sanborn's coffee was not only dated to insure freshness, but promised to never go "flat in the cup." Sunsweet "tenderized" their prunes, and Cream of Wheat was the "energy breakfast cereal." General Mills, with their popular "kitchen-tested recipes" packed in every flour sack, advertised that 282,268 women switched to their Gold Medal brand in one month alone.

Nevertheless, it was obvious to young couples in 1932 that two could *not* live as cheaply as one—despite budget recipes and rock-bottom food prices, and despite Eddie Cantor's assurance that potatoes were cheaper so "Now's the Time to Fall in Love." Consequently, the marriage rate dipped 22 percent to an all-time low.

Other vital national statistics were falling sharply. Even in those pre-pill days the birth rate dropped 13 percent. And divorce, down 18 percent, became a luxury supportable only by the café society set. One estranged Manhattan couple, unable to afford separate domiciles, took their cue from Clark Gable and Claudette Colbert in *It Happened One Night* and hung a blanket down the center of their one-room walk-up.

If adversity was the glue that bound most families together during the thirties, then entertainment made life more bearable.

Faced with the stark reality of a seemingly endless slide into economic disaster, it is not surprising that Depression family entertainment took the form of fantasy and fad—as well as fun.

The great escape began a few weeks after *Variety* billed the stock market crash with the show-biz headline: "Wall Street Lays An Egg." Midget golf was the first craze to tee-off in 1930, becoming a $125 million industry within a year.

Such indoor sports as jigsaw puzzles and a cutthroat real estate game called Monopoly wiled away empty hours. But whenever four people got together, contract bridge was likely to be the game of choice. In 1931, while employment dipped lower and apples could be had for a nickel on many street corners, Americans paid $10 million for bridge lessons.

It was the silver screen that provided the ultimate escape, however. Gangster films, like the controversial *Scarface,* became Public Entertainment Number One since their themes were as fresh as the daily headlines. Horror films *Frankenstein, Dracula,* and *King Kong* were smash hits at the thirties' box office, as were their opposite number, the musicals. Annual *Gold Diggers* and "Kids, let's do a Broadway show" flicks never seemed to tire ticket buyers. At the peak of the genre, Busby Berkeley time-stepped his chorus girls right into America's heart, displaying their talents from exotic sets which made the bleak world outside recede just a bit farther.

But it wasn't just gangsters, G-men, giant gorillas, or chorus girls that drew families to the Bijou. For the price of a fifteen cent ticket, bank nite at the movies gave people with nothing to lose a chance to hit the giant jackpot. In one case, the pot reached an unheard-of $1,000; and the slow turn of the ticket cage on stage was enough to send the audience's collective temperature soaring. One observer remarked: "Their eyes were those you see around a roulette table."

When bank nite ran into trouble because of lottery laws, dish nite took its place. Many a family ate beans from gaudy china patiently collected one at a time, week upon Depression week.

And the thirties had its own "All you ever wanted to know about sex," only it didn't hit the best-seller list. The book came sealed in a plain brown wrapper. "Is sex ignorance driving the one you love into the arms of another?" asked the brazen direct mail ads for *Sex Harmony and Eugenics.*

But it was less likely "sex ignorance" that drove out lovemaking during the Depression and more likely the pounding, national, economic "headache."

One wife, interviewed during a serious labor strike, said, "You should see him come home at night, so tired like he was dead, and irritable. He's a good, kind man, but the children don't dare go near him, he's so nervous and his temper's bad. And then at night in bed, he shakes."

"Yes," agreed another woman, "they're not men anymore, if you know what I mean."

In spite of the anxieties of life in Depression America, most man-woman relationships continued to plug along more or less as usual. For many, the primal urges to mate, marry, and propagate had to take second place to eat, sleep, and work. Nevertheless, they made up and broke up in and out of wedlock; wrote love novels, poems, and songs; were silly and noble—much as they had always been and still are.

They made the best of the worst of times . . . at least they were in it together.

Chapter One

ROOTS

MY MEMORY OF WOMEN in the 1930s is mostly the memory of my mother. No matter how many years pass, fixed images of the two of us remain in my mind like so many neatly mounted psychic snapshots.

Under each of these pictures are mentally engraved captions: "Mother giving me a soda bath when I had measles"; "Mother warning me to go easy on the butter 'cause it was forty cents a pound"; "Mother red-faced when I bombed as a Pilgrim in the Thanksgiving pageant."

There were other things she did. Most of them had to do with money or the lack of it. Every Friday night after we children went to bed, she and my father hunched over the kitchen table, dividing a small pile of bills and coins into yet smaller piles. They kept their voices low, but the tense, secretive tones always made me want to listen. In a two-room house, that wasn't difficult.

Between paydays, she had a litany she repeated whenever my younger sister Reno, my baby brother Richard, or I asked for anything that involved money. "You'll just have to learn to make do," she would say with an exasperated sigh. "Money doesn't grow on trees."

She was often exasperated. My father worked nights in the Cities Service oil fields which started across the street from our company house. He had to sleep days—in a two-room house—with three children aged seven, five, and four. Mother's job was to keep us quiet.

She had only one woman friend that I remember. "It's because

I'm from the East and more reserved," mother said once, explaining her lack of entry into Oklahoma oil camp society. She was really just farm girl shy.

My sister Reno and I had no such problems as dozens of ready-made playmates tumbled from the row houses every morning. She and I went our separate ways as soon as we could walk. Reno played with dolls, sold Penny-Ade drinks, and, in general, behaved—mother said approvingly—"like a little lady." On the other hand, I was a stereotypical tomboy, and no one—least of all mother—hesitated to tell me so in those openly sexist times.

I played baseball with the boys in a pasture when the bull was off doing whatever bulls did. For some variety, we had impromptu games of kick-the-cow-chip, after first determining that the chip to be kicked had the proper age.

Once I asked about bulls and babies and such things. "When you're older you'll understand and we'll talk about it again," mother said, following a lecture on seeds and eggs and fertilizing. When I was older I did understand—enough to know I didn't want to talk about *that* with mother.

Reno and I had an uncanny knack for riling each other, with me usually getting the best of her, and her snitching on me. "I don't know what I'm going to do with you girls," mother said at least a dozen times a day. I don't think she ever did.

Until I was seven it did not bother me that we were poor. We weren't too different from our friends. True, I didn't have as many comic books as Lloyd Shockley or take piano lessons like Barbara Curry; but we always had peanut butter for sandwiches and fresh mint leaves for iced tea. The only rosebush in camp grew in an old rubber tire in our backyard.

But when I was seven I began to understand that "making do" almost always meant "doing without," and I developed an insatiable desire for everything in the 1938 Sears, Roebuck & Co. catalog.

Mother hated dirt. She stuffed rags in window sills and under doors to keep sand out, but still the choking dust filtered in, settling in layers across the polished floors. But there was an even bigger hazard, living as we did in the middle of the Oklahoma oil fields. She cried the day her hand-scrubbed sheets were speckled with oil from some wildcat well blowing its head off.

"WHAT WOULD YOU DO if there was another depression?" I asked
Reno late in 1974 when I visited the four northern California acres
she and her husband had staked out for their new country home.
My sister and I had started treating each other as people in our
mid-twenties. This transition from sibling brattiness had led to
real tolerance and eventual friendship.

"For one thing," she began, "I would learn to grow a garden and
can food. I suppose we'd keep a few animals, but we'd eat less meat.
Yeech! Who'd want to slaughter cows, especially ones you know?"

We decided that all the talk about a new Depression might be just
nostalgic yearning for the trappings of childhood coupled with a
latent middle-class urge to drop out, like 1960s hippies.

" 'The Waltons' have made me forget what it was really like,"
said Reno. "It wasn't a big family around a table radio and everybody saying good night while Bing Crosby crooned 'Pennies From
Heaven.'

"Maybe that's why I yearn for a kind of pseudo-depression life-
style. I bake bread which I never used to do, go to garage sales, and
we all wear more practical clothes."

"But that's not WPA," I said, "or soup lines or teachers not getting
paid. How would you make do? What about your big house, the
camper-truck, and all your *things?*"

"What would I do?" she asked herself. "Tighten my belt and
keep going, I guess. The thought of another Depression doesn't
frighten me, and maybe that's a little frightening in itself. Sometimes I feel that we all have too much, and that somehow it would
be *good* for us as human beings to sacrifice and begin again, working
shoulder to shoulder."

"My God, Reno," I said, "you make a depression sound absolutely inspiring—like something you could order for $3.95 out of
the *Whole Earth Catalog.* We were just kids in the thirties. We
really didn't know what it was like to be women with families and
responsibilities."

Reno agreed. "If you want to know how thirties women coped,
why don't you ask them?"

I did. And I found women who survived, day-to-day, the worst
economic holocaust this country has ever seen. During the past year,
I've talked with many "make-do" women. Few lost money in the

stock market collapse of October, 1929, or lived in abject poverty. Most of them, like most of us, were middle-class women who managed, somehow, to get by.

They had an unassuming courage, but they would be first to scoff at any accolades. "We had no choice," they said. "We just did what had to be done one day at a time." Perhaps, that is after all, the classic definition of courage.

This book is not full of demographics, sociological studies, or fictionalized women who represent what we already know about the 1930s. It portrays the thirties woman as she actually was; for the first time it tells her true story in her own words.

To begin, I went to the first thirties woman I knew—my mother.

BLANCHE EDDY'S STORY

There was a question hanging over our heads: What would we do if your daddy lost his job?

I was married in 1930, and for the first couple years we didn't have it so hard. Your daddy had his thumb blown off in a well explosion. The company paid him a thousand dollars for it, just so much a month. He used the extra money to build a little house just north of Oklahoma City.

How I hated that house. It sat on a sandpile. Sometimes the wind would be so thick with sand I couldn't see across the street. Sand was everywhere. It seeped into our food, our water; I can taste the grit in my teeth yet.

Who could grow anything in that country? No grass, no vegetables, no flowers. I tried marigolds in a window pot that first year we lived there. The hot wind shriveled them up the first day.

Lots of men working in the oil fields in those days built small, portable houses on company property. This type of house could be built for $200. They had gas lights and cold water—no indoor toilet, though. The company would let you have your water and gas free. Nobody had electricity. Everybody used gas because there were gas wells every few yards.

Every family in the oil fields wanted to move into a company house. They were bigger, had hot water and indoor toilets. Whenever anybody moved, we waited to see who got the company house. This was determined by a list. Even if you had seniority with the company, you still had to wait your turn on the list.

Company houses also became vacant when men got laid off. I always thought your daddy would be next to go. He was only a roustabout, the lowest job on the scale. There was a continuous fear he'd get caught in the next layoff. He'd always say: "No, we can't buy that, I might be laid off." That's the way we lived then. There was always that question hanging over our heads. What would we do if he lost his job?

Maybe it was me, but we women in the camps never mixed too well. I never became very friendly with anyone except for Neola Query. We started a sewing circle once, but it fell through. Some of the husbands didn't want their wives to go. They thought we gossiped too much. But I never heard any gossip when I went.

Still we women found ways to help each other. We always passed on clothes. A neighbor lady gave me almost all your baby dresses before you were born. And magazines were shared because they cost a dime or more. There used to be a lot of good stories in them for women. There was always a new recipe going around the camp. Salmon was cheap—three cans for twenty-five cents. And we made it every which way—patties, loaves, sandwiches, salads—everything out of salmon.

We women didn't have a lot of extra time for visiting, you know. It took all day to keep house because we did everything the hard way. Once a week I spent one whole day and part of the night ironing. Oh, I ironed a lot of things that didn't have to be ironed. All the diapers, for instance, and the sheets and pillowcases. I even starched sheets and pillowcases. I know that sounds crazy now, but I wanted to do it. That's me, I guess; nobody made me.

By the time your brother was born in '35, we had a small company house, but your father was only on six hours a day, four days a week, and making eighty dollars a month. It cost fifty dollars to have a baby in the hospital, so I had to have him at home.

A woman who had helped at other births came for the last few hours. She wasn't a midwife and had no anesthetics. My labor lasted a day but when he started to come, he came fast. The doctor was very late getting there, and your daddy was furious. I could hear him yelling out on the sidewalk as the doctor pulled up to the house.

Richard had laid in bed tied to me for twenty minutes because the woman didn't know how to cut the cord. Years later, I heard babies could be brain damaged if the cord wasn't cut within fifteen minutes after birth. But, thank God, nothing happened to Richard.

As bad as it was for us, I remember others who had it much worse. In Oklahoma City, long lines of people waited for soup; and a large shantytown grew up under the viaduct alongside the Canadian River. Poor folks just took canvas or cardboard cartons—anything they could get their hands on—and threw up a house. From the bridge, it looked like a jungle of junk. Water was piped in by the city, and the shanty people would get their water from a faucet with buckets. I never heard anybody call them "Okies," though.

One winter morning we heard a baby had frozen to death in shantytown. I wondered why its mother couldn't have warmed it with her own body.

Hoboes passed by all the time, and if I had anything I'd feed them out on the porch. I didn't always have extra, but when the young girls would come, I'd invite them in and try to give them something —maybe a peanut butter sandwich. They were so young—maybe twenty—maybe younger. I'd want to ask them where they were from and where they were going, but I didn't.

I remember looking out the front window one day. A woman went by the house; she was brown as she could be from being out in the sun—brown as an Indian. She didn't stop, but I remember her because she was carrying a little baby and she was pregnant. I can remember that clear as anything.

Chapter Two

WOMAN AND THE FAMILY

WHEN YOU'RE SEVENTY YEARS OLD like Pearl Thorley, you have a mind crowded with memories. But if you've mothered sixty-three orphan children plus three of your own, like Pearl Thorley has, your memories can become a confusing jumble. "Sometimes, I can't put names and faces together," she said. "There were so many children . . . so many sweet memories.

"Oh, I'm telling you, it's hard to give up babies you've raised for two years. I've shed buckets of tears after the social worker left, knowing I'd never see them again."

PEARL THORLEY'S STORY

It was sink or swim together—and sometimes I thought it was all against the tide.

Hardwood floors . . . that's what I remember about our first apartment. It was almost ritzy, but then my husband got put on short time and finally ended up with three days every other week—that's six days' pay a month. Ended up, we had to move to something cheaper.

We took a duplex in Medford, about seven miles above Boston, for twenty-five dollars a month. It had eight rooms—two rooms each on four floors, since it was backed up to the bottom side of this hill. I used to worry about fire on the upper floors because you'd have been killed if you jumped out of the top floor. But the worst part was the bathroom. It was on the third floor so you needed to start a little ahead of time to make it. I can't tell you how many times the kids didn't.

I had one little boy when I applied to the New England Home for Little Wanderers. I knew I could take care of youngsters when I couldn't do much else, and it would be a little extra money—only four dollars a week, but at least it was another paycheck coming in at the end of the month.

I thought they'd forgotten me when they called, asking if I still wanted a child. By that time I was seven months pregnant with my second one, and I didn't think they would let me have him. But they did.

Sometimes I had as many as seven kids at a time, but I didn't make a lot of money. Remember I had to clothe and feed them out of that four dollars.

Two weeks after I took the first boy, everything just seemed to go to pieces. My husband had a hernia operation. The foster child got convulsions. My son came down with scarlet fever, and I had him in quarantine up on the third floor.

For six weeks, I was the only one who could come in and out of my son's room. I changed clothes as I went in and as I came out. Boiled all his things so that the boarding child wouldn't catch it.

We got out of quarantine on Saturday and my daughter was born on Monday. The hospital I was supposed to go to—Lawrence Memorial Hospital—wouldn't let me in because of the scarlet fever so my doctor did some telephoning, and a small, private hospital finally said they'd take me if I took a bath, shampooed my hair, and put on all clean clothes.

The alarm woke me up Monday morning and I knew this was the day. So my mother shampooed my hair and I went to the hospital with it dripping wet. The baby was born an hour and a half after my alarm went off. I barely made it—almost had her in the taxi.

The next summer—that was '33—I had to go to the hospital myself and have my appendix out and some inside work done. I hadn't recovered from that when my oldest child got polio. I was a wreck! If you looked at me I'd cry. Up and down the stairs, and me so nervous I was going to pieces.

'Course nobody would come and help me with the polio—nobody.

See, you had to hang a sign that said POLIO on the front door, and when people saw it they'd cross right over to the other side of the street. Our church decided they would take up a collection and get somebody in to help me, but even they couldn't find anybody willing. My doctor finally told my mother, "That girl needs help. You go in. It's all right." So she came when she could and gave me some relief.

But you know, the milkman put the milk out in the backyard and ran back to his truck. Wouldn't even pick up his bottles or his money. I had to keep track of everything and pay him when it was all over.

About '35, I guess it was, things got some better and my husband bought a small press he put up on the fourth floor. He was a printer, and he got a good deal on the press—the kind you pull the handle down on. We named it "The Yankee Press," because we were both Yankees. He'd get jobs printing tickets and church bulletins and things like that. I helped him fold and I'd sort the type on the dining room table at night. Later on, they let me into the Men's Vocational School so I could learn to set type.

It was all hard work, but it was sink or swim and we were sure swimming, both of us—and sometimes I thought it was *all* against the tide.

IN THE FALL OF 1946, Laura Buhekuhl got a letter from a former neighbor who had moved on west. "With the way you people work," the letter said, "you could do a whole lot better leaving Missouri and coming to California." She took the letter and walked out to her husband who was bringing in their soybean crop.

"Well, the tractor had just broke down when I got there," she remembered, "and he was hot and disgusted. When I told him what the letter said, he throwed a wrench on the ground and yelled, 'By golly, let's go.'"

Buying a Ford truck with the proceeds of their crop sale, they migrated, like so many others before them, to California. But they never returned to farming. While her husband worked in construction, Laura became a licensed vocational nurse.

"I retired from that a few years back," she said, "and we went to New Zealand to see our son Dale.

"Now that's a beautiful country. I think it is a lot like this country used to be years ago—the way I remember it anyways."

LAURA BUHEKUHL'S STORY

What did we do during the thirties? We had babies, that's all we had. We did without lots of things, but that wasn't one of them.

For delivering my third baby, the doctor charged me $6.50. Now since he'd charged me $7.50 each for the first two, I figured he was giving me a break because I was such a good customer.

I've always been a worker. I never missed a day in my whole life of milking six to eight cows morning and night, raising gardens, chickens, and even taking care of the hired hands when we had 'em. I done all my own baking and cooking, and I never thought anything about it because that's the way my mother did it and her mother before her.

My kids—all of 'em, from the time they could sit up—went to market with us. That was in Hannibal, Missouri, ten miles from our farm. Those kids saw me take the eggs and cream to sell, and then they saw me get the groceries. They'd see there was nothing left over.

You know, my youngest boy, he was kinda spoilt, and my husband would say, "That boy won't never amount to a hill of beans." But you know he did, and I think it's because of early training. Once you get 'em a good start, ain't nothin' going to change that.

My older boys would work a whole day driving a tractor or mowing the cemetery for fifty cents, and come home with the skin all wore off their hands from cuttin'.

I raised four boys and a girl in the thirties. I am glad I only had one girl. I could keep up with the boys, but that girl was a goer. One time when we moved, she got behind this truckload of furniture and it backed right over her hand. I didn't know she was back there 'til she screamed. But you see, she was always doing things like that because she had this powerful desire to help. Bound to help, she was, no matter what.

When I went to the hospital for an operation, although she was only nine, she could catch a chicken, dress it, and cook it for the men. She was so ambitious, if you didn't watch out she'd take over everything.

Like I said before, there's no point in letting kids play around until they're sixteen years old and then want them to work, because they just won't know how. They've had no experience. See, ours worked with us from the time they were babies. I used to put them in a washtub and take them to the garden with me. I'd let them sit in that tub and I'd get an old rope on it and I'd drag it between the rows with me as I worked—so I'd be out there with them, and they'd see what work was like.

I always believed in keeping an eye on my children. I had one two years and one six months, and I was pregnant again. So I had cows to milk, see, and I'd take the oldest one with me and set him on a little box by my side while I'd milk, and the baby I'd lay out in the salt trough—where we put salt for the cows. Now this one evening, I hear Melvin squallin' out there, and I ran out, and he was layin' there with this old cow licking his face. Well, you know, he always had a rosy complexion, and I told him it's from the old cow licking him.

Another time, I was milking—it was hot that evening—and I saw this big sow coming up from the pasture and she had her little ones with her. Well, ordinarily I didn't pay any attention to the sow, but when she came through the gate she saw my daughter settin' there in the yard and she didn't recognize her. Well, now, that sow started right toward that baby with her mouth open. Up I jumped and ran and splashed that whole pail of milk right in her face. Turned her around just a few feet from the baby. If that sow'd grabbed her, she'd have tore her all to pieces. I tell you a woman has to keep her eyes on her children all the time.

Oh, those kids—it's one thing after another. Once the girl run into barbwire and got cut on her lip. You know, I never got upset about things like that. Why, I just picked her up and held her head while her daddy drove her to the doctor. I was just glad it didn't hit her in the eye. My mother always said, "No matter what happens, it could have been worse."

One time, one of the kids fell into the big water tank, and he would have drowned if it had been up to his daddy. The kids came yelling that the baby had fallen in the tank. My husband tried to break open a barn door that he had nailed shut in the winter. Well, now, I just set my milk bucket down, ran to the other end of the barn and out the door and instead of opening the gate, I just jumped over and got there in time to pull the kid out—and his daddy was still in the barn trying to get out. You know, he don't use his head!

Those kids was always getting poison oak in the summer, but I had a sure cure. You put one-half whiskey and one-half sour cream on it three times a day. The whiskey kills the poison, see, and the cream keeps your skin soft.

I guess the worst time was when my oldest boy was three and a half, and he took the Hinckle pills. You know, I always had a lot of trouble so I kept Hinckle pills as a laxative. I came into the kitchen this one day and found him lying on the floor. He was all red in the mouth and his head was throwed back and his eyes were rolling. I saw this empty Hinckle bottle on the floor. They got strychnine in them, so I called the doctor quick and he told me to tickle his throat with a feather and give him all the cream I could get down him. I tried and tried but I couldn't get him to vomit, so I called the doctor back and he said all right, he'd be right out. Now, two doctors came and stayed all day. They did everything— pumped his stomach, got him through the convulsions—and they pulled him through. When they started to leave my husband said, "Doc, how much do we owe you?" And Doc said, "I think ten dollars will take care of it."

You know we had exactly ten dollars saved. Had it back in a little hidey-hole under the stairwell. It was all we had, but we could pay all we owed. Now don't tell me God isn't looking out for those that take care of themselves.

"I HOPE I HAVEN'T INTERRUPTED your favorite television program," I said apologetically because I was late arriving for our appointment.

"No," she answered, turning off the set. "That was last night. 'Gunsmoke' was on last night."

Bertha Norton is a Maidu-Wintu, descendant of Indians who once extended from California's northern coast inland to the Sierras. Maidu basketry was a unique and highly developed technology.

"I don't even know how to make baskets or beads," Bertha confessed.

BERTHA NORTON'S STORY

I had my baby the old way—walking miles 'til it was just ready to come.

The year 1930 was when we went to Santa Rosa picking prunes, and we were camping out here and there. My family and my sister and her family went in a caravan group.

We followed the harvests—prunes and hops—'til the family got typhoid fever. The water was bad. We didn't have the camps like they do nowadays; we had to camp where we could. It was damp; spiders and mosquitoes were all over the place. We had to use water where somebody else had camped. That's how my husband and my two little daughters got typhoid. Couldn't get 'em into hospitals there even when my little girl had meningitis. Yes, there was prejudice. Definitely.

So we went back to Chico because the water was better. The farmers took better care of the water . . . put it in tanks where it was purified.

But most of the time in the 1930s we lived in the mountains. George prospected for gold on the Yuba River. Found enough to keep us in flour—maybe a dollar a day.

My father used to stay with us sometimes and he'd shoot jack-rabbits for the pot and sometimes coyotes for the bounties. Sometimes George would get on WPA and make nine dollars. That helped out a lot.

We had a tiny little car. I think we paid thirty dollars for it but it wouldn't always run.

We didn't have no garden. We used to have these beans we gathered on the ranches. They'd give them to us—horse beans and limas. And we gathered lots of mushrooms. There were lots if you wasn't too lazy to get out there, and watercress, too, up there in the mountains.

When we needed clothes, we'd go to the Salvation Army in town and buy dresses and blankets.

Prejudice never bothered me. I just didn't see it. My dad used to say, "You're so ugly, you should have been polite." But nobody ever says, "She's an Indian." They always just say, "Hey, there's Bertie." I never gave a thought to who was white, black, or brown.

It is true, I do not remember much of the Indian ways. When I was a little one, I went to the sacred dances. Oh, I been to all those dancing places. You are not allowed to mention any names because they are religious. Sometimes I'd see my papa go into a sweat lodge. I'd yell, "Momma, papa is over here." She'd put her hand over my mouth and tell me that wasn't nice.

But I don't remember much more of that. And I just don't give prejudice and such things much of my time.

Back in the thirties, we used to eat a lot of acorn soup with jackrabbit. It's so good, and it's healthy for your stomach.

After I gathered the acorns, I ground them in a meat grinder 'til it was like cornmeal. But it was bitter, so I put it in a great big gunnysack and then I'd put some warm water in there and keep putting water in until all the bitter got out of it.

Sometimes I used to make bread the way my mother did. You get a big rock to put in the fire while it's baking and the rock spreads the heat out. That rock is called, "the heart of the hunter." Oh, you could slice that bread—it gets dark—and you could have meat with that, and you'd never get hungry.

When I was expecting my third daughter they were giving different ones a little help—blankets and things—the government was. Do you think we could get anything? We didn't get a thing! My cousin helped. She was a midwife but she believed in the ancient methods, and she had me walk. I walked miles 'til that baby was just ready to come.

"I CANCELED MY NEWSPAPER last month after forty years," she told me as we sat in her son's living room. "Maybe I shouldn't have done it, but I don't have time to read it anymore.

"People had more time back in the thirties. Now they're watching television all the time. We've got a half dozen of them around here, and I think it's the ruination of the American home. There's no family life as we knew it anymore."

DORIS LEMASTER'S STORY

It was a hard life, raising turkeys. But I had a good husband. If a woman has a good husband, she can do anything.

My husband was a streetcar conductor in Oakland when we went to the country to help out my folks with their turkeys. Had we realized how bad things would get, we would have stayed put—street car conductors kept their jobs. But we didn't know there was going to be bad times—not as early as 1930.

We had a backer—Rouse Poultry in San Francisco. Mr. Rouse would get us started, and then he got the top when we sold: he got first money and then we got what was left. You know, in those times there wasn't always much left. One year it cost us more to raise them than what we got!

Our vegetable garden and my canning and the pig my folks raised for us was all that kept us eating that winter. Botulism? We didn't know enough about it to be afraid, and we got along fine.

It's hell to raise turkeys. Oh, they die of everything and you're never sure of your crop until you get a check for them in your hand. Anything can happen. Yes, ma'am. We had "roup" go through them—just wiped us out.

We had to vaccinate them for every kind of thing. Had a needle, like a big darning needle, and we stuck it in the vaccine and then poked it through the web of their wing. Oh, it was an awful job doing that on 1,500 of 'em.

Once they all got sick; we had to nurse each bird individually. They were just like babies; we'd work 'round the clock and even hire a woman for fifteen cents an hour. Some years we purty-near went under.

When my two boys were young, we all went to the rice fields in the summer with the turkeys. My husband and I each had a dog we'd trained to herd them. You can't do a thing with turkeys without a dog. Oh, they'll only pay attention to a dog.

Didn't take them to the fields until they were what they call "shooting a red"—that's when they're big enough to take to pasture.

Built us a little knock-down cabin by a stream and put up a tent for the boys. They stayed in camp while their dad and I took the turkeys out—those birds loved the rice up in the fields. It was after the harvest, you know, but there was lots of grain left behind on the ground. At night we'd give them a little shell or grit—stuff they had to have.

The turkeys had a roost surrounded by a wire fence we put up, but in the morning, we bounced out about four o'clock—the minute we heard those turkeys dropping off their roost. We'd have to get up and go—fast—leave our kids in bed and grab a handful of cereal. We'd stay out with the turkeys until about midmorning, then we'd bring them in because it got too hot for them. Then when it would cool down later in the afternoon, out we'd go again, until evening. And all this time those birds were eating and eating. Sometimes if we knew of any green grass anywhere, we'd herd them down there. They liked that.

It was a hard life—raising turkeys. But I had good boys. I had a good husband. He's gone now. We lived together thirty-nine years. You know, if a woman has a good husband, she can do anything.

It wasn't all bad. We had our good times, too. When work was done, we'd get in this little old Model T—we always seemed to have a little gas—and we'd take a picnic supper and go to the river for a swim. And I mean we went every night in summer. And when it got dark we built a bonfire, and there was other families there. We all knew each other.

We had a radio on a battery in our car, and we'd take it out and bring it to the fire. When it ran low we'd just charge it up in the car again.

Sometimes we'd spear salmon. It was against the law to do it since they were going up river to spawn, but we pickled them in jars and used up every bit.

Everybody had to help and take help in those days. It was just like going up the Alcan. If everybody doesn't help everybody else, you'd never make it. Families stuck close together, too. Sure, there was fights, but our pleasure was being together.

I remember after we sold our turkeys we'd go into Folsom for a night out on the town. Paid five cents for a big, thick hamburger and ten cents for a milkshake or a soda. Then we'd go to the picture show—all of us—even the babies. The show had this crying room in the back on the second floor. It had a glass front for the mothers to see the picture—because a woman couldn't leave her babies behind in those days when they were nursing.

MARION CONRAD, AT EIGHTY-FIVE, lives in a marvelous two-story English Tudor home on the edge of a great university complex—the intellectual atmosphere that stimulated her for decades. A nutrition expert, she has written two books on food allergies, and is working on a third.

MARION CONRAD'S STORY

This country was so different for families traveling in the thirties.
You stayed with local people and ate the food of the region.

We had a unique opportunity in '34. My husband, John, had just finished his Ph.D. in agricultural engineering . . . his specialty was soils and plant nutrition. He was one of the first. So before he began his teaching career at Cal, they told him to get out and around the country, visiting experimental stations and colleges to find out what was going on in his field. We decided to take our twelve-year-old Jack out of school for seven months and make it a family trip.

In a way, it couldn't have been a worse time to do such a thing—right in the middle of the Depression and all—but we took our Model A and headed first for Montana, near the Canadian border. It was the most marvelous year for young Jack. I kept him up in arithmetic and reading—I had been a high school teacher—and then he taught himself more U.S. geography and history than most people learn during their entire lives. He became such a good map reader that he did all the navigating for us. We had oil company maps and he'd plan our route a day in advance and go over it with his father every night. He had a lot of little hobbies that kept him amused during the trip. One was the population of cities . . . to this day, he can tell you the 1934 population of almost any city you're interested in.

The roads in those days were not the way they are now, and there weren't many motels, although in the East they had what they called auto courts; sometimes these were little better than primitive log cabins. We camped beside the road when we couldn't find a tourist home or a hotel.

We went through the dust bowl during the middle of their terrible drought. We saw those sad people. And at night you could hear their animals crying—in Kansas, Nebraska, Iowa, and some of those places. The beasts were really starving, and there didn't seem to be anything that could be done about it.

Crossing the country, we went north clear up to Maine. John's mother had grown up on Penobscot Bay and his cousins lived in one of the most beautiful little towns named Casteen—high on a promontory overlooking the Atlantic Ocean. Those old captains' homes—great, square houses—they were beautifully designed. There was a fireplace in almost every room, upstairs and down, and huge elms around the place that had been planted by his long-ago, sea-captain ancestors. That gave the boy the greatest sense of his heritage.

When we left New England, we followed the fall colors the whole length of the Atlantic Coast. This country was so different for families traveling in the thirties. You stayed with local people and ate the food the region was famous for. For instance, in the South there were antebellum houses that were turned into tourist homes, and I think it only cost us about $1.50 a night—for the three of us—with an absolutely gigantic dinner and breakfast thrown in.

Once we stopped in Greenville, South Carolina; there must have been twenty tourists in the home that night. One of them was an authentic Southern colonel. Some of the fellows baited him a little. That was all he needed, you know, and we heard more about the Civil War and "damn Yankees" than we ever thought we would.

My boy Jack and I had a wonderful time, even though John was busy at the colleges and experimental stations most of the time. We saw all the historical places and visited state capitals . . . we got to know what this country was all about. We did silly things too—kept an elaborate record of the number of white horses we saw in each state. Montana won west of the Mississippi, and Vermont won for the East.

One of the nice things I remember about travel in the thirties—because I've done a lot of traveling since—is that nothing was crowded, not the roads or the hotels.

There were disadvantages, too. We often had to act as our own mechanics and carry extra gasoline . . . just in case we didn't come across a gasoline station for miles.

In the spring of '35 we came home, back through New Mexico and Arizona. We stopped and visited people along the way—by this time we were getting to be so well known that the people from one experimental station wrote on ahead about us. We had friends waiting.

SHE LIVES IN A LARGE HOME today on the best side of town, and worries about her weight. In 1943 she was the first black woman to integrate a war plant in Chicago. "I just went about my business and did my job, a good job," she recalled. "Those other women— white women—didn't know how to act around me at first, but we soon got to be friends. I accepted them, most of them anyway, and they accepted me."

PAULINE'S STORY

Young black couples knew the Depression was the time to get ahead—property was cheap and you could buy security for the future.

I came to Chicago to live with my aunt in 1930, and I began to do substitute teaching in Gary for about a year. But there really wasn't enough work because teachers weren't staying home sick . . . they couldn't afford it.

Next I went to work at Montgomery Ward. Because I had college training, they thought I was smart enough to wrap packages. But I left there after a couple of weeks and got a job in a linen supply house—that paid more—wrapping towels.

By this time, too, I had met my husband. My cousin was married to his brother, and one day he came over to get some tickets from my aunt. I was there and we talked—he was about nine years older than I was—but I thought he was a pretty sensible fella, which he was. So we married in January, 1932.

At first we lived with his sister because she had a boardinghouse she was struggling to keep filled with tenants. That's the only way she could make it. But I got pregnant two weeks after I got married, and then I wanted a place of my own. So we got an apartment where our daughter was born the next November.

We rented in this building until 1935 . . . then we started buying it and eventually another one as well. One building helped pay for the other that way. It was hard trying to keep things going because we had borrowed the money to put down. So here we were paying off both loan and mortgage.

Many of our friends were doing the same thing. We knew that a depression was on and it was the time to try to get ahead if you could. We used to talk about how to do it. Prices were down and property was cheap. It was the best time to buy some security for the future.

Two years later, I had a son. There was a lady I kept in the house, you know, and she sort of helped with the children. It gave her a place to stay and it also helped me. I went back to college some of the time, even though by that time I was considerably older than the other students. I'm glad I did, because it helped me later toward my degree. But my main interest at that time was in improving myself.

I also worked with organizations that were trying to help people in need. Later, some of them were labeled subversive, but I never saw anything like that. They were mostly interested in improving black neighborhoods. Once we were trying to get a place there that was called Bacon's Casino to offer children on the South Side some kind of playground or activities.

This same group—I can't remember the name although I think it had something to do with actors and actresses or something—offered cheap insurance and so my husband and I took that insurance out. Later we had to give up the policy because this organization was on a list.

My husband was a postal clerk, making $2,100 at the time, so we had a stable income, but a great many people didn't. There was poverty all around. So my husband and I helped establish a co-op grocery store near where we lived, based on the ones in England. The co-op store bought in large quantities and spread the profit, but we didn't take our profit because we were trying to build it up.

We mothers used to take our kids and go to Washington Park in nice weather and listen to the speakers. Once Marshall Field came and I remember he said that it was the duty of people who had wealth to share it with people who didn't. And Paul Robeson was one of the speakers. He sang songs and I listened to him say that he had traveled all over the world—and he named the countries

—but he said, "I did not feel like a man until I went to Russia." He meant color-wise. He felt that there were no prejudices there.

I think there were stirrings then among black people. There was another thing the people were doing. Landlords would move people out of their homes . . . set the people right out on the sidewalk when they couldn't pay. Well, there was this group—like the Panthers or something—they would go out and set the people right back in.

You'd walk down the street almost any day and furniture and clothes and things would be piled up in the front and you'd see old women sitting there with nowhere to go . . . so we'd just set them right back in, and I helped do that, too.

MARY MONAHAN BELIEVES there will be another depression. "Oh, the government claims they're fortified against it," she said, shaking her head. "But I don't know. They don't even have enough money now to pay off Social Security.

"I think it will take another president, like Roosevelt, to get us back on the right track."

As an afterthought she said: "The next depression will be even harder on the unemployed than the thirties were. I remember my mother would sit those poor folks out on the sun porch and feed them. Not today. No way. Today if you get a knock on the door, you're too scared to let them in."

MARY GRACE McKENNA MONAHAN'S STORY

Once I traded a big sack of relief flour for oranges. I was pregnant and had a terrible craving for fruit.

After mother died, my father sent me to live with my aunt in Pittsburgh. He could see that I was terribly depressed, and he scraped up five dollars, I think it was, to send me.

I met my husband there and we were married in 1936. He had a job working in a bakery for sixteen dollars a week. It wasn't bad but it wasn't real good, either, because he had been to Carnegie Tech. He'd always say it took two years of college to learn to make a pie.

We didn't have a bathroom of our own for years and years. There's always been a housing shortage in Pittsburgh, but in the 1930s people were renting out their bedrooms for twenty-five dollars a month and a whole houseful of people would have to share a bath.

Just like most of our friends, my husband was out of work half the time so, when I got pregnant, we had to go on relief. But it was a different kind of relief in those days. I mean, you didn't go on relief without working. It wasn't a handout. They put him to time-keeping at the Bellfield School of the Blind—he was timekeeping for all the other fellows that were on relief and working there. That paid $7.50 a week and we got food supplements besides. Sometimes they gave me way more than I could ever use—great big sacks of flour—and so I'd trade it to someone for something I needed. Once I traded for oranges. I had a terrible craving for fruit when I was pregnant. And they gave us canned milk and raisins and lots of real butter. Even my friends who weren't on relief couldn't afford butter, so I'd trade that too.

Those days you did everything to save a penny. Pennies mattered because they were worth something. My next door neighbor and I used to shop together. You could get two pounds of hamburger for a quarter, so we'd buy two pounds and split it—then one week she'd pay the extra penny and the next week I'd pay.

And I remember, we used to cut each other's hair. It must have looked awful, but we'd put it up in coffee can curlers and think we looked like Joan Blondell.

Once in a blue moon my husband would have his hair cut. The barber would come to the house and do it for a quarter. This is the way he made it, going to people's houses, 'cause he couldn't afford to open a shop.

Oh, I hear all kinds of talk about how the Depression brought out the good in people. I don't remember much of that. Talking about people having and people not; you know, we sat outside on the stoop a lot in the evening and there was this policeman's family living across the street and he made thirty-five dollars a week. Their kids had more than the next and, you know, those kids were mean. They would have candy and they would eat it and maybe leave a little in the wrapper. But would they give that to kids on relief? No! Those poor kids would be sitting, looking at them eating and those rich ones would just take that candy and throw it in the dirt right in front of them. They were just plain mean is all I can figure out.

THE CRUNCH OF MY TIRES on her gravel driveway was the signal for several protective poodles to start barking. Two of them competed for her lap all during our conversation.

By the time I left, it was obvious to me that Evelyn Christiansen had realized her wish to settle down. Pictures of children and grandchildren lined the fireplace mantel. The small frame structure had the comfortable clutter of a house long lived in.

"He is still curious about other places," she said, motioning toward husband Bill, "but now he just talks over his citizen's band radio instead of going there."

EVELYN CHRISTIANSEN'S STORY

He always wanted to see what was on the other side of the hill, and I never said 'no' to anything he ever wanted to do.

When the twins were six months old, my husband was working in a Thom McAn shoe store in Valparaiso, Indiana. They said they could give him a raise—he was making eighteen dollars a week—but they would have to take his help away. He didn't like that so he came home and said, "Let's go to Texas."

We bought an old 1927 Reo club coupe to make the trip, and they took my wedding ring as a down payment on the car. They said they'd send it back to me when the car was paid for.

Now the old Reo was built different than most coupes because four could easily ride in there. It had a seat for the driver and along the back was a seat for two people, then there was a jump seat which folded down. We bought a homemade trailer for our clothes and stuff and started off—with the twins and our dog Midgie—and about thirty-five dollars in our pockets.

San Antonio was where we went first; we rented a little cabin for seven dollars while my husband looked for a job. He found one the very next morning at Joselyn's Shoe Company, but he wasn't there three months 'til they transferred him to Los Angeles. Three months after we got to Los Angeles they transferred him to Long Beach.

At that time, people just got shifted around every place and didn't have too much to say about it. But I got to tell you, the worst place —no doubt about it—was Long Beach. This one real estate lady asked me if I had any children, and when I said "yes," she said, "In Long Beach, we consider children the same as animals and it's hard to find nice places that will rent to you."

Boy, I was pretty hot under the collar after that. I took off out of that place walking and found a nice place just down the block—the whole bottom floor of a house, furnished, for twenty dollars a month.

We were just two blocks from the ocean, and at night it got cold all year long. I had to light my gas heater even on the Fourth of July. Wouldn't you know, I was just settled in there when he got a better job offer from a company in Fresno. We packed up and moved. The day we got there it was 114°. The twins and I spent the first two weeks lying on the bed panting. I couldn't go out to do any shopping until after the sun went down.

But I got lucky in Fresno. Found an Indian girl through the Indian Agency who came and helped me with the twins and took care of the house for $2.50 a week. By this time my husband was working for Silversteel Metal Crafts, selling cookware. I'd go with him and together we'd prepare demonstration dinners for people. After they ate, he would give his sales pitch while I was in the kitchen cleaning the dishes.

That winter we transferred again, to Leevining, where they were putting through the water flume to Los Angeles. We could go out in one afternoon and make one hundred and thirty-five dollars in commissions. You see, on a construction site, people don't have any other place to spend their money but the bar, so salesmen do great.

The worst thing though was we didn't have any place to go, either. We got snowed in. When the snows came, nothing and no one could get in or out of that town. The mail came over the mountain by dogsled. Two or three families all bunked together to conserve wood.

There were about two things left on the shelf to eat when the road opened. We went out of there right behind the snowplow.

I can't count how many times we moved those years. He always wanted to see what was on the other side of the hill—see if the grass was greener. But grass is grass. One reason we always got along was that I never said no to anything he ever wanted to do.

After Leevining, we went over into Nevada and ran a tailor shop in Virginia City. My husband's father had been a tailor, and the fellow that owned this shop let us use a huge house on the hill rent free in exchange for my work. I would do all the hand-pressing and the repairs.

About this time the Indian girl wanted to go back to her people, so we sent her and took an older girl from the orphanage in Carson City to help with the house and the twins. Paid her two dollars a week. But one weekend her friends came to visit her, and she was so homesick she went back with them.

That left me with my hands full, I'll tell you; but we didn't stay in Virginia City too long . . . a lawyer came down from Reno and offered us a job running a tailor shop he owned. Now, my husband never could refuse a better offer so we packed up and off we went to Reno.

But after a few days there, I don't know . . . something happened. Anyway, we were out on the street with no pay. No nothing. Stranded.

We called the Red Cross and they said they would give us one night's lodging. One of the people there went to John Foy—he was a state senator then—and told him what a mess we were in. He sent for us and got us tickets for a free Christmas dinner and one for New Year's, too; but he couldn't find us work.

Finally, on New Year's we told him we were going to hitchhike back to Indiana. He said, "You can't hitchhike with those children," and he got the Salvation Army to get us tickets on the train home. They had a deal with the railroad; they could get tickets for half-price.

That was Jan. 2, 1939. The only problem was that the senator couldn't talk the Salvation Army into paying for our dog Midgie, and we couldn't leave without her. So I hocked my wedding ring (my poor wedding ring was always the first thing to go!) to pay Midgie's freight fare back home on the same train with us.

An hour before train time, Midgie began to have puppies, and we had to wait for her to finish so we barely made it to the station on time. We turned up there . . . instead of the one dog on the ticket, we had ten. But the freight-master just looked and didn't say a word.

FORTY-FOUR YEARS HAVE PASSED, but when she talked about her two lost babies, tears spilled down her cheeks and sobs wrenched the words from some chasm of hurt deep inside her.

A GIRL FROM MICHIGAN

The court declared them neglected children and took them away from me. They were adopted out. I never saw or heard of them again.

What did I know when I was eighteen? Just what somebody told me. I trusted people then.

Everybody was getting laid off in Pontiac in 1930, including my husband, and us with two babies. When my father wrote from New York City saying he could get him a job, we packed up and left the next day.

My father didn't like my husband, Lester, much and he liked me even less. He wanted a boy when I came. Later when his son was finally born, both the baby and my mother died. After that, I went to live with my grandmother, and I didn't see my father again until we went to New York in 1930.

I don't know why he got us back there. I doubt that he really tried to get my husband a job. One day Lester came home and said he had found a good job in New Jersey. He packed his bag and said he'd send for me in a few days. He lied to me. He just took out and hitchhiked back to Michigan and left me there.

My father didn't want me either, so he sent a man with thirty-five dollars who told me I was supposed to catch a train back to Michigan. My father never came himself, never even said goodbye.

The man he sent put us on the wrong train. So I ended up in Boston in the middle of the night with two babies—six weeks and thirteen months old.

I had to carry both of them so I hired a red-cap to put our suit-cases in the waiting room. He wouldn't do it unless he got twenty-five cents. I don't think I have ever felt so alone. I just sat there and cried into a baby blanket until we finally got on the right train. Nobody helped me; nobody cared what happened to me.

When I got back to Pontiac, I went out to my grandmother's house and stayed with her for a while; but she had a sister who was an invalid so she closed up the house and went to take care of her. Now, there was no place for me and my babies to go.

This great uncle of mine—he was married to the sister my grandmother went to take care of—put me in a little apartment. "I'll take care of you," he told me, "but the children are Lester's responsibility."

He had it in his mind that we would get married when his wife died, but he was about forty-seven years old and I was only eighteen. I had known him since I was a little toddler, and I just couldn't think of him that way. So his help didn't last too long, you know.

In the meantime, I got a cousin who was an attorney to file for a divorce, with the help of my grandmother, of course. She had to sign since I wasn't of legal age. It cost fifty dollars and he took my wrist watch to pay for it. Gave it to his wife that Christmas.

I got the divorce—no trouble—and was awarded seven dollars a week alimony and seven dollars for both kids. But Lester never paid any of it, not once.

After that, I stayed with this one and that one. I tried to get a job but I couldn't do anything. I tried to get on relief but they said I was supposed to be getting alimony from my husband.

While I was looking for a job, I left my two children with some friends; at least I thought they were friends. But they went to the law and said my children were neglected. When I asked, "Why did you do that?" they said, "We thought it would get you on relief and that would be a way for you to get money."

I was subpoenaed into court on it. I told them I just wouldn't neglect my babies. I told them all the things I'd tried to do, all the things I'd done to keep them with me. But the judge said I had no established home and no money, and so he said, "Young lady, I have no choice but to declare these as neglected children, and take them from you for their own welfare."

I went to my cousin the attorney for help, but he told me it would be better all around if I signed and gave them up. They were adopted out right away, I was told. I never saw or heard of them again.

What was I to do? I begged the judge; I would have got down on my knees but everything was on his side.

"TIMES SURE HAVE CHANGED," Erma Gage said with a wry smile. "Back in the 1930s, my sons wore patched blue jeans to school and felt embarrassed about it. Now my grandsons insist I put patches on their blue jeans when there aren't even any holes."

ERMA'S STORY

I stretched everything to make ends meet, but some of the ends just wouldn't meet. You can only stretch things so far.

My husband was a sheet metal worker. He'd been working steady, but when the hard times came he was just off and on, off and on.

I got a job helping out in a grocery store across from a school. Made sandwiches for the kids during their lunch hour. Made a little money that way, and got some good sandwiches for my own kids. Otherwise, my kids made bean sandwiches—just mashed up beans and put them between bread.

My aunt and uncle lived next door and used to help out with clothes for the kids. And sometimes when I was late with the payment—we was buying our house from them—why, they helped us out that way, by waiting for it. But we always made it up later. I saw to that.

Seems my house was always full to the rafters. What with our three kids and his dad and my mom and sometimes his brother—all not working. We had a long lot, 160 foot back, and he put the whole thing in garden—pole beans, squash, tomatoes, and even a few hills of potatoes.

I don't think we ate salads in those days. We had radishes or green onions right out of the garden, but we never seemed to have salad. I think he tried to raise lettuce, but it didn't turn out so good.

We ate lots of macaroni and spaghetti and I could make three pounds of hamburger go a long way. I used to mix a pound of butter with a pound of margarine and, if I didn't tell 'em, people didn't know the difference. And I didn't tell 'em.

I figured every which way I could to make ends meet—turned

shirt collars, watched for specials—but some of them ends just wouldn't meet. They just couldn't be stretched far enough to meet.

The worst of it all was the kids. I wanted to give to them and help them more, but I just didn't have the money to do the little extras. You know, it made me feel terribly bad, but as I remember, they were very good about it.

I did what I had to do. I seemed to always find a way to make things work. I think hard times is harder on a man, 'cause a woman will do something. Women just seem to know where they can save or where they can help, more than a man. It's just a worry for him, and he feels so terrible when he can't take care of his family.

My husband got very despondent, you know. Oh, he'd say you can't have this and you're not getting that, and I don't want to hear about this; just fighting against it all the time. A woman, like I said, can take more. I always said that she can stand more pain. Take, for instance, when a man gets sick; why everybody within yelling distance has to wait on him. But a woman, now, will go along with pain and never say anything. Least that's how it seems to me.

Chapter Three

AS AMERICAN AS GREEN TOMATO PIE

MANY THIRTIES WOMEN threw away their old make-do recipes as soon as hard times ended—but a few kept their favorites and are anxious to share them again.

FRANCES RIDGWAY

Christmas time in Michigan always meant goose (which we raised), cranberries, and green tomato pie. I remember wading December snowdrifts to get home—and mother would always have a piece of hot green tomato pie waiting for me on the kitchen table. It was a cheap version of mincemeat pie, but I always thought it was better than the real thing.

There were eight of us, so mother made about seven pies at a time, but you can cut the recipe in half.

GREEN TOMATO MINCEMEAT

1 pk green tomatoes	2 t cinnamon
½ pk apples	½ t cloves
½ c butter	1 box raisins
5 c white sugar	1 c cider vinegar

Grind tomatoes and apples, mix with other ingredients, and cook for two hours. Place in nine-inch pie shells and bake at 375° until done. Makes six or seven pies.

FRAN NELSON

When I was first married in 1938, we'd often run short of money before payday. When that happened, I would make bread pancakes with a cheese sauce over them—my husband loved them and they were cheap, yet filling.

BREAD PANCAKES

2 c stale bread crumbs	2 t baking powder
2 c milk	½ t salt
2 eggs, beaten	pinch of pepper
3 T flour	

Soak crumbs in milk overnight; keep in a cool place. Add eggs and dry ingredients sifted together. Beat until smooth. Pour batter by spoonfuls onto hot griddle. Cook until brown on both sides. Serve immediately with:

CHEESE SAUCE

2 T butter	dash of pepper
2 T flour	1 c milk
½ t salt	¼ c grated cheese

Melt butter; blend in flour and seasonings; add milk gradually; cook until thickened, stirring constantly. Add cheese, stir until melted; serve at once. Four servings.

HELEN SPARKS

For young marrieds we were really adventurous when it came to food. For instance, I used to make a mayonnaise cake once a week ... I know it doesn't sound good but it was so delicious. ...

MAYONNAISE CAKE

1 c mayonnaise	2 c flour
1 c sugar	1 t soda
1 t nutmeg	1 c boiling water
1 t cinnamon	1 c raisins
dash of salt	½ c nuts
3 T cocoa	

Bake in loaf pan for one hour or more at 325°

PEGGY O'DONNELL

At least the food in this country was good during the Depression. Until World War II it was fresh, unadulterated, seasonal, and well cooked. I don't remember ever seeing my mother use a can opener. We had fairly simple Indiana meals—fried chicken, veal, biscuits, red-eye gravy, cherry pie—but the ingredients were the *best*: pure country butter, fresh eggs, home-canned cherries, real buttermilk . . . none of this chemical stuff.

Anyway, my mother believed in feeding her family good, nutritious food so when her kids got out in the world they could survive if they missed a meal or two. And it worked. I never had a cavity and when I left home and went to work, I lived on a pretty abominable diet for a while. I even had to do without sometimes. But I survived and was in good health all the way. I think it's all due to the good food my mother served me when I was growing up.

BLANCHE EDDY

I used to listen to Aunt Susan on WKY in Oklahoma City. She came on Monday through Friday at 10:30 A.M., and I'd always stop my housework and write down her recipes. Over the years, her voice changed a dozen times but the recipes were 'most always good. One of them I remember getting was called a "poor-man's cake" and variations of it were passed around for years.

POOR MAN'S CAKE

1 c sugar	2 c water
2 c raisins	2 t cinnamon
1 t cloves	1 t nutmeg
½ c lard	pinch of salt

Boil all ingredients 3 minutes. Cool. Add 2 teaspoons baking powder, 1 teaspoon soda, 3 cups flour. Mix and bake in medium oven about 45 minutes.

A THIRTIES COOK

When we cleaned out a bowl we said we'd "hoovered it"—that meant we'd scraped out every last bit.

ANNA BARNES

Back then, they didn't have dry yeast and sometimes in the summer we couldn't afford ice to keep cake yeast—so this was a great way to get yeast-like bread without it.

SALT RISING BREAD

2 medium potatoes, sliced	1 heaping T cornmeal
1 heaping T flour	1 t salt

Pour boiling water (just enough to cover) over all this and stir. Set in a place overnight to keep just warm. If it has foamed over in morning take out potatoes. Add about

1 T salt	1 t soda
1 T sugar	

Thicken with flour, set in warm place, and let rise. Add a pint of warm water (not too warm or you'll kill your rising). Add enough flour to make stiff dough. Shape in loaves, knead well, let rise in warm place again, then bake about one hour in a moderate oven.

ANNE WALTHER

We lived right at the end of the railroad line in Cody, Wyoming, and often I cooked for a dozen section hands. In the winter, I'd make head cheese after my husband had butchered hogs—it was sure inexpensive and delicious.

HOGSHEAD CHEESE

Boil a hog's head until it falls to pieces. Remove from kettle, draining off the liquid. Chop and season to taste with salt, pepper, and sage. Then return meat to the kettle and add one-fourth as much liquid in which it was boiled as meat. Simmer over fire twenty minutes and turn into a deep basin, placing a weight on it. When thoroughly cold, cut in slices and serve.

AGNES BENSON

Back in the lean years, when I was workin' on Oklahoma farms, this was a favorite of everyone.

SWEET CHUNK PICKLES

Take small or large cucumbers soaked one week in salt brine (1 cup salt to 1 gallon water); drain, then soak in clear water 24 hours. Cut in slices or chunks. Add boiling alum water (3 tablespoons alum to 1 gallon water). Let stand 24 hours. Drain, then add clear boiling water, let stand 24 hours. Drain, then add syrup—made of 1 pint strong vinegar, 1 pint sugar, and 2 tablespoons celery seed —tied in a bag. Bring this to boil, then pour over cucumbers; let set 24 hours; drain and reheat syrup each day for four days. Each day add ½ cup sugar.

On the fourth day pack cucumbers in jars, then pour hot syrup over and seal. If brine gets weak and short, add more vinegar.

MAGGIE MOFFITT

We used this recipe in the early spring when we didn't have good, fresh apples. You know, they didn't have ways of keeping apples good all year 'round, so in the spring if I could find them at all, they were mealy and tasteless.

I don't know if I actually saved any money on this pie but it was a sure conversation piece.

MOCK APPLE PIE

1½ c sugar	1 T lemon juice
1½ c water	12 soda crackers, broken
1½ t cream of tartar	into quarters
1 t cinnamon	2 T margarine
dash of nutmeg	pastry for two-crust pie

Combine first five ingredients and cook five minutes. Add lemon juice and cool thoroughly. Line pie tin with pastry and put soda crackers broken in fourths on top. Dot with margarine. Pour cooled mixture over crackers. Top with crust. Bake in a 400° oven for ten minutes, then 375° for 25 minutes.

ELZENA LAMB

I got this recipe back in Steele, Missouri, when I was working as a WPA housekeeping aid. My family has loved it for forty years.

CABBAGE APPLE SALAD

½ head of cabbage   ½ c raisins
salt to taste   salad dressing
4 apples

Shred cabbage, add salt, cut unpeeled apples in small pieces. Mix with cabbage, add raisins and salad dressing—mix well. Add nuts if you like.

OTHER COMBINATIONS

Chopped carrots, green peppers, grated carrots with cabbage.
Diced beets, chopped onions with cabbage.
Chopped cheese, onion, carrots with cabbage.
Oranges, cut in small pieces, with cabbage.

MARGARET BROOKINS

I was born on a Karok Indian rancheria in northern California. This is the kind of bread we made in the 1930s and long before.

INDIAN BREAD

4 c flour   pinch of salt (Indians
⅛ t soda   learned to use salt from
2 rounded T lard   the white man.)
                         water

Mix ingredients with hands; add lard, working well with fingers. Add water 'til biscuit dough consistency. Knead about 5 minutes. Pat down into an oiled baking pan and push into shape with knuckles. Score with knife so that it will break easily. Bake 'til brown in 350° oven.

MY SEARCH FOR MAKE-DO RECIPES from the 1930s ended at General Mills' Betty Crocker Kitchens in Minneapolis. A young woman with the improbable name of Nancy Sweet researched my request.

"According to our files," she said, "the Depression brought desperate pleas for help. The kitchen staff spent two weeks in the early thirties working out recipes and menus which would provide well-balanced meals for families eating relief food.

"The plans won national acclaim from nutritionists and social workers and were used by women all over the country.

"I'd like to add a word of caution regarding the recipes. They're over forty years old, after all, and products and methods have changed since then. I think you ought to mention that they don't necessarily meet today's standards at Betty Crocker Kitchens—but they do give a fascinating history of what women were cooking in the thirties."

The following are one week's menus and their recipes (for a family of six) on a very low food budget or relief subsidies.*

MINIMUM BUDGET

SUNDAY

BREAKFAST	DINNER	SUPPER
Prune sauce	Beef and kidney pie	Cream of tomato
Farina, milk, coffee	with vegetables	soup
cake	Chopped cabbage	Toasted cheese
Milk for children	with vinegar and	sandwiches
Coffee for adults	sugar	Bananas
	Chocolate pudding,	Milk for children
	milk	
	Bread and butter	
	Milk for children	

* Courtesy the Betty Crocker Kitchens, General Mills, Inc.

MONDAY

BREAKFAST
Oatmeal, milk,
bread, and
molasses
Milk for children
Coffee for adults

LUNCH
Potato soup, crackers
Scrambled eggs on
toast
Orange gelatin
pudding
Milk for children

DINNER
Macaroni, cheese,
and tomatoes
Onions and bacon
strips
Raw carrot strips
Bread and peanut
butter
Prune pudding with
sauce
Milk for children

TUESDAY

BREAKFAST
Tomato juice
Fried cornmeal
mush with bacon
and molasses
Milk for children
Coffee for adults

LUNCH
Vegetable soup
Bread and peanut
butter
Milk for children
Apples

DINNER
Ham hocks and
cabbage
Boiled potatoes
Bread and butter
Rice with raisin
sauce
Milk for children

WEDNESDAY

BREAKFAST
Tomato juice
Farina, milk
Pancakes and syrup
Milk for children
Coffee for adults

LUNCH
Creamed salmon
with hard-cooked
eggs on toast
Spinach
Toast and honey
Milk for children

DINNER
Split pea soup with
ham bone
Lettuce
Rye bread and
cottage cheese
Thin cranberry sauce
Milk for children

THURSDAY

BREAKFAST
Orange juice for
children
Oatmeal and milk,
bread and butter
Milk for children
Coffee for adults

LUNCH
Corn, eggs, and
bacon scrambled
together
Scalloped tomatoes
Bread and butter
Cocoa for all

DINNER
Veal stew with
carrots, onions,
peas, and potatoes
Bread and butter
Fruit roly poly
Milk for children

FRIDAY

BREAKFAST	LUNCH	DINNER
Sliced oranges	Carrot soup	Codfish balls, salt
Cornmeal mush and	Bread and peanut	pork gravy
milk	butter	Raw carrot strips
Milk for children	Stewed prunes	Mashed turnips
Coffee for adults	Milk for children	Bread and butter
		Suet pudding,
		vinegar sauce
		Milk for children

SATURDAY

BREAKFAST	LUNCH	DINNER
Oatmeal with	Spanish rice	Baked beans
raisins, milk	Rolls and butter	Brown bread and
Bread and butter	Fruit sauce	butter
Milk for children	Milk for all	Cabbage slaw
Coffee for adults		Baked apples

MAIN COURSE MEAT (OR FISH) AND VEGETABLE DISHES

BEEF AND KIDNEY PIE—Remove outside membrane and fat from 1 pound kidneys (beef, pork, veal, or lamb). Split lengthwise and take out fibrous part with a sharp pointed knife. Soak in cold, salted water 1 hour or more. Chop 6 onions and 6 carrots. Brown a little of the onion and carrots in 2 tablespoons drippings or other fat. Add 1 pound beef (any cheap cut). Sear well on both sides. Cover with boiling water, add salt and pepper, and simmer until tender. During last half hour cook kidneys, 6 potatoes (cut in small pieces), 1 sliced turnip, and the remaining carrots with the beef. Remove beef and kidneys from liquid and cut in small pieces. Make a gravy by thickening 4 cups of the meat stock with 5 tablespoons flour blended with 5 tablespoons hot drippings or other fat. Stir until thickened. Season to taste. Place all the meat, vegetables, and gravy in a deep baking dish. Cover with top crust made with 1 cup Gold Medal "Kitchen-tested" flour, 1½ tablespoons shortening, 2 teaspoons baking powder, ½ teaspoon salt, and ⅓ cup water. Bake 20 minutes in hot (450°) oven.

MACARONI, CHEESE, AND TOMATOES—Use 1 pound macaroni, the pulp from 1 No. 3 can tomatoes, 3 onions, and ½ pound cheese.

HAM HOCKS AND CABBAGE—Use 2 pounds ham hocks and 5 cups shredded cabbage.

VEAL OR LAMB STEW WITH VEGETABLES—1 pound lamb or veal breasts (or any stewing meat), 6 potatoes, 6 carrots, 3 onions, and 1 No. 2 can peas.

CODFISH BALLS WITH SALT PORK GRAVY—Wash ⅔ pound dried codfish in cold water and tear into shreds. Dice 6 potatoes. Cover fish and potatoes with boiling water. Cook until potatoes are soft. Drain through strainer. Mash thoroughly in dish in which they were cooked. Add 1 teaspoon fat. Roll in flour and fry in drippings from ¼ pound salt pork. Thicken drippings with a little flour and add 2 cups milk (or more) to make gravy.

CORN, EGGS, AND BACON—Use a No. 2 can corn, 4 eggs, ¼ pound bacon, ½ cup milk, and 2 tablespoons butter substitute.

SPANISH RICE—Cook 1 cup rice in 1 quart boiling, salted water until tender. Brown 1 onion (chopped fine) in 4 tablespoons fat. Combine with ¼ cup green pepper or pimento (chopped fine), ¼ cup diced celery, and 2 cups canned tomatoes. Add cooked rice with 2 teaspoons salt and ⅛ teaspoon pepper. Place in a greased casserole and bake thirty minutes in a moderate (350°) oven. This dish may be cooked on top of the stove.

SOUPS

CREAM OF TOMATO SOUP—1 quart milk, 1 No. 2 can tomatoes (juice and pulp), 3 tablespoons fat, and salt.

POTATO SOUP—1 quart milk, 6 potatoes (cooked), 1 onion grated, 2 tablespoons fat, and salt.

VEGETABLE SOUP—3-pound meat bone, 3 quarts water, 3 potatoes, 1 turnip, 3 carrots, 3 onions, 3 stalks celery, 3 leaves cabbage (all cut fine), and seasonings.

SPLIT PEA SOUP—Soak 2 cups split peas overnight in plenty of water. In morning, drain and add 2 quarts fresh water. Add a ham bone and 1 onion (cut up). Cover. Bring to boil and simmer slowly four or five hours until peas are soft and liquid partially cooked down. Rub through coarse sieve if desired. Blend in 3 tablespoons flour mixed with a little water. Dilute with water as desired. Season with salt and pepper.

CARROT SOUP—Grate 6 small carrots and mince 1 onion. Cook carrots in an open kettle in small amount of water. Melt 1 tablespoon fat, add onion, and stir in 1 tablespoon flour. Gradually add 1½ quarts milk stirring until smooth. Add carrots and reheat.

DESSERTS

PRUNE PUDDING—Sift together 2 cups (sifted) Gold Medal "Kitchen-tested" flour, 4 teaspoons baking powder, ½ teaspoon salt, 2 tablespoons sugar. Cut in 2 tablespoons fat and add 1 cup milk. Drop a layer of this soft dough into a greased pan or pudding mold and cover it with a layer of cooked prunes (2 cups cooked prunes in all will be needed). Add alternate layers of dough and prunes having a layer of dough on top. Cover and steam 45 minutes. Turn out on serving platter and serve hot with Prune Sauce.

PRUNE SAUCE—Mix 6 tablespoons flour with ⅔ cup sugar. Add 2 cups cold prune juice (in which prunes were cooked) and 1 tablespoon butter substitute and cinnamon. Add 2 tablespoons vinegar and cook until thick.

RICE WITH RAISIN SAUCE—Stew 1 cup raisins in 2 cups water and serve hot as sauce over 4 cups cooked rice.

FRUIT ROLY POLY—Make a sauce with ⅓ pound cranberries, ½ cup raisins, and 1 apple, cut up. Drain off the juice and save it for the pudding sauce. Sift 2 cups Gold Medal "Kitchen-tested" flour with 4 teaspoons baking powder and 1 teaspoon salt. Cut in 2 tablespoons fat. Add ¾ cup milk. Roll out in oblong shape, spread with well-drained fruit. Roll up like jelly roll and place on one or two pans on a rack over boiling water in a large kettle or covered roaster. Cover tightly and steam without lifting cover for half hour. Serve hot with fruit sauce.

FRUIT SAUCE—Use fruit juice thickened with 4 tablespoons flour or 2 tablespoons cornstarch (to 2 cups juice).

SUET PUDDING—Mix together 3½ cups (sifted) Gold Medal "Kitchen-tested" flour, 1 teaspoon soda, 1 teaspoon salt, 2 teaspoons cinnamon, 1 cup suet (½ pound) chopped fine, 1 cup milk (sweet or sour), 1 cup molasses, 1 cup chopped dates, and 1 cup raisins. Fill greased basin or pudding mold two-thirds full, cover tightly, and steam three hours. Serve hot with Vinegar Sauce.

HOT VINEGAR SAUCE—Mix 6 tablespoons flour and 1 cup sugar with 2 cups cold water and 2 tablespoons mild vinegar. Cook until thick and add 1 tablespoon butter substitute and a little cinnamon or nutmeg if desired.

Chapter Four

OF MARRIAGE
AND MEN

"YOU'RE JOKING," I said when a friend recommended I talk to her. "Nobody is named Sadie Belle."

I was wrong. There is a Sadie Belle, but she does not fit my vision of a Li'l Abner character. Charming and delightful—two words she uses a lot—describe her well. Obviously living above Social Security level, she and her husband maintain a spacious apartment, tastefully furnished with Louis the something or other. Her husband, Mr. Nelson—that's what she calls him—a long, lean man in a starched white shirt, sat nearby while we talked. He sat by quietly, responding only to her requests for verification of a date or a half-forgotten name.

By this time, I have become wary of thirties' husbands. They tend to inhibit a frank interview, or worse, take over.

"I have had a wonderful time being his wife," she said, and I understood she makes the same statement whether or not he is in the room. "He gave me a salary the first Saturday night we were married—almost fifty years ago—and it's been doubled every Saturday night that I've been good. Of course, it was zero to start with, but it makes me feel awfully good to have it doubled every week."

And though they must have laughed at that old joke hundreds of times, they laughed again.

SADIE BELLE NELSON'S STORY

We wives would just be tremendously tense during fire season, especially when we'd look up at the mountain all in flames and know our husbands were there.

I was teaching home economics in a small high school in Iowa when we married, so I think that background in relation to those lean years helped me a great deal. Although, frankly, government people didn't suffer greatly during the Depression. We were making $2,800. It didn't go up, but it didn't go down, either.

It was a good time for me because we made delightful moves due to Mr. Nelson's job in the forestry service. We lived comfortably and we always became a part of every community. The only real problem I can remember was the fire season and the possibility he would get hurt.

Our first move was to Mt. Shasta, way up near the Oregon border; it was a little lumbering town then. During the summer season, which was long, hot, and dry, hundreds of hoboes—I suppose we called them hoboes but they really were just unemployed men moving from place to place trying to find work—well, these hoboes would come through town. Sometimes there were 300 of them on one train, and they would deliberately set fires so they would be hired to put them out. The Shasta canyon was a natural for setting fires because it was shaped like a box.

We were living in a small house on the main street right across from the railroad station. There were big trees around the station and after the forest service had taken the men off the trains to work on the fires, their bedrolls would be hanging in the trees—those huge trees looked as if they were filled with rather ungainly but colorful crows.

Hoboes didn't bother us at all. I recall one night a funny little man came to my door and wanted an onion for his stew. He told me he had everything for the stew except an onion.

I suppose I'm a worrier by nature. I think I had worry built into me during those years. Mr. Nelson was in charge of the fires and it was his duty to be the last man home, and I didn't like that much. All the other husbands came home very jauntily and he came in the very last—days afterward because he waited until the fires were completely out. And they were not ever completely out during the summers. Or at least it didn't seem so to me.

The fire season was just tremendously tense for the wives. When we looked up at the mountain all in flames and knew our husbands were there, *each* of us thought that our man might be trapped.

The month before our son was born in June of 1931, Mr. Nelson was fighting a fire just down the canyon and he got caught in it with a Mexican who was helping him on the line. The fire jumped in front of him and behind him so they just lay down on the ground and a little rabbit came down and stayed there alongside them 'til they got out. During a forest fire all living things stick together like this.

After that experience, Mr. Nelson doubled his life insurance.

As I said, we made some delightful moves. Once we lived in Nevada City in a second floor apartment which was extremely comfortable and cost the grand sum of sixteen dollars a month. Unfortunately, we shared a bathroom with another family; it was on the *third* floor—in the attic. So one simply climbed to the attic and hoped that one could sing loud enough to keep all intruders away while bathing. The bathtub sat in the middle of the floor and had no partition around it. It was the same feeling as taking a bath on Main Street.

Nevada City is an old gold rush town, and I think all those towns are fascinating. During the thirties, the North Star and Empire gold mines were operated by English capital, and the English people who managed the mines were charming. We dressed for dinner almost every night.

Another nice thing I remember about Nevada City is that we lived on Piety Hill, and to get home we walked up Tribulation Trail. During the early days all the ministers had lived there, just as all the bankers had lived on Aristocracy Hill.

We never bought a home during the thirties. We rented. There was a superstition among forest service people that one should never buy because the minute one did, away you went.

I suppose our Weaverville house was my favorite. It was eighty years old at that time and had a marvelous rosewood Steinway grand—a big square one with the fattest legs. The story was that they had brought it over the mountains by mule wagon. All the furniture in that house was delightful.

One thing—those old mountain towns had a special etiquette that, at first, I didn't understand. They had wonderful, rousing dances. Never were there balls like there were in Weaverville, and all the gals dressed to the teeth. The children came too and were parked along the wall. Now I had never been asked to dance by a man I didn't know or hadn't been introduced to, at least. At college, our programs had always been filled by our escorts and so the first night I went to a dance, I made a faux pas. One of the local men came up to me and asked me to dance and I said very properly, "Well, you'll have to ask my husband." That was very bad manners for Weaverville, and I got off to a bad start.

But it was all great fun and at midnight the dancing stopped and we ate. Such banquets! They were absolutely scrumptious. Long tables filled with ice cream cakes piled high with whipped cream, great bowls of potato salad, hams, turkeys, and all the trimmings— feasts as I look back on them.

Oh, we were aware, of course, that there were apple sellers and soup lines. We read about them, but they didn't seem to touch our lives. We were really quite isolated. In those small communities we learned to be self-sufficient, even making our own fun, organizing dancing and socials of all kinds. The Catholic church would help the Protestant church, and the Protestants would help the Catholics when they had something special. You had a real community feeling —it was a real brotherhood of man.

While we lived in Weaverville, there were five forestry service telephone lines coming into our house, and I was the telephone operator. I remember being in the house after dark—it was on the edge of town—taking calls and a coyote would be howling right outside. I think that must have aged me prematurely.

But most all my memories are happy ones. We had good friends and our wishes were comparatively simple. We did a lot of enter- taining—fun was inexpensive. And we had a good marriage—we were close no matter what. Mr. Nelson would always try to let me know where he was if he could. Once when he was working on a mountain near Weaverville, we used mirrors to flash messages to each other. I didn't know the code, but we flashed back and forth. Just to say hello. . . .

I remember one especially gourmet meal in our married life that surpassed all others. We went across Trinity Mountain through Hayfork and into a little ranger station. We knew it was going to storm badly, so we pressed on late into the night until we got to this little camp, cold and tired and somewhat dispirited. We built a roaring fire and I found some cold potato soup which we heated.

It doesn't take anything under glass to make a gourmet meal—only two loving people and a fireplace.

ONCE, YEARS AGO, I knew other women like her—big hands with red knuckles from too many hours over a washboard, and a sun-faded, dry complexion that Midwestern blondes seem to put on with their years. If she wore a print cotton dress, I thought, instead of a pantsuit, she could step into any made-for-television 1930s movie.

I liked her weeks before we met. "I just want you to know," she told me with some emotion on the telephone, "that even if we never talk anymore—even if I don't see you, you have given me a new insight on my life. I thought I had been so ordinary."

She isn't ordinary. Unless courage, persistence, and good humor are ordinary. I don't think they are, but I didn't convince her. She pressed a quart jar of home-canned preserves into my hands as I left. ". . . For your time," she said.

KATHRYN HASKELL PERRIGO'S STORY

We pulled together—literally. When we cut fence posts I pulled my end of a crosscut and he pulled his.

My papa passed away in '33, shortly before we moved to Boone County, Missouri. At the time my mother was forty-six years old and I was her last child and the only girl. She went down to Kansas City and went to work housekeeping for people. So I had to live with first one brother and then another. They had both been married such a short while and I felt like I was intruding. All in all, I just decided, if I don't have a home any other way, I'll just get married and make one of my own. Big decision when you're fifteen, you know. You're going to lick the world!

I think I was an old fifteen. Girls grew up fast in those days. But I don't know if I could have made it without my mother-in-law She was a gem—one in a million. My husband was the youngest and he was a mama's boy—which probably helped my mother-in-law to accept me. She passed away a year after we were married but she gave me all the support in the world. If I had any questions, I could go to her easier than to my own mother.

At that time, my mom was just a bit inclined to be bossy and she was rather tiffed about my getting married so she told me, "If things go wrong, don't come crying to me." I was very stubborn and I made up my mind I never would. I never did. I decided I would not admit defeat.

Now, my mother-in-law was a person who loved fish, and she loved catfish best of all. Being in the area of the tributaries of the Missouri River, there was a creek below the house where we used to hand fish. It wasn't legal, but in the spring the catfish will nest under rocks and logs and you just go down in the water and reach under and take them out. They'd weigh maybe four or five pounds. They're awful ugly but, oh, they're delicious.

We fried 'em in cornmeal batter. Most of the time we caught them and took them to my mother-in-law's house and fixed them for her right there.

My husband and I pulled together, literally, all our lives. We worked and we struggled and we tried hard. We'd go out to cut white oak fence posts and I pulled my end of the crosscut—a six foot crosscut saw—and he pulled his. I always worked right with him whenever I wasn't pregnant.

In those years a woman didn't worry about gaining weight. You never had time—you were too busy. Sawing is the best exercise there is for your waistline and I sure had a good one.

I don't think farm people ever had the problems that city people had. We cut wood nearby, and we had a garden where we could raise something to eat. So we didn't have to be cold or hungry.

And it's absolutely surprising the number of things a woman can do to manage. I made my boys pants out of old coats, and a ten-pound flour bag was a pair of training pants when they were babies. I never bought five pounds of anything 'cause you got that in a paper bag, and I didn't have any use for a paper bag. I baked my own bread and I got to be a pretty good hand at making biscuits.

Our first house—I thought it was beautiful when I first saw it— was a very small one and very old. We had an outhouse and a well, although we usually pulled up a dry bucket. Fortunately, we had a spring below the house where I did my washing on a washboard.

Rather than carry the water to the house, it was much simpler to take the clothes and go down there. I had an old iron wash boiler that we put on rocks, so we could build a fire underneath. I'd boil 'em and rub 'em and then carry them to the clotheslines. I washed that way for ten years.

I believe marriage was much less difficult then for one reason. You really didn't have choices. You accepted what you had and you made the most of it rather than to think, ". . . if I had something better, I'd such and so." Because you knew you couldn't have it anyway. You knew you had just the best you could get.

I don't want you to think it was all hard work. We played a lot of rummy and pinochle, and on a really big Saturday night we'd square dance to our own music. We'd go to different houses and somebody had a fiddle, or somebody had a banjo and a washboard. There's a world of things you can do if you don't wait around for somebody to do them for you.

And we never thought of leaving our babies behind. We'd take 'em and put them all in one bed—there'd be a whole bed full of wriggling babies with chairs stacked 'round the bed so's they wouldn't fall out.

I recall we women visiting each other a lot—more than now. We quilted together. We hardly ever talked without doing something with our hands. I had a close neighbor that put a quilt on the quilting frame, and it was always there and there was always five needles threaded and a like number of thimbles on that quilt. So if you went in and decided to sit and talk, you quilted.

In those days, if you needed someone, you had someone to talk to. I mean we talked about everything—we poured our hearts out. We didn't worry about psychiatrists—we were each other's psychiatrists.

When I had my first baby, I wasn't quite sixteen years old and my mother wanted me to come to Kansas City to the hospital. Now, there I found out I was this fantastic milk cow! I not only fed my own, but sold mother's milk back to the hospital for ten cents an ounce. With the carfare they gave me, I made $1.80 a pint—twice a day.

By the time I was eighteen, I had two children. Thank God, I had the first boy potty-trained before the next one came. I never had two in diapers at once—thank God for that! But I never had a diaper that had four corners, either. Each diaper had holes in the corners where they were on the clothesline, because in the wintertime they froze and then when I pulled the clothespins off, I pulled off a chunk of cloth—'til those diapers kept getting littler and littler.

I'm just jumping all around as I remember things. But like I said, in those years a woman canned out of the garden. If you didn't can it in the summertime, you couldn't eat it in the wintertime. My husband could find wild berries where other men couldn't. I'm one of the few people in the world that ever ate a fresh wild raspberry. We usually didn't can with sugar because we couldn't afford it. So we canned without and then put a little sugar on at the table. They were just as good that way.

Now canning vegetables is different. I could never get twenty dollars together for a pressure cooker, so I just had to boil them for hours. One batch a day was just about all I could ever get through with.

I tried to manage things the best I could. There was no electricity, so I did my ironing by heating the iron on the stove. The days I ironed, I baked bread—because the stove was going and I didn't waste anything.

For two years, I made bread with everlasting yeast that I borrowed from a neighbor. I kept it going; I remember how to do that. Each time you mix your bread sponge you pour out about a pint of starter and then you feed it a little flour and sugar and warm water. Then you set it in the back on the stove 'til next time. I told you, I got it from a neighbor, and she got it in turn from a neighbor who got it from her mother-in-law. No telling how long that everlasting yeast had been around.

All those years my husband worked like a Trojan. He used to trap a lot of fur bearing animals in the wintertime. Mostly he hunted with dogs, but he had some traps. He used to hunt mink. I've seen some beautiful mink in my day, but I never could keep it. I got quite good at helping skin. And maybe I even had them right in there on the kitchen floor skinning them, when it was too cold outside.

But he would work hard, like I said, getting up and walking cross-country through woods and fields. He knew every animal den in that country. I'd get up and get his breakfast about three o'clock in the morning. He was usually gone 'til dark. Sometimes he'd get home with just enough light to saw wood for heat the next day. Or, if I could, I did it. That was a daily chore, sawing and splitting wood. And we both did that work. There was no "his and her" jobs on the farm. We both did all the jobs, as we could.

You know, sometimes in the spring and early summer fresh meat was a little hard to come by. We had a cured pork, but fresh meat we just didn't have until our chickens got big enough to eat. So he'd take a .22 rifle and shoot cottontails, which were delicious, let me tell you. I'd go hunting with him when I wasn't pregnant, especially squirrel hunting. I'd get to be the squirrel dog rattling a bush on the other side of the tree so my husband could shoot 'em.

Once we had a rather odd situation. I saw this darn little cottontail about two-thirds grown go across the yard and some way or other manage to squeeze underneath the top of the well and fall in. I thought—if it stays in there it's going to ruin our water. So right away I got a bucket and a rope and lowered it down and fished out the rabbit.

When my husband got back I found out he'd managed to shoot two cottontails. I got half as many as he did and I didn't even leave the house. We laughed about that for a long time.

We learned to eat squirrel, rabbit, wild ducks, fish—all those. We ate just whatever nature provided. There really was no point in sitting down crying 'cause you didn't have any fresh meat, while there was wild meat out there running loose. Once, a darn mink was coming and eating our ducks off the pond. But we laid for him and got him. He ate our ducks, but we ate off his hide! So you see, we were in competition with them. It was kind of them or us, and the first one gets it.

HER GRANDMOTHER came to America from China on a sailing schooner as a "picture bride" whose marriage was arranged by a broker on the basis of a photograph.

Constance Chang works part-time for a San Francisco travel agency. At sixty-eight, she is beautifully groomed and an international traveler.

CONSTANCE CHANG'S STORY

I couldn't get a job. Finally, I did the only thing a woman would do—I got married.

My father was very liberal. He wanted me to have a college education, even if I was a girl. But my mother was reluctant because I was the oldest and I was supposed to stay at home and help her until I married. Father prevailed and I went to Cal at Berkeley and graduated in '31. I got a letter in sciences and majored in economics with a minor in political science. But halfway through my last year everything went wrong for my father, and he couldn't help me anymore. I found a job that paid twenty dollars a month and was able to finish.

When I graduated, there were only eight Oriental girls in school, and not one in my major. I think I studied what I thought would please my father. He was in business, and he was very interested in politics, especially the Chinese Nationalist government. We had similar interests then—my father and I—but I grew out of it.

So here I was in San Francisco with a degree, and I thought it would make a difference. The first job I applied for was at American Insurance Company. I expected maybe a clerical job, but there were none there—those jobs weren't open for Oriental people at that time. Then I tried a ladies' apparel shop as a stock girl. That wasn't even open to me. Oh, they don't tell you right out to your face—but you have that feeling. Finally, I did the only thing a woman would do . . . got married. Ha!

Sure, I found a solution but I was still anxious to get a job. After a few months I found work at a Chinese variety store—the National Dollar Store. There were Caucasian sales people but it was run by Chinese people. That's the only reason I got that job, I guess.

San Francisco's Chinatown was a very small area then. I don't think we could go above Mason Street. That was outside our area. We seemed to take it. We had no resentment or anything that I remember. Just took it as a way of life at that time.

My husband and I rented an apartment. It was small because we did not plan to have any children. The feeling then was that it was just too rough to have children.

He did whatever he could for a time, but then he started a bus line running from Chinatown to the delta where a Chinese settlement is. And he did very well with that.

I made eighty-five dollars a month and everybody thought I was wonderfully paid. I remember I worked long hours so when I came in from work I wouldn't want to cook. We'd send out for pork chops, hot biscuits, coffee, and apple pie—all for about forty cents. We didn't always eat traditional Chinese food because we had been Americanized by then.

But the best part for women was we just put our trays and dirty dishes outside our door, and the next morning they were gone.

Chinese people love to talk, and so we were very social and got together a lot. We belonged to a family association, and we'd have dinners on holidays. Chinese people love to eat, too.

The women played a lot of Mah-Jongg, but I was never interested in sitting for hours at a game.

I remember after the Japanese invaded China—during the thirties—we had rice bowl parties. They were benefit parties to raise money for the Chinese government.

But the best time was Chinese New Year's when the whole of Chinatown got together. It was like a carnival. Merchants would decorate their stores with red good-luck banners and all along Grant Avenue there would be pink and red flowers for sale.

It's a tradition that you must have a clean house and new clothes for New Year's. Also you're supposed to pay all your debts and give lucky money, called Li See, to all little children. In the 1930s it was hard to live up to traditions that cost so much.

But the best time was the parade—the New Year's parade when the Golden Dragon, the Gum Lung, was a block long and everybody you met on the street wished you the best for New Year's.

Chinese people also love to stay up late at night. And we always had a snack before we retired. So about nine or ten o'clock we'd call the operator—operators in Chinatown speak Chinese—you didn't have to tell her a number, you just told her the name of the restaurant you were calling. Well, we'd call up and have noodles or rice gruel delivered.

Sometimes I'd even go out about midnight to visit my aunt for a talk. There was a great deal of hustle and bustle on Chinatown streets then—people would go out to talk or have a bite to eat or go to the theater.

I was considered very modern by my husband's family. Girls were still being confined, and some marriages were still arranged. So their attitude—that is, the women's attitude—was often one of envy. They thought I had a lot of freedom.

LOIS FARLEY'S HOME, like Lois Farley herself, is a curious mixture of yesterday and today. The sunny rooms painted in modern pastels seem an odd museum for the heavy, stained furniture which has been in her husband's family for more than 150 years.

"I respected my in-laws," she said. "When they died I couldn't bring myself to get rid of their things. And I'm glad now I couldn't because my grandchildren have a sense of their past. So many young people today don't have that."

LOIS FARLEY'S STORY

We drew up a paper saying everything we owned would belong to both of us. For 1933, we had liberated ideas.

When I married him, he was supporting his family on a small farm. His brothers went off and had their families, and they left him to take care of the old folks.

The first problem we had to work out was that he was a Roman Catholic and I was a Protestant—so before we were married we had to go to the priest for permission. His family would never have recognized our marriage, and he never could have gone home if we hadn't been married in the Catholic church.

So we took our instructions; but we made a private compact between us. I promised never to proselyte him and he promised never to proselyte me. And we also decided we'd let our children choose their own religion for themselves. But, of course, the priest didn't know that.

The religion thing caused him to leave the Knights of Columbus and I had to quit the Eastern Star. In those times a Protestant wife wouldn't be welcome at KC functions, and vice-versa with the Eastern Star. So, rather than cause any trouble, we left.

One thing I insisted on and he went along with: we drew up a paper saying everything we ever owned—anything and everything

—would belong to us both. We had a lawyer draw it up for us and file it with the legal records office.

Yes, I guess you might say that for 1933, we had liberated ideas.

I moved into the farmhouse with him and his parents. They had no electricity, no running water, and the "chic sales" was in the back-yard—but they had no mortgage on any of it.

My husband was like that all his life. Vermonters believe in hold-ing their heads up, not owing or being owed. I mean that is their attitude—"I'm my own man."

We had our milk and our chickens and eggs. We raised vegetables and everything we could; we did for ourselves. We sold the good vegetables and ate the "buggy" ones. That sounds bad, but that's a way of getting by. My husband worked on a big farm nearby for thirty-five cents an hour and was glad to get the job. That's the way we got money for store items—now don't laugh—our grocery bill was eight dollars a month for the four of us.

A little flour and salt and some sugar—that's all we needed. I remember our favorite dessert during the Depression when we couldn't afford a lot of sugar for cakes and such, was a kind of milk pudding. I'd put a container of whole milk in the oven early in the morning. It was a wood stove, so a small fire was kept burning all day. After twelve hours or so, it had formed the consistency of pudding and the milk sugar after this slow heating process had be-come very sweet. I'd take it out and grate a little lemon over it or sprinkle a little cinnamon on top. Delicious!

A WOMAN NAMED CLARA

I lost my home in 1933. That year they cut my husband's salary ten percent. He was in the safety department in Oakwood-Dayton, Ohio—that means he was a fireman and policeman both.

I wanted to try to hold on to the house by just paying interest like so many people were doing. But my husband said, "No, if we can't pay all we'll just give up." Which we did. . . .

It's hard on a woman to lose her home. I really felt we could hold on, but my husband was always so conscientious . . .

So we rented from then on. We never did buy a house again.

During the thirties, my husband took a correspondence course to be a lawyer. He got good grades and worked for years and years, every spare minute. Just three months before taking the bar examination, Ohio passed a law saying a man had to go to college to be admitted to the bar. I pleaded with him to go to another state so he could be a lawyer. But he wouldn't. He gave it all up, and he always felt bad. . . .

It seemed like I didn't have free time ever. I couldn't do my housework days because my husband was sleeping, and I would try to be quiet. But after the children would be put to bed, I would do my work—washing and ironing and cleaning.

I just kept on going during those years. I always took care of the children and my home. And I kept my husband's routine because he was a very strict disciplinarian and insisted on a well-run home. The reason was that his safety work was very important to him, so I helped him with his studies and kept things going smooth.

MILDRED HUFF is an old-fashioned woman. She wears her best dress when she goes visiting.

On the day she visited me, her husband Al—at her insistence—had driven 200 miles so she could be interviewed.

MILDRED HUFF'S STORY

At night I'd take the children down to meet "Big Bertha"—
that's the bus that brought the men down from Boulder Dam.
Sometimes we'd see the ambulance and I'd pray it wasn't Al.

Ever think something's coming to an end when it's really just beginning? When we left Wisconsin for Nevada in March of '32, I thought we were going to the other side of the world. My husband, Al, had had pneumonia real bad and his dad who lived in Searchlight, Nevada, had written for us to come on out. He had a service station he said we could run.

So we packed two little kids, three and four, in an old Hudson car and pulled a trailer loaded down with a thousand pounds of furniture and stuff—everything we owned.

It took us thirteen days, because we hit a big snowstorm in Greeley, Colorado. You know it hadn't snowed all winter 'til we left, and then it snowed all the way. Outside of Greeley, there was a big truck stuck on the highway and we stopped to give them a hand. They didn't have a shovel, so Al helped dig them out with ours. By that time the wind was blowing hard and it was a regular blizzard. The truckers tied a chain to our car and helped us into town. It's a good thing they did, because that day a school bus got stuck near there and eight little kids froze to death.

We stayed there two days and then went on. Most of the roads were dirt in them days. Especially through Arizona. I never seen such roads—got stuck in the red clay mud several times around Flagstaff.

When we got to Searchlight, Al's dad had a service station-cafè, but he was also bootlegging. After a while, Al applied to get on at Boulder Dam which was being built at that time.

We moved to Boulder City—which wasn't a city at all, but hundreds of company houses. Ours was much like the rest, although some of the higher ups had nicer ones. One big room—that's what we had—with a partition between the kitchen-dining room and the living room-bedroom. And then it had a two-sided porch that we covered with metal awnings. When it would get so blistering hot, we'd let water run on them to get the air cool.

We had a bathhouse and outdoor toilet. It was a dandy—a double holer—and we had a separate shower in there. But the water was so hot in the summer—'cause the pipes were laid only six inches under the ground—you couldn't take a shower 'til night.

Al had terrible working conditions—of course, you couldn't do much about those things then. He drove a truck in a tunnel and the air was so bad from the fumes that he came home with a pounding headache every day for a year. He never got a day off, either. Seven days a week he worked—all straight time—and if some guy didn't report for the next shift, Al had to double over. And he couldn't say no, if they asked him, unless he wanted to lose his job.

Lots of times when it was hot at night, I'd take the children and go down to meet Big Bertha—that's what they called the bus that brought the men down from the dam. Sometimes, I'd meet the ambulance coming from the site, so I didn't know whether to go home or go on down the line. You never knew who the ambulance was bringing. You just prayed it wasn't your husband.

They had a school for the kids there, and the six companies with contracts on the dam went together and built a store and a poolroom where they sold beer. But there wasn't really a lot to do. It was a godforsaken area, just desert and sand, and most of the husbands were gone all the time. They only got paid for eight hours, but they were gone twelve hours—the extra time was for getting to the dam and back.

It was sure hard to have any social life with all the husbands away, working shifts. We women played cards and we'd sew together. Sometimes we went to the store, if we had money. Or we'd draw script.

They issued us script whenever we wanted an advance on wages. Everybody was broke, so you drew script and they were only good at the Six Companies' Store. It seemed to me they got most of their money back.

We only managed to save $150 in three years there. It was hard to hang onto money, especially because there was no bank there. A couple of bachelor fellas my husband worked with, who couldn't hold their money, would ask me to be their banker. "Now don't give me this money, no matter what," they told me. But you know they'd get drunk or something and then they'd come around and say, "I want my money!" And, I'd say, "No, you can't have it. I sent it into Las Vegas to the bank." They'd always come around later looking a little sheepish and thanking me for not giving them their money when they asked for it. Some of them young guys got out of there with a lot more money than we did.

Of course, you couldn't blame 'em for it. About a mile or two outside Boulder City there was a place called Railroad Pass and they had a lot of gambling there and girls, too, because prostitution was legal in Nevada.

After three years, I wanted Al to quit. We had hardly any home-life and it was just getting so dangerous I was always scared for him. And I was right. A few days after he left a landslide buried a bunch of men right where Al had been working.

So we took the $150 we'd saved and Al bought this old dump truck. It had no windshield and no cab, but he got a job hauling ore. It was at a mine that was developed years earlier, but they'd found a vein about an inch wide. Al hauled ore to Oatman, between Kingman and Needles on Route 66. Sometimes at night I went with him, and that's when I seen the Okies broke down all over. We'd stop and help 'em, what we could—tow 'em into Needles or give 'em a gallon of gas. I found out what being poor was like then. We'd had hard times—one Christmas we were down to only three dollars—but nothing like that.

Later we had a cafè and bar near there, and those Okies would come in looking like they hadn't had a bath for a year. You know, they would only work a few hours a day, just to get enough to spend in the bar and have fifty cents for gas to get to work the next day. They were happy-go-lucky, but you wouldn't believe how they lived. They were provided houses that had tent tops, and they chopped holes in the floors for bathrooms instead of going outside.

Once we came on some old Okie truck that had gone off the road down an embankment. Oh, that was terrible, hearing people crying and calling to each other and we couldn't get anybody to help 'cause there wasn't anybody riding on the road at that time of night, hardly. Finally, what we did was to go on in and send some help back for them, but a couple died. Poor devils.

TELEPHONING ME A WEEK EARLIER she said, "I read—where you were writing a book about women during the 1930s. Will you—can you—come out please? I don't have much—time left."

Squeezing the words out between gasps and wheezes, she left me little doubt about what she meant. She was dying or thought she was.

A retired bookkeeper, not yet sixty, she lived in a run-down tract house near a sign that read: NOT A THROUGH STREET.

"I have about six months—the doctor says I only have 9 percent of my lungs left—four packs of cigarettes a day, you know," she said, smiling through jerky sentences, sitting upright in a black, vinyl recliner. At night she slept sitting up so she could breathe.

The room was untidy. *Encyclopaedia Britannica,* an entire set, was scattered about her chair with torn pieces of newspaper marking places here and there for future reference. A certificate of membership in Mensa, an organization for people with an IQ over 148 hung on the wall above her chair. She told me she had converted to Catholicism the year before.

"If I had even a year left," she said, touching deep wrinkles in her face, "I'd have it lifted. See, here's—a picture—of me—when I was twenty-six. I thought I—was so ugly then, but I'd give any-thing—to look—that way again."

As an afterthought, she asked: "Will you not use my name? There are a few people still—around—who might be embarrassed. Use my *professional* name."

GINGER LAKE'S STORY

We were in New Orleans, my first husband and I, when I first turned out. It was his idea. He couldn't get work or sell enough needles for us to eat on. What else was there that was honest?

I left home when I was seventeen. My family was on relief, and it seemed all we did was fight. One day my older sister and I got into it . . . she took a sweater of mine and lied about it. When I called her a liar, momma hit me right across the mouth. You see, momma thought words were bad—not what you done—but what you said. And "liar" was a bad word in her book.

I just hit the road. I guess I had a spirit of adventure—you have to, to hitch rides in the rain after dark. Within a few days, I hooked up with the Jack Hoxie circus. I mean I took care of his baby while he and his wife worked. He'd been a big western star in the silent days, but when I met him he wasn't much. He didn't give me a regular bed, but let me sleep in the back of his Cadillac. You can imagine how that got to be after a few weeks: I was sleepy all the time. This one night he found me asleep and the baby crying, so he sacked me, up around Pennsylvania somewhere.

That's when I hitchhiked down to Norfolk, Virginia, where my big brother was in the navy. I was dying to see him. Oh, I wished I was a boy! All we talked about during the Depression was joining the navy for a minority cruise, staying on twenty years, and getting out with a pension while we were still young. I thought that would be the most wonderful thing . . . that looked like real security then. 'Course I'd never seen an ocean, you know.

In Norfolk, I got a job as a waitress, and I got a boyfriend. First real boyfriend I ever had in my life—and a gentleman. He only had one eye and he wore a black patch over the other, but I liked him very much. I even met his sisters, went to their house for dinner, and they invited me places with them. Now, that's when I had a nice social life for a few months. If I didn't have this sense of adventure, I might have stayed there and married that boy.

But one day I just took out for Great Falls, Montana. In those days, I was wild to travel. My family didn't get to travel like people do now. If we could ever afford to drive or visit during the thirties, we always seemed to visit relatives.

There were lots of girls on the road in those days, and lots of men who would stop and give you a ride. I didn't have any trouble . . . I could travel faster hitchhiking than taking the train. It took me thirteen hours to go from Norfolk to Pittsburgh and twenty-nine hours on to Chicago, but then it got a little slower. Anyway, when I got to Great Falls, I hooked up with another circus; well, I knew they were there, and I got this job cleaning "donikers;" that's toilets.

Now the circus in the thirties was a big event. It was the place where people took what money they had to spend it, and where the tips were the most. People just always throw their money around at a circus, somehow.

Usually, it was the "crips"—the cripples—who had the doniker concession. I worked for this crippled woman named Mavis, and she taught me the ropes. I did the cleaning, and she'd get their money on the way out.

That's how I met Jackie—my first husband. He was one of the "crips"—had one arm. I guess we lived together for about a year before we got married. There's something awful about marriage—it just ruined everything. You'd think I'd know him, after living with him, but I guess I didn't. I don't know. I think I was still laboring under the delusion that any marriage can be made a success by a woman.

If the woman is the only one who works at it, then that's too high a price to be paid. I can look back and I see that I could have made a good husband out of him—if I would have just picked up a chair and beat the livin' daylights out of him about once a week. But that's no way to live—so I didn't. The thing that came between us was the way he would talk. You see, people could talk me into things. I could never say no to him, and have him drop it. I either let him talk me into it, or else he'd keep arguing about it until I'd go crazy.

But I had some interesting jobs with the circus. Once I was a barker for the two-headed baby. 'Course, I'd talk like it was alive, and the pictures on the tent showed it in a highchair eating with two spoons. But it was dead and pickled in a jar inside.

Then I played the "lady in the bed" game, and when you do that you're on top in those circuses. I was in this bed, see, that's on an arm. If a person threw a ball and hit the target, then I got dumped out of bed onto a mattress below, wearing nothing but silk scanties and a bra.

My husband got me that job, and fortunately, the young man that put the act together didn't mess around with women at all. He had his mother interview the girls and she was the one that told me I'd have to wear silk scanties and a bra. If he'd asked me, I might not have done it. I was still kinda shy. But his mother . . . ? I kept asking her if I couldn't wear a bathing suit, but she said no—silk scanties and a bra or no go. What I ended up doing to satisfy myself was wearing *two* pairs of panties. I had hair shoulder length then and it was reddish and probably looked even redder under the lights, and it had a permanent. I really think I looked glamorous up there with my makeup on and all. Everybody said I did anyway.

That winter we ended up in New Orleans, Jackie and I, and that's where I first turned out. I suppose that I have always thought I was adaptable and, undoubtedly, I was maybe a little *too* adaptable. But I don't think I could have done it if he hadn't introduced me to what we used to call the landlady, which you probably call the madam. It was all his idea at first. But I don't blame him; this was 1936, remember, when plenty of guys with two arms were out of work. He couldn't sell enough needles for us to eat on. What else was there to do that was honest? I couldn't steal.

Think of it as a way to make money and think that we had been poor and broke and, frankly, I would just as soon live on that as I would the results of his selling needles. To me that's begging, and what I did was something I owned that I could honestly sell to somebody that wanted it. When he took his packages of needles around, the people just gave him a dime to get rid of him; they didn't even take the needles. I mean, gee, it might be a good way to get enough for gas money out of town, but that was all.

I wish I could remember her name—that first landlady—she was real friendly. They were all nice people that I met there.

Well, Jackie had gone to her and she told him it was all right to bring me around to talk to her. I explained I thought I was ugly and didn't think any man would look at me, especially the way I looked then—'cause I didn't have money enough to buy any makeup. If I'd had any lipstick—or money to buy any—I could have got a waitress job. But you can't even get that kind of work without lipstick.

Oh, she was kind, and she assured me that I'd probably do just fine. She showed me the bedroom and how to use that purple stuff—some kind of disinfectant, you know, in a pan, and I sort of took it for granted that you would take a douche between each time. She said no—you don't do that—you don't have time to.

She told me she charged a dollar, and I'd get half.

At first I worked days. She explained to me that the fellas that you got in the daytime were mostly older men and they were more gentle people, and I wouldn't have such a hard time breaking in—and I wouldn't meet so many bad ones.

The only competition I had in the daytime was a rather plump girl, thirty or over. But she was real neat looking and she was nice, too. She and this landlady kept talking to me and saying they were sure I could make it. The fat girl said she never had any trouble making money. She used lots of this violet toilet water. . . .

After awhile I got more confidence and the landlady decided to change me to nights. When I went to work nights, I began to make as much as forty dollars a week. You see there was a time limit, you really weren't supposed to let them stay but fifteen minutes. I didn't have to watch the clock all the time, because there was this Negro woman who came and knocked on the door if one stayed too long.

You know, I worked every night. I don't think I had sense enough to ask for a night off—after all, I didn't really consider it hard work.

Now work to me is like picking potato bugs off a vine, outdoors in the heat when the perspiration is rolling down your face and on the way it's getting in your eyes and stinging and burning—and your hands are full, and you've got a bucket of live potato bugs in one hand and a stick in the other you're knocking the bugs off the vine with—now that's work!

I never really had that much trouble with the men. The way this place fronted, you got kind of nice types. It looked like a soft-drink stand and I stood behind the counter and gave out Cokes. Now, if they were strangers, I'd say, "Would you like to have a date?" and motion toward the back or something. If they didn't catch on and seemed kinda stupid, I said, "Well, it costs a buck." When I got wiser, I'd say it cost two dollars if I thought I could get away with it. But I was honest. I never rolled a drunk or did any of those awful things that you hear about people doing; I never hurt anybody.

Later on, when I was at a house in Galveston there was a young girl in there who had a man come in; he just wanted privacy to take dope. Well, she detested dope so she took her heels off and hit him on the head, laid his skull open . . . then came out and bragged about it.

I only stayed there in New Orleans one winter. Jackie only wanted me to do that in the wintertime—just to save up a little money and have a stake for the carnival season.

Like I say, I was very adaptable and I always tried to please people, including my husband.

One time in the afternoon when it was getting along about time for me to leave and he was getting a little bit amorous—well, I said no, we haven't got time. But then I got real affectionate all of a sudden because I really felt that way. And I said, but that's all right—go ahead, it'll make me feel good! And then I tried to explain that I could work better when I felt good—or that I could make more money when I felt good . . . I don't know . . . something like that. But that made him mad. He drew away then. He felt like I was asking him to get me hot for somebody else, you know.

But most of the time things were fine. He might buy something that I thought was too extravagant and that he didn't need, but I mean he didn't run around with another girl and spend my money on her or anything. . . . I don't think I would have put up with that, but then I don't know what I would have put up with.

The next winter I went to Jo Mae's in Galveston—it was one of those steam room things—and it was more convenient for me to stay at the place and live there and sleep there. So I bought Jackie a little trailer and he parked it nearby. Sometimes we'd take a little vacation when I got my "flowers." That's when you have your menstruation period. Now, that was a revelation to me. I'd never heard it called anything but "the sickness." Momma always called it "the curses." But flowers—now, wasn't that pretty? By golly, they hadn't given time off for that in New Orleans, come to think of it. You just wore a silk sponge—you used to be able to buy them in the drugstore—and you put this little silk sponge up in there, see, and you went right ahead working during that time.

One of the first girls I met in Galveston said when someone gave her a bed jacket—"Us whores don't have any use for things like that." That surprised me a little, that she would call us whores, but she explained it was a good name. "Chippie" was bad, because they were cheap and just chippie-ing around. Whores were honest.

In Galveston, I met my second husband. He saw me nine times and then he just took me out of there. It didn't bother me to walk out on Jackie at all—the fact that anybody thought you shouldn't walk out on your pimp was really astounding to me. One of the women took me aside and talked to me like that. I didn't see any reason why I should tell him anything. I just said, "Tell him I'm gone!"

It took me a year to get my divorce, but we got married, my second husband and I, and lived together twenty-one years until he died . . . see, he was nineteen years older than me.

Most people think whores don't like men, but that's not true. I love men. I need men. I'm crazy about men.

Oh, I don't mean in a sexual way. I'm not really sure I ever had an orgasm.

THE 1930s have been on Helen Meret's mind.

"Shopping is as frightening today as it was in the thirties," she told me. "How do poor people eat? I tried to buy a pound of rice at the store the other day. It was eighty-nine cents . . . I was shocked . . . rice is peasant food."

Helen lives alone since her husband Tom was killed while they were vacationing in Mexico. A bulletin board—covered with pictures of him, their children, and grandchildren—separates the small kitchen and living room.

"I always got along," she said with the pride of accomplishment. "I was the youngest of four children and grew up with everybody telling me what to do. It was natural that I learned early to accommodate myself to other people."

HELEN MERET'S STORY

I love Jewish rye bread. When we moved to New York to live with Tom's mother, I once overheard her complaining to my husband, "But she's always buying bread!"

When we got married we were both going to Carnegie Tech. A Pittsburgh newspaper wanted to interview us because we were one of the first married couples going to college together. We thought that was a silly idea—an interview. Besides my college life didn't last long. I got pregnant so Tom finished and I had the baby.

When Tom graduated in '33 we had no money and no job. Our parents felt it would be better if we lived apart. My mother wanted me to stay in Pittsburgh with her, and his mother wanted him to come home to New York alone. I think that's when I discovered I was married to a very unusual man. He told me nothing would touch us. We would be with each other and no one was going to break us up. He said nothing—family, economic conditions—nothing would ever separate us.

So we went to New York and moved in with his mother, Uncle Phil, and younger brother, David. We kept track of everything we spent so that some day we'd be able to pay her back. We lived there rent-free because there was no work for him in New York. Originally he thought when we went there that he would be able to get a job with the firm he had worked for every summer for years. He picked up all his drawing instruments and went downtown to the office and found it was closed. There was no work for architects in 1933.

So he did whatever he could—walked the streets and even sold insurance door-to-door—that kind of ten-cents-a-week sort of policy. One day he fell on the ice and did something to his knee so he couldn't even do that.

There was nothing for me to do at that time but raise a baby. And when you raise a baby in New York City you spend all your time outside, walking it or pushing it around in a buggy.

I remember I got up at four o'clock so I could get the baby's diapers done and out of the way before Grandma Lena got up. And I helped with the housework.

But mostly I played bridge with other young people out of work —two lawyers and some others. Everybody was out of work except the teachers. Before the Depression they had been on the low end of the professional scale; but all of a sudden they were high because they had work.

Really, I got along very well with his family. I wasn't deprived. Though I remember one thing I couldn't get enough of—fresh bread. When I moved to New York we used to get this wonderful Jewish rye bread. I overheard my mother-in-law say to my husband, "She's always buying bread!" That hurt. I knew she thought I was spending too much money. But then she was very kind, too, because I smoked and she would make sure that I had money for a pack of cigarettes—even though she hated my smoking she still would do that. So you see, one thing balanced the other, and I appreciated the good more than I resented the little innuendoes.

I had no bitterness. The most wonderful thing was that no matter what happened, Tom and I remained together, and we had that steady faith that there would be better times ahead for us.

And after four years, the time came. He got a job designing the new Queens County courthouse and our income jumped from zero to fifty dollars a week. We found a one-bedroom apartment at 60 Carrol Avenue in Yonkers. It was a lovely apartment with a small park in the back. We furnished the whole thing for under forty dollars with temporary furniture that we were going to get rid of later. Of course, I had it for years, you know. But life was beautiful because we were alone together and had many friends. All our friends lived within an income so when they came over they brought their own treats—and everybody did seem to end up at Tom and Helen's. When we could, we shared with them, and we thought those days were the greatest. Nothing touched us then.

We could even afford a babysitter occasionally, and I would go down to where Tom worked to meet him and we'd go to the Met—top balcony, last row. They were the cheapest seats in the house, but they were special to us.

You know what our big wish was? That someday we would be making so much money we'd have to pay income tax. In those days that meant you'd really arrived.

"MY HUSBAND AND I were divorced in 1940, and I went to work for Union Oil as a secretary," Eve Greeney told me, sipping coffee at her kitchen counter. "I never remarried.

"After I retired, I was afraid to stay on in the city by myself. You can't go out at night. It's just like being a prisoner."

She lives with her daughter's family near an Air Force base, bicycles instead of drives, and worries that the United States will go communist if there is another depression.

"My family sometimes thinks I'm a radical," she said, "but I worry what kind of world my grandchildren will grow up in."

EVE GREENEY'S STORY

My husband used to say: "I just hate to tell you anything because you get so excited and then when it doesn't materialize, you're way down."

When "talkies" came in, musicians had a depression all their own. My husband had been playing in pit orchestras for the Fanchon and Marco Shows—he was in on the tail end of vaudeville. But when talkies came, they came fast, and there were hundreds of musicians out of work in Seattle.

Because, you see, nightclubs and roadhouses were closing right and left. There was just no business, or not enough. It was sad to see men like Freddy Hizer, who had been a child violin prodigy, walking the streets or driving a garbage truck. I'll never forget, he used to laugh and call it the "salad wagon."

My husband was luckier than most. Greeney—everybody called him that—had a nice voice and he was an arranger and played trumpet. When times get hard, I guess the people who get jobs are the ones who can do the most and have the most versatile talents.

He was one of those, so it wasn't long 'til he was emcee of the KOL Karnival Hour, and he became a very popular local celebrity. For that, he made twenty dollars a week.

One time he took me to one of those "bucket of blood" speak-easies—they really did have sliding peepholes—where he was well-known. People would crowd around and want to buy him drinks.

That kind of life never appealed to me. I always had to get up early and go to work—any kind of work. I was a waitress, a switch-board operator. I did all kinds of jobs, anything I could get. When everybody would gather around Greeney, I usually sat over in a corner and I was very shy. I wasn't really noticed and pretty soon, if I could get him to take me home, we went home . . . but that was hard to do because he loved that life. He loved the attention, just ate it up and *drank* it up, too, I might add. But it wasn't very glamorous as far as I was concerned.

Wendall Nyles, the famous announcer, was originally from Seattle; once he came back and tried to talk my husband into going to Los Angeles. That's just when the networks were beginning to take hold, about 1932. He thought about it, but the union laws were very strict then. You couldn't take steady engagements for six months if you moved. And then, too, he was a big shot where he was, but in L.A. he would be a nobody. I'm sure he must have thought about that. So he didn't go.

Several other big deals came our way. Once, this booker said the Cafe Hotel in Shanghai, China, wanted a trumpet man. They wanted him to be good-looking, a singer, and single. Now this booker kept encouraging us. "We'll see. If they're pretty hard up, they may overlook the fact you're married." Best of all, they offered to pay him 300 "mecks" a month. I can't remember what a meck was in U.S. dollars, but we thought we'd be in the money. The booker kept saying, "They'll come across, I know they'll do it."

We were both really high, and everybody called to congratulate us. Greeney sent me to the Chinese consulate and I got a lot of information on living in China. Wow, we got built up, but the whole thing fell through. They wanted a single man so they could put two men together in a hotel room and they just wouldn't go for a married man.

Another time, we were all set to go to Johannesburg, South Africa. You know, I'd never been twenty miles from Seattle in my life and this was exciting beyond my dreams—like going to the moon. We even had our pictures taken down on the dock waving goodbye to the KOL band. That time our big backer just disappeared and left us with egg on our face.

I would just be crestfallen when this would happen, and I felt like life wasn't worth living. My husband used to say to me: "I just hate to tell you anything because you get so excited and then when it doesn't materialize, you're way down."

But my biggest problem was I didn't really know anything about music. I made such terrible mistakes that were humiliating to my poor husband. I remember on one occasion I heard the fellas talking about Grieg's Concerto and one evening this piano player came over waving a piece of sheet music, yelling: "I've got it!" It was Grieg's Concerto and I suppose I just heard what he said with half an ear. After he played it, it was so beautiful that I was really impressed and wanted to say something nice. "So that's Greek's Concerto," I said, very knowingly. Everybody laughed but my husband. He was so embarrassed. I kept explaining, "That's what I thought they said. It sounded like that to me."

A RETIRED nursery school teacher-owner, she has never been in good health since her three miscarriages: two of them in the 1930s. "But I'm not having any more operations," she assured me, listing her four major surgeries. "I'm dying with everything I got left."

VIVIAN RAYMOND WESTON'S STORY
Mormons believe marriage and home are sacred . . . what you can't change you learn to live with.

The only place we could rent was a little attic—one big room and off to the side a little room. The little room was our pantry and we'd put all the food we got from my husband's family in there —cabbage, apples, carrots, and potatoes, enough to last all winter. One winter they froze, and I had to peel snowballs for months.

We could only stand upright in this room about three feet through the center, because after that the roof started to slope sharply and you'd have to walk bent over. I had this little table where I washed dishes, and I'd have to stand with my head tilted over to one side.

But, you know, we didn't really mind. We laughed about it. When you're young and in love, hardships are jokes. And, too, I think Mormons tend to believe marriage and the home are sacred. So you learn to accept problems. What you can't change you learn to live with.

From 1930 to 1933 my husband went to United States Agricultural College in Logan, Utah, and we lived just any way we could to stay alive and keep him in school. Did odd jobs and picked potatoes and what we could. I didn't know that there were hazards to being pregnant and doing hard work, so I went out picking potatoes to try to help out. I thought I was a heathy, strong girl, but on the way home from the field I stopped at his grandmother's place because I had so much pain across my back. She said, "Honey, sit on the oven a bit." She had this old-fashioned oven that let down and you used to be able to sit on it and warm your back. I was sitting there— the worst thing in the world for me to do—and hemorrhaging. When she saw what was happening, she got me to bed fast.

It was a small town. There were only two doctors. One refused to take care of me because I wasn't his patient and couldn't come to the hospital. The other said he'd come as soon as he delivered a baby.

He came, but it seemed like hours. He told me if it had been ten minutes more he couldn't have saved me 'cause I'd lost too much blood. The fetus didn't come, so he had to take it. And I always thought that's why that other doctor wouldn't handle me because it was considered, I guess, like an abortion.

We did everything to get my husband through college. After we lived in the attic we moved to this little house and I mean it was little. Just one room. Cost us six dollars a month and my husband worked as a night watchman from two to four o'clock in the morning. We didn't own an alarm clock. All I had was my wristwatch. I'd have to stay awake until about a quarter to two, so I'd be sure and get him up. He'd be so tired. He never got enough sleep, studying and going to school and working, too. I'd have to get in behind him and just push him onto the floor and even help him dress. But he earned fifteen dollars a month for that job and that's what we lived on; that's *all* we lived on.

We had a stove, a bed, a table, and a couple of chairs. In the winter, my icebox was a washtub hung outside the window against the house. I'd buy a dime's worth of hamburger, divide it into three balls, wrap it up, and put it in that washtub. It would freeze just as good as in a refrigerator and I'd take it out and fix it different ways. It would last us a week. The lady next door gave us some vegetables and skim milk. We lived on that.

About the third year he was in school, all my clothes wore out at once. My shoes had holes so I kept putting pasteboard in the bottom, until the shoes finally fell apart. Then when I'd go to town, I'd wear my rubbers—nobody could tell there weren't any shoes under there—then pretty soon the rubbers wore out. My dresses all got threadbare across the bust. That summer my mother came to visit me and she got real mad: "Why didn't you tell me you were having such a rough time of it?"

Toward the end of our years there, our money problems did ease up a bit. My health still wasn't very good. I was anemic so when I got pregnant again I told the doctor I had been dizzy and my head kept ringing. He told me he didn't know whether I'd be able to carry the baby full term, but he said I just might if I ate lots of sauerkraut and liver.

My husband bought a whole case of sauerkraut and every time he was in town, he would go see the butcher and load up with liver. I hated liver. I couldn't stand sauerkraut, but I ate it—twenty-three cans of it—but that last can I dumped out. I just couldn't eat it. Right on schedule, I had the healthiest baby the doctor ever seen.

There wasn't a lot of time for amusements. But this elderly couple next door used to invite us in every Friday night to play "Crazy Annie." I guess it's a little like Old Maids, only Crazy Annie was the queen of spades. It was a Danish game, and I never played it since, but we used to have the most fun. And, oh, did we look forward to Friday night because they always had dessert . . . applesauce with whipped cream and thick slices of sweet brown bread with butter on it.

Sometimes I'd get to go to the movies. I'd go to the Billy Curl Show—that was a theater in Logan—a strictly western house. I didn't particularly like westerns but it was only ten cents. Since we didn't have two dimes, I'd go while my husband sat in the lobby and studied until I came out. Then we'd walk home.

We always tried to save where we could—even if it was only a nickel. For instance, when we'd get our groceries, we couldn't afford two bus rides so I'd sit in the hotel with the bags and let two buses go by, then I'd catch the third. That always gave him time to walk to where we lived and meet me. All of that to save the extra bus fare. A nickel was just that important.

One thing I forgot to tell you. When I was pregnant, the doctor also told me to get out and walk in the sunshine, and so that summer I'd go out walking all I could. I walked the street and the mountains with my lambs.

I had raised two little lambs and they'd follow me, just like in the nursery rhyme. I'd wander around the ditch-banks with them and watch them prance along and play all day. They were the sweetest things, and I loved them.

I tried everything to get someone to take them when we were leaving, since they couldn't come with me. But they had to go, they had to go. My father-in-law sold them to a butcher who came through town. To see my lambs thrown into a cattle truck and hauled away was horrible, just horrible.

I remember afterwards, I went down to this country store where my lambs used to go with me and the man said, "Well, I don't see Pete and Jack with you, today." I just broke down and blubbered. I told him what had happened, and I said, "It was just like selling my sons."

What a silly thing to say. What that man must have thought.

IN HER EIGHTIES NOW, Ella Weesner is a small woman with a head of thick, white hair cut very short.

"Now I don't mean to say my husband was a bad man," she said, looking a little worried. "I just mean to say he was a very proud man. And sometimes when a man is that proud it makes it hard on his family. Can you understand that?

"After the Depression was over and the girls had grown and gone, things was easier. We had some better times together till he died."

ELLA WEESNER'S STORY

All that worrying made him spiteful. When I'd call him for dinner, he'd just ignore me.

He couldn't find work anywhere but he didn't want me to work, either. He was too proud. His pride caused us to have to do without when it wasn't really necessary.

We never had a Christmas tree. At school they'd let the poorest kid take the class tree home, but my girls never did. Their daddy wouldn't have stood for it. Somebody else always got the tree.

I remember we decorated the living room lamp one year—with paper rings and an angel that my girl Teola colored at school.

Now he was a hard worker, my husband—a conscientious man. He just never learned to give an inch. And he never knew what clothes meant to a girl. It was just no use asking him for a new dress.

I felt real bad when my girls started high school in Sioux Falls. Seems there were two groups of girls—lawyers' and doctors' daughters who had nice clothes, and the ones, like my daughters, who didn't have anything.

Can you imagine they voted on a best-dressed girl right in the middle of the Depression? Still makes me mad to think the teachers would allow such a thing.

You see, my husband could have had some jobs but he never liked to work for anybody. He wanted to be his own boss. He wanted to be the head of everything—including me.

Those hard years caused a lot of arguing. I remember we would argue like mad. It was money, always money. He would sit around and be so depressed because there was just nothing he could do. He was an ambitious man who really wanted to get ahead.

Well, all that worrying made him spiteful. I remember he'd be listening to the radio and I'd call him for dinner, and he'd just ignore me. He'd hear me all right, and that's when we'd get into it.

But I'd always give in. It seems I had to give in to keep peace. There weren't any divorces in my day.

I used to listen to the radio a lot—programs like "Ma Perkins" and "Stella Dallas," and I'd cry. The tears would be rolling down my face while I did my housecleaning.

I could just put myself in those women's place and imagine how they felt.

A MONTANA WOMAN

I had all seven of my babies at home. The sixth one was a breech birth, and I had a terrible time. The doctor came and said the baby would never live, and I probably wouldn't either. I heard him talking outside to my husband. But we did pull through—both the baby and me. Then I told my husband I didn't want any more. I was scared to death I would get pregnant again; but in those days the husband had the say. A woman didn't know any way to stop having babies; we had a whole flock of 'em before we knew how it happened. We didn't talk about such things among ourselves—not even women together—so if anybody had any information it was never passed along to me.

The man was the master; the only thing we knew that would stop children was abstinence, and no man is ever gonna go for that.

I had babies as long as I was able—past wantin' to. But the men had all the say-so. It sure looks to me like they coulda used a little better judgment, I think.

BORN INTO A NEW YORK CITY German immigrant family, Anna Griffin devoted the years between grammar school and marriage to hospital work. Two influences—her mother's Teutonic housekeeping and the hospital's sterile standards—created problems for her later. "My Kansas in-laws acted absolutely offended because I starched my housedresses and wore white gloves," she said. "They considered me some kind of show-off, and we never got along."

Today Anna lives near her daughter, Charlotte, and they visit each other every morning.

ANNA GRIFFIN'S STORY

When we could pay the electric bill, Ray would turn on the radio and we'd dance all over the house. . . .

One Sunday morning at breakfast—it was the summer of '33— I saw Ray looking sad. At first he wouldn't tell me what was wrong but I insisted and it all came tumbling out. "I just feel like I have to go home to Kansas," he told me.

I said, "Well, your vacation comes up in September; why don't we take the train to Wichita then?" When we figured it up, that was too expensive so I said, "All right, why don't you take a leave of absence from the bank?"

He didn't think he could get one because jobs were still scarce in New York City and he was earning twenty-nine dollars a week—a big salary in those days. He was surprised when they said it was OK—without pay of course.

That last Friday night he brought home his final paycheck and a long stemmed red rose for me. He'd saved out of his lunch money that week and paid fifteen cents for it in the subway. He was always a thoughtful, sentimental man. He called me his "charm." You see, I was his third wife so I was the charm. Oh, we had lots of adjustments to make because we both came from such different environments; but we worked at it.

Now my biggest problem was that he loved to eat, and I had never learned how to make even a pot of coffee—mama was one of those German women who would not let anyone in her kitchen. Ever!

Anyway, where was I? Oh yes, this Friday night he came home from work, and I'd sold all the furniture. That surprised him, but I explained that was the only way we were going to have enough money to make it. I knew in my heart we weren't ever coming back, anyway.

The next day he took the car in—it was a Star—and the mechanic scared him to death. "It's got a cracked block," he said. "You'll never make it to Kansas. Wherever it gives out, just leave it and catch the bus."

What else could we do? We went on. We couldn't buy another car. We'd sold our furniture and our friends were having a going away party for us that night.

We got some money as gifts from our friends and my dad slipped me twenty dollars when I said good-bye—my parents just knew I was going to be killed by Indians.

We left on Saturday morning with eighty-six dollars. All our bedding and suitcases in the bottom of the back seat were built up to make a bed for our daughter, Charlotte. A bunch of our friends trailed along behind us for awhile, and a good thing, too. The car broke down and they pushed us to the nearest station. The points needed adjusting or something. Finally, we were on our way; they said good-bye in New Jersey and turned around.

By that night we reached the border of Pennsylvania. We found a camping ground for cars, cooked our supper, put our bedding on the ground, and then left before daylight the next morning.

That trip turned into a nightmare. We cussed that blasted car up every hill. It took more oil to get us to Wichita than it took gasoline, and that car would stall on every incline. One day I told Ray it looked like we were going to have to push the darned thing clear to Kansas.

On top of that, the roads weren't good. There was no Pennsylvania Turnpike then. We had no money for a hotel so at night we would stop at an all-night filling station that had a café and get permission to park in back and sleep. People were sure nice; they'd let us use their restrooms and bring us a big bucket of hot water in the morning to wash in.

But I didn't get anything more than a "spit bath" for a week, and that was harder on me than sleeping on the ground.

When we got there, we stayed with his family 'til he got a job. It was like a new world to me. I'd never seen a bathroom in the backyard and a pump on the back porch. I thought I would have to become a regular pioneer woman, but Ray soon found work and we bought a house down the street that had a bathroom inside, where it should be.

For a few years everything went well for us. Ray worked for the best dairy in Wichita, servicing hotels and restaurants. He made twenty-five dollars a week plus commission. But then when it looked like everybody else was coming out of the Depression, we had ours.

My papa died in my house while he was visiting that year. Woke up one morning saying he felt constipated and I cooked him some prunes. Later on, he stopped by the kitchen to tell me it looked like they were going to help, and went on into the bathroom. About five minutes later I heard this heavy thump, and somehow I knew it was papa and I knew he was dead.

Well, he had fallen off the toilet and wedged against the door and I couldn't get him out of there. I was very upset and crying and I didn't know what else to do, so I called Ray. He said he'd be right home after he got a replacement for his route.

So he came home and helped with laying out papa on the bed, and called the doctor and everything. Then after that was taken care of, he went back to work only to find that the man who said he'd get a replacement for him *hadn't,* and all his customers were calling in mad. He was fired, you know, right on the spot, and nothing he said made any difference.

Then the bad times started for us. He couldn't get a job, and we couldn't get on relief because we had a home, and *we were too clean.* That's right. The case worker told us we didn't *look* like we needed relief—my house was too clean, my kid was too clean, and I wore starched white aprons. Cleanliness was a virtue where I came from, and I never got over being penalized for it.

I remember Ray would walk sixteen blocks to town every morning and pick up any job he could—maybe helping out in a filling station. At noon he would collect his pay and stop at the grocery store to buy bread and a little package of lunch meat. If he hadn't come home like that, Charlotte and I would not have eaten lunch many days.

But Ray always seemed to find some odd job to make a few cents —and sometimes he would find all-day jobs, but still he would walk home at noon so we could eat. He'd no more than get home, until he'd have to turn around and go right back again.

In spite of all that, he was a happy man. Always singing and laughing. I could hear him whistling down the block before I could see him.

We managed to hang on to the house, by scrimping and scraping and selling our things off one by one. And my brother in New York, who worked for a coffee, tea, and spice liquidating house—well, every month he would send us five pounds of the best coffee and tea and spices and cocoa, and my sister-in-law would send a new housedress with an apron to match or maybe some very colorful linen dishtowels.

Those packages came just like clockwork—even our mailman would say, "It's getting close to when you get your package."

What really saved us was the city weed tax on empty lots. There were three lots next to us. Ray wrote the owner asking could he clear their weeds and plant a garden. Back came a telegram, "Please plant garden." A neighbor bought the seed and we did the work and split the produce.

We had a closeness between us. Every evening after supper when

Charlotte was in bed, Ray and I would get together at the kitchen table and we'd discuss our situation. Once in a while one of us would come up with some crackpot idea to make some money and that helped a little bit. And if the electricity wasn't turned off—which it was when we couldn't pay the bill—Ray would turn on the radio and we'd dance all over the house from the living room into the kitchen, down the hall and back again.

Then one day we heard that there were going to be federal government jobs opening up, so Ray put on a business suit and a white shirt left over from his days at the bank, and went down to the Alice Hotel to apply for what turned out to be the first FHA. Men were picked for their appearance and so he was one of a hundred chosen out of literally thousands who applied.

His job was to go house to house, business to business, taking a poll in writing as to what they needed done to their property in the way of repairs. He was to try to get people to sign up for government mortgage money . . . long term and low interest.

Sometimes he had to encourage them, and sometimes browbeat them into accepting money; a lot of them actually refused to have anything to do with it. They thought it was some kind of gimmick. I even went with him sometimes to try to impress the wives with the idea that this was a real opportunity to fix up their homes.

A CHICANA WOMAN

Some people used to ask me how I could live with one man so long—I say, "Because when he come through the front door, I go through the back door." See, I use to work in the night shift at the cannery.

That's the best way you can live with your husband without having a lot of headaches. When somebody ask: "How come you have so many kids?" . . . I say, "Well, every now and then I don't make it to the back door."

PART TWO
GROWING UP FEMALE IN THE THIRTIES

LINES FROM THE 1934 POEM, "Land of the Free," written by Archibald MacLeish* could sum up the spirit of young thirties women: "We don't know, we can't say, we're wondering . . ."

He could have added, "but we are not afraid."

The year MacLeish wrote those words 21 million young Americans were searching the scarred landscape for a place—an identity. One who found it was Betty Coed.

Who was Betty Coed? She was the popularized female counterpart to Joe College in scores of thirties movies, ads, and stories. As more colleges became coeducational and jobs became scarcer, thousands of young women entered college who might otherwise never have considered higher education.

By 1932, over 372,000 young women were studying, many going on for graduate degrees. They received two out of every five masters degrees and one of every ten doctorates during the thirties. Scholarly pursuits for women, considered unnecessary (if not downright unhealthy) a brief generation earlier, became an accepted part of the American college scene.

Although tuition and expenses could mount to $1,000 a year at prestigious Eastern schools, small land-grant colleges charged as little as twenty-five dollars tuition a semester. And during the latter part of the decade, many students received grants from the National

* Archibald MacLeish, *Land of the Free,* (New York: Harcourt Brace Jovanovich, Inc.)

Youth Administration, an arm of the WPA. Grants could take the fòrm of monthly stipends for after-class jobs or outright loans.

Betty Coed had considerably more freedom than her predecessors, but once on campus she was still faced with a bewildering array of Victorian rules regulating her life. One woman's college insisted: "Students will not be permitted off campus without hats, gloves, and all appurtenances of complete street costume." Chaperonage was common, and the least hint of scandal could result in disgrace and dismissal.

It's surprising that Betty Coed had as much fun as she did. But she did. Blanket parties, rumble-seat rides, "necking" (done but not discussed), sports, and bull sessions—all provided a well-rounded, if somewhat physical, social life.

But the most fun of all, especially after 1936, was dancing. Even the smallest school could hire a monthly swing band . . . and nightly radio and record hops probably lowered more than one A grade to a B.

How did she budget her time? Not much differently than male scholars, according to a five-year study published in 1937. A college woman spent her time: (1) sleeping, (2) sitting, (3) in class, and (4) studying, in that order. The report explained that when a young lady was "sitting," she was generally socializing or talking. What did she talk about? *Life* magazine revealed her favorite topics were: personalities, sex, careers, and religion, in that order.

Though most thirties coeds may have expended their energy on only four problems, experts at Stephens College for women in Missouri compiled a monumental list of 7,400 women's worries. In an effort to solve them, the college designed a "modern curriculum" where Stephens girls were taught the science of beauty, dress, and voice—all in an atmosphere *Life* described as "swank."

While some women's colleges continued the finishing school philosophy of an earlier day, most maintained high scholastic standards.

Not that fashion wasn't important everywhere in academia. After 1935, the sensible campus brogue gave way to saddle shoes and anklets. Cardigan sweaters were buttoned up the back (even in *Vogue*), and worn with a scarf. Shorts and slacks were in, especially in western colleges, and the silk dress and long formal were as important to pack every September as underwear.

To complete the fashion picture, Betty Coed, like most women, was sold on products which vanquished Madison Avenue's unholy trinity—body odor, pink toothbrush, and chapped hands. She bought Mum so that classmates wouldn't "suddenly recoil," Ipana for "that tell-tale warning on your toothbrush," and Hinds Honey and Almond Cream because "he loves the touch of silken smooth hands."

For those young women whose figures may have ballooned in response to midnight dormitory snacks or endless sorority teas, the thirties had its own fad diets. The Hollywood diet consisted of citrus fruit and a prepared toast along with modest amounts of raw vegetables and coffee. Dr. Hay's diet banned "antagonistic" foods —in other words, protein *or* carbohydrates could be eaten, but not both at the same meal. This diet also advocated daily cathartics and enemas—which could put a positive crimp in a girl's social life if the diet hadn't already. Along with these, a coed could try the less rigorous tomato and egg diet, the lamb chop and pineapple diet, or the potato and buttermilk diet. Whatever the weight-losing plan, most diet articles of the day ended with the caution that Leta Lee, Barbara LaMarr, Renée Adorée, and Louis Wolheim—all famous Hollywood stars—had died from overdieting.

Despite the frivolity that was a delightful part of every thirties college career, 50,000 purposeful adult women with degrees in arts and sciences spilled into the job market every June. Those who had no secretarial skills were counseled into business colleges to acquire them. Those who had no clerical aptitude could find their way in sales. "We like the college type when they are attractive as well as brainy," commented the vice-president of a large New York City department store.

Apparently the operative word was "attractive." An employment agency in the same city advised a 1936 Vassar grad that "the tilt of your chin might be more important than the speed of your typing and shorthand."

Most capable women graduates faced the prospect of under-utilization in the tradition-dominated and contracted employment scene of the 1930s. Nevertheless, in spite of their frustrations, they had equipped themselves for fuller lives, to know better the business of living in a make-do world.

But most young thirties' women didn't go near a college except the "college of hard knocks." For them, the American dream had gone cockeyed. They were underemployed, unemployed, and some thousands of them had turned to the hostile highways. Most, however, stayed at home—experimenting with life and learning to type.

Politically, they had been radicalized by unionist, socialist, and communist propaganda. In an interview of twenty-six young people published in 1937, the words "proletarian," "masses," and "revolution" dominated their remarks.

Young women, particularly later in the decade, were more realistic than had been their older sisters. They had seen the faces of rural women caught in Margaret Bourke-White's lens, heard of the striking garment workers marching arm in arm down New York's Fifth Avenue, and perhaps even read one of the many books critical of the American way.

But they diluted their realism with large measures of fun—just "getting together," playing cards, dancing, or talking wildly off the tops of their heads. Nor were they above fantasy, since every young woman of the thirties knew a dozen classic Hollywood success stories—Hollywood was the only place in which the dream was still intact—where from nothingness and nobodyhood a woman could be lifted to riches and success overnight.

Younger girls (they weren't called teen-agers until later) lived in the familiar limbo between baby fat and curves, reading such incredible "true life stories" as: *The Girl Who Made Up a Baby* and *She Was No Longer a Woman Above Reproach.*

Preteen girls of the thirties had the greatest identity problem of any recorded decade—they had the Dionne quintuplets and Shirley Temple. The quints, smiling and healthy and five, endorsed breakfast cereals that no right-thinking kid would eat. But it was Shirley who made many a little girl's life hell. It was reported she had exactly sixty-five curls, which set off a boom in children's permanents—or at least brought about a daily singeing with the curling iron. Adding further to the trauma of growing up female in the thirties, were the would-be stage mothers who dipped into meager Depression paychecks for tap lessons. It's no wonder. The adorable

Temple tapped down innumerable staircases—never missing a beat —in movie after movie.

For years after, tap dancers showed up at school assemblies, amateur shows, and talent contests—their slap kicks and spiral turns a staccato reminder of the 1930s fad.

Deep into the decade, young women found more and more freedom. They could smoke without ruining their reputation (their health was not yet in question)—Wings, if they only had a dime, but Lucky Strikes or Camels if they were flush.

An ad campaign appearing in many women's magazines depicted a glamorous society matron in a Saks Fifth Avenue frock, smoking a Camel. The message implied: smoking was for the sophisticated or those who aspired to that desirable grace.

Drinking, while hardly condoned, was nonetheless an attractive sin—enough to prompt this warning from Margaret Culkin Banning in *McCall's* November, 1935 issue: "Liquor isn't kind to women. It ravages their looks and their loves and their homes. The truce you girls make with it now . . . may be all right if you never trust it. But don't think it will ever be your friend."

Growing up female during the Depression decade was youth without precedent. Old faiths had decayed; Victorian traditions were gone; patterns of behavior were no longer stable. A society, falling apart, granted women more freedom and yet more accountability. Instead of sharing the responsibility for her sexual honor with men, she had to work out her own salvation. The burden made her the most "self"-conscious woman in the country's history.

Chapter Five

BETTY COED

KIRSTEN VANDENBERG is a stylishly dressed, neatly coiffed woman with light, sparkling eyes and a North Sea complexion—a gift from her Danish mother.

I visited with her one Saturday afternoon, two weeks before Christmas. Sitting in the midst of cards, wrappings, and decorations, she said: "It's been such a long time, I must apologize for my memory. So many things have happened since then."

KIRSTEN RICHARDS VANDENBERG'S STORY

The college women I knew were ambitious . . . serious about it. That doesn't mean we didn't have lots of fun, but not what you would call frivolity.

Thornton Township Junior College near my home in Harvey, Illinois, was one of the first junior colleges in the country, and that's where I started in '33. I had graduated from Thornton Township High School and the college was right in the same building.

My father was my teacher in English and German. He spoke six languages . . . or maybe seven. I remember sometimes he was paid in Standard Oil coupon books, which he could cash at a discount.

There was never any question but that I was going to college. My mother who died when I was eight, was a teacher; my grandfather was a professor; and my aunt was a doctor. It was just assumed that I would go to college—no question.

I knew that two years of junior college would be it, if I didn't get outside help. Thank heaven, I got a scholarship to the University of Chicago for my junior year.

The summer before I started at UC, I worked at the Chicago World's Fair in the Tyrolean village selling some kind of German licorice candy. You wouldn't believe the crowds of people; they just didn't stop coming even though the fair was in its second year. The monorail—it must have been one of the first—was famous. It had two little cars, one called Amos and one called Andy. They had a fabulous science building, but everyone thought the monorail was the last word.

I got my scholarship based on a six-hour competitive exam. It was renewable the second year if I maintained a certain grade average.

But I didn't quite make it. I had pretty good grades, but they weren't tremendous. I really got desperate about my last year until my aunt, the physician, stepped in at the last minute and paid my tuition. It was $300 a year and that was terribly high.

One of the reasons my grades weren't so high was that I always had about four or five jobs going at one time. During my junior year, I got an NYA grant. I think it was fifteen dollars a month, for which I typed a manuscript for a history professor who was writing a great, huge book. I also worked in the cafeteria, in the checkroom in the women's clubhouse, took care of kids, and worked on the desk in the dormitory.

The girls' dorms were really inexpensive living—they were converted men's dorms and didn't have a dining room. But we did have hot plates in the basement where we cooked meals.

Pitching woo? Sure I remember that term, but mostly we talked in terms of necking and petting. And there was a fair amount of that going on. I know, but uh . . . you were fairly careful about it because, for one thing, abortions were darn hard to get in those days. I remember one girl that got in trouble and she managed to get an abortion. She later married a well-known journalist but she was considered "not nice" even after that. Nobody liked her. And the attitude at Chicago was much less condemnatory than it was in many places. A girl from my hometown got into this sort of situation and her parents . . . Lord, it was a major tragedy.

I didn't have much in the way of clothes, but then I didn't need too many. I had one formal gown, and I could borrow shoes and a purse. We traded our things; there was a lot of that going on.

At the University of Chicago they gave a comprehensive exam for bachelor's degree candidates. And when you graduated, what determined your ranking was your exam, not your course grades. It was a two-day exam, and the pressure was really tremendous. They weren't objective questions but long essay types. It was a physically grueling thing, and my eyes were beginning to bother me. And, oh boy, that two-day exam about threw me. I immediately went to the eye doctor and got glasses.

In spite of everything, I graduated in '37 and even managed to come out Phi Beta Kappa.

That year a friend of mine talked me into joining a sorority, and I've always been glad she did. Chicago had a very unusual sorority system; it was strictly local and there were no houses so it didn't cost a lot.

My mother had died when I was very young. My father brought me up, and I had never picked up the standard social practices that a girl was supposed to learn—like how to give a tea, how to make hors d'oeuvres, and things like that. Besides that, I got to go to dances and social things that otherwise I wouldn't have gone to.

We used to give teas in the women's clubhouse. Once I remember we invited the mothers, and once we had a reception for someone . . . I've forgotten who. But I remember, I talked my present husband into coming and he was mad as hops because he didn't want to. And I got to one football game in all the time I was there, and I think that was the last year they played ball. The score was eighty-seven to nothing or something like that, so maybe that's why they quit playing. Chicago had really more of an intellectual atmosphere than sports or social anyway. I think it has that reputation and it's true.

During the Depression, college students were very labor conscious, and the big thing to do was to go and picket. I never did, but I had many friends who did. I was always too busy and then it was a group that flirted a little with communism. It was just a flirtation; it never got serious. But it's certainly true that communism was very attractive in the thirties. Pacifism was another strong movement, at least until we started getting so many professors escaping from Nazi Europe. Then pacifism wasn't such a popular idea.

I remember hearing Norman Thomas speak on campus. I even voted for him once. He was really rather intellectual and not a rabble rouser type. He never did have much real popular appeal . . . wasn't the right personality. And Josef Benes spoke—you know the president of Czechoslovakia. He was an inspiring man.

After I graduated there was never any question but that I would go on and do my graduate work in American history. Most of my friends went on to graduate school; at Chicago it was a tradition. It was an accepted thing that a woman would have a profession at least until she married.

It took me three years to get my master's because I had to go to work full time. I worked for Time, Inc. in circulation on the night shift, and then after a year I got a research assistant job and did that for the rest of the time I was there.

I had been trying and trying to get that fellowship, and that was the first time I ran into the attitude that I was different because I was a woman. I remember I was talking to one professor, and he kind of looked at me and smiled. He said, "Well, you know, let's face it, you're going to get married, and it isn't fair for you to take a fellowship from a man."

Outside of that one incident, Chicago was probably better than most, so far as attitude toward women was concerned, because it was very intellectual and we were accepted if we had something intelligent to say. Didn't make any difference, except that once.

During the thirties when I went to college, the women I knew were ambitious—and serious about it. That doesn't mean we didn't have lots of fun, but there wasn't a lot of what you would call frivolity. There may have been on other campuses, but not at U.C. One of my girl friends became a professor of social service, another a personnel officer for the navy. They did things.

One of our biggest complaints at that time was against the size of the university; we just thought it was a big, impersonal machine. There were about 6,000 students there then.

IN THE WORLD of the white South where I spent my girlhood, blacks were Negroes, and they entered and exited from my life in a series of cultural exchanges, much like the comings and goings of the modern Moiseyev Dance troupe. On Brotherhood Sunday, the minister of the Negro Baptist church across the river switched pulpits with our own Dr. Ring. Services were always crowded with the curious those Sunday mornings, and our choir would tediously present their version of well-known spirituals in a musically ecumenical effort of welcome. I remember the astonished comments after the service would always center around the Negro minister's speech which was as cultured and erudite as our own good reverend's.

During my high school years, we exchanged assemblies with George Washington Carver High—across the river. My friends and I—the jazz liberals of the day—thought their band was the grooviest, and we brought our auditorium down with applause. Once I went to *their* high school as part of a program. I remember walking down the corridors past a gauntlet of unfamiliar black faces, experiencing the shock and aloneness of my difference. I smiled at them, what I hoped was a friendly smile.

Thirty years later, while sitting comfortably before a log fire in Eva Rutland's home, I talked with her and Isabel Gassett, her friend from college days in Atlanta. Both are black women of achievement: Eva, an author; Isabel, a political appointee in the governor's office.

EVA RUTLAND'S AND ISABEL GASSETT'S STORY

Eva. We were protected . . . all through college my daddy would say, "Don't go to places alone."

Isabel. A white man who might not dare accost a white girl is safe in his advances on a black girl.

Isabel. I didn't feel any great contrast between the Depression years and the twenties. We didn't have much to begin with so we didn't have much to lose. It must have been pretty bad, but somehow we didn't feel poor; we had about what everybody seemed to have at that time.

As for the girls I went to college with . . . whose parents were maybe professional people . . . I didn't have any feeling that they were privileged.

Eva. That's right, I didn't even think about it.

Isabel. No, you didn't, and when they had their parties we were invited. When we had ours, they were invited.

Eva. It was the overall identification with school, I think.

Isabel. The difficult thing to explain to you is that segregation, as it was practiced then, was like the weather. Just like I know we're going to have cold days in the winter, I accepted segregation. You know you don't go jumping up and down and cussing the elements because the sun isn't shining. Well, the pattern of segregation in my childhood in the South was an accepted thing, like the weather.

Atlanta had a unique complex of schools and colleges for blacks. Going to Atlanta University was the biggest thing you could aspire to, and economic status was not a part of that. I was treated just like the girls whose daddies sent them up from Savannah to live on campus. We all dressed alike, because there were strict dress rules: middy blouses and skirts so that there would be overall uniformity, lest some girl feel that another was dressed better. The wife of the president, Mrs. Adams, watched what you wore to be sure you were not bedecked with necklaces and earrings and inappropriate things. I didn't realize then that she was trying to show us that the embellishments have no meaning, they just get in the way of education.

Eva. And it was a great era for education. Most of the teachers had been in universities in New England and had worked 'til retirement. They loved to come south for the winter. So that meant we had solid, experienced New England people . . . they taught us the meaning of solidarity, fairness, and emphasis on the intellectual. They were white, elderly men and women but they were marvelous teachers. There was no distance between us.

It was an unusual situation because nowhere else did we ever see white people. Our neighborhood was solidly black. There were two black areas of Atlanta connected by a streetcar which carried only black passengers, and there was no contact with whites; there was no reason for it. So we built up this tremendous security among our own people.

Isabel. There was a deep sense of community and a deep sense of family. I think it was unique to Atlanta because I remember visiting Savannah and Durham where I ran into a different atmosphere.

All our universities—there were four of them for blacks in Atlanta—had been founded by the American Missionary Association after the Civil War. I heard my papa and cousin talking about how the first classes were held in boxcars after Atlanta was burned.

Eva. Yes, and there was a high school for blacks in that complex because the public high school was not built until the late twenties. I remember my mama thought the new high school must be a terrible place where there was a lot of fighting.

During that time, the Rockefellers were great contributors to the universities, and one of them would always come to commencement and stay in our dormitories—not in downtown hotels. We thought that was just tremendous, so I think this kind of thing plus our elderly white teachers prevented the hatred that many blacks had for whites.

Isabel. Many a black girl and boy were able to work their way through college because of the Rockefeller endowments. They would work in the kitchen, the dining room, cleaning the halls . . . and sometimes it would take five years instead of four to finish, but they would finish.

I had to take care of my daddy and four brothers, so the school gave me special permission to leave campus around noon and even miss the chapel period. I would run home, dropping by the grocery store, and start dinner. Sometimes I'd kill a chicken and get the beans cooking, do whatever else the house needed, and then rush back to school just in time for Latin class.

Eva. It wasn't all work though. We had parties, social parties that were done in the right way. I had a debut in '37 when I finished college because I finished very young.

It was beautiful. The mothers of the girls gave several small parties in their homes, then topped it off with a big dance at the Top Hat which was the top of the Odd Fellows building. It was owned by black people and had a dance area on the roof.

Isabel. I was there and it was grand: a reception and a band and punch, and everybody was dressed. . . .

Eva. That's right. The men came in tuxedos. . . .

Isabel. . . . yes, done up right. That is one of the things I think Southerners are most particular about, the proper dress for the occasion.

Eva. We were protected all through school and college. My daddy would say, "Don't go places alone." The idea was if you were a black girl outside your area and a white man decided to insult you . . . nothing could be done. My family made a complete life within the black community; our doctor was a black man, and so was our dentist. My whole world was absolutely, comfortably, beautifully black.

Isabel. Some of the girls wanted to work downtown as waitresses, you know, and I asked my daddy if I could—to earn extra money. Daddy said, "You will never go to work downtown. Not the way white men think about black women."

Eva. Yes, a black woman was free prey, you know.

Isabel. You see, a white man that might not dare accost a white girl is safe in his advances on a black girl. Why? Because in court her papa or brothers or any black man—even a black lawyer—wouldn't dare stand up against one white man.

Eva. The answer to all that was to protect us from it ever happening. Yes, and when we were students . . .

Isabel. . . . when we were students, it wouldn't occur to us to do what students later did. I don't know whether I should apologize for it, but it just didn't exist in our hearts and minds at that time. Imagine a bunch of black college students going into Woolworth's and sitting down there. Why Woolworth's had been there for years and years; we were so trained and segregation was so engrained into our way of life. . . .

Eva. It's not that we weren't proud. We were. I remember going to church and singing the beautiful spirituals, and at school the Negro national anthem. It's the most beautiful song; James Weldon Johnson, one of our first black poets wrote it. I don't think there was a black Atlanta college student who didn't know the words . . . we learned every verse and every word.

*Eva and Isabel. Lift every voice and sing
               Till earth and heaven ring,
               Ring with the harmonies of Liberty;*

Let our rejoicing rise
High as the listening skies,
Let it resound loud as the rolling sea.
Sing a song full of the faith
that the dark past has taught us,
Sing a song full of the hope
that the present has brought us.
Facing the rising sun
of our new day begun
Let us march on till victory is won.

Isabel. It's very stirring—the melody is as strong as the words and the words are very beautiful. But it doesn't have the same meaning for our children today. You see, it was something that was ours alone. . . .

Eva. Yes, white people never heard it, except maybe the Rockefellers or people like that.

JOINING THE RANKS of many of the other Betty Coeds from the past, Ann Markam assured me: "I never wanted a career. My ambition was just to get married and have a house filled with kids.

"But after my husband was killed, I taught school. If I hadn't had a degree, I would have had a very difficult time. I've been able to take care of myself and my children when they needed me."

She remembered her first encounter with the "Okie" stereotype: "I can't explain it, but I hadn't been aware of the migrant situation. When I got to Los Angeles in the early forties, I constantly ran into people who didn't believe I was from Oklahoma. I spoke very properly from all the college speech training I'd had, and they expected someone from the *Grapes of Wrath*."

ANN MARKAM'S STORY

We had tag dances with the girls doing the tagging. We couldn't invite young gentlemen ourselves. The invitation had to go through the college administration office, and they checked up on the boys first.

You know, when my family's farmhouse burned down for the second time and my father borrowed money for a cotton crop in '38, I didn't really expect to go to college. If I hadn't had a scholarship to Oklahoma College for Women, I couldn't have gone. The scholarship was for twenty-five dollars which paid for my first year's tuition, and I remember there was even three dollars left over for the second year.

I lived in with a family and worked for my room and board, just during the first year since I couldn't stand it any longer.

I went to school in the morning and took care of two kids in the afternoon and did all the housework and cooking. They treated me like a servant. I stayed four days into my Christmas vacation baking cakes and candies for their relatives and friends. They gave me four dollars for that and acted like they were giving me the Denver mint!

Oh, there were some pleasant times, but I just felt very much taken advantage of in that situation. The mother was very young and her husband traveled during the week, so she got lonely. To make up for his absence, she got involved in all kinds of community activities and shifted a lot of her responsibilities to me. Besides all I had to do, I sometimes took care of her husband's retarded sister and she was always offering my services to take care of neighbor's children. So it seemed like they just sort of piled things on me.

But there was no other way I could go to school, at least that first year. You know, I *had* to get an education, otherwise I wouldn't have put up with those things.

After that one year, I spent two and a half years waiting on tables in the college dining room and living off campus in a rented room. I got twenty-five cents an hour for that work, but it was enough. There was an NYA house and some of the students had grants, but I never did. I was a good student and my minister wrote a letter for me, so I got the job waiting on tables. . . .

College was a lot of fun but I wasn't the wild type. I didn't have my first date until I was nineteen. My fun was centered around the church. I came from a very strict Methodist background; the Epworth League was the only club I joined.

I was in a lot of plays. Acting was the bright spot in my college life, even when I had to play a man's part. I had a deeper voice than most girls, so I always got stuck with the man's role.

Occasionally we had tag dances, with the girls doing the tagging. There was never enough boys to go around, so we were allowed to invite young gentlemen we knew. We couldn't invite them directly ourselves—that wasn't proper—we had to go through the administration. The college would send them a bid to the dance, and they wouldn't even know who sent it. It really was quite a strict college. They always checked up on the boy's reputation first.

I wasn't very ambitious. I certainly had no desire for a career. All I wanted was to learn about other people and what the rest of the world was like. I originally tried to major in speech, but my background had been rather limited, what with growing up on an Oklahoma cotton farm. There was a lady in charge of the speech department who didn't think I was acceptable. I was good enough for my speech class teacher but not for her. I was supposed to get on my knees and beg her, but I'm not that kind of person. Some of the girls gave her gifts; well, I wouldn't have given her one if she'd been dying. I didn't have any money anyway. So, I ended up as an art major with a speech minor.

I lived in a dormitory my last semester and it was a different kind of life than I had ever had before. I was very fond of the housemother and she liked me too. She was a white-haired old lady that nobody had any time for. I always spent a little bit of my day chatting with her.

It always pays off to be nice; she let me break rules where she wouldn't allow others. If I got in late or my room was messy—and boy, it got messy—she'd never say anything.

ONCE AGAIN I TURNED and drove down the dirt road between neat strawberry farms. TSUKAMOTO, the mailbox plainly read. How could I have missed it twice? Perhaps I was thinking of Mary Tsukamoto.

If she hired a press agent, her reputation couldn't be improved. She is noted for her work on the International Committee on Childhood Education, and in Elk Grove, California, the mention of her name among a group of her fellow teachers leads to an explosion of adjectives. "Wonderful." "Fantastic." "Brave." "Best."

It was early afternoon when I pulled up to the small farmhouse and parked alongside the old barn that had been converted into a garage. Mary had returned from San Francisco that morning where she receives monthly acupuncture treatments for rheumatoid arthritis. She held her right arm in a permanent "L", fingers twisted.

Being Japanese, she told me, means she remembers the 1940s better than the 1930s. "When they declared the West Coast a war zone, we had to leave fast. I was made director of evacuation in Florin, and I had to get 2,000 people ready. Women were crying because the FBI had arrested their husbands; people couldn't decide which belongings to take. What would happen to their farms, to their homes?

"My husband and I were sent to the relocation center in Jerome, Arkansas, and we did not come back again until July, 1945—a month before the war with Japan was over.

"We had to feel around to find out if we'd be welcomed back. For a long time we didn't go anyplace for fear we would run into someone who wished we hadn't returned.

"My husband and I were very lucky. Bob Fletcher, the fire chief, was a good friend. He kept our grapes alive all those years so we had a farm to come back to. Many others lost everything, and the banks foreclosed while they were in camps."

Mary Tsukamoto finished her last year of college in 1950 and began to teach. "It's hard to talk about my years at College of the Pacific in the thirties," she said, "without talking about my entire school experience. It was much different for me than for a Caucasian child."

While we talked, we ate mochi (rice cake) and drank tiny cups of hot, green tea.

MARY TSUKAMOTO'S STORY

There were not too many things I could major in at College of the Pacific because the counselors said I would never be able to get a job.

In 1925 my father brought us from Fresno to a farm in Florin. I was ten years old. We had always attended school with Caucasian children; Fresno had been more of a melting pot, with Armenians and Italians. I'd never encountered discrimination—oh, there were embarrassing moments when people made unthinking remarks, but somehow, I didn't see it as my personal problem.

All this changed when I went to the Florin grammar school where I soon found out that everybody had a Japanese face. Of course, I spoke English but many of my classmates were aliens—their parents spoke only Japanese—and they were growing up in a strange bicultural world.

At recess they would speak Japanese. They were scolded for that, as it was bad to speak Japanese at Florin grammar school.

It's kind of hard to explain just what I felt. I remember feeling a little bit ashamed, a little bit bewildered. And at that moment I began to feel for the first time that maybe there was something the matter with me.

Many children were held in the lower grades for two years until they learned to read and write English; there was no such thing as a bilingual program then. All the teachers were Caucasian.

So you see, in 1929 when I graduated from the segregated school, it was quite a shock to go to the Elk Grove High School which was mixed with all kinds of people.

At the same time, I was interested in my education. Among Japanese families, education is important. My parents felt they had suffered by missing their education in Japan because of poverty. My father felt a powerful need to educate his children and was always willing to give us a lot of time to study although he had to work even harder on our strawberry farm.

To be fair, I think the teachers tried their best to involve us in high school activities. They encouraged us and yet we were shy. I felt inadequate. I tried to go to the class parties and things, but it was hard. I was always aware that I was Japanese.

Of course, I was especially aware of the people who didn't care for Japanese, as you could sense they didn't want us there—even some teachers—so we were careful not to tread on anybody's toes. I was always apologetic about being around.

We knew of the Depression. It became harder and harder for my father to eke out a living. As the time approached for me to graduate, there seemed little chance that I could go on to college.

It's really a long story, but during my last years at Elk Grove I had a wonderful English teacher, Mrs. Mabel Barren. She also taught public speaking. Now, I don't know why I took public speaking, but I did. One time the assignment was to prepare an oration on California history and the best speech was to win a prize. I was told I won. Later, I was called to the principal's office and he told me that because of my background, I'd been refused the prize by the Elk Grove Native Sons and Daughters of the Golden West.

I was innocent. I did my assignment. I had no ambition to win —no plans to be part of an oratorical contest where they didn't want me. My teacher, Mrs. Barren, was upset about all this, more shocked and hurt, I think, than I was.

But there was nothing she could do. I knew then that there would be places where I couldn't go, where doors would be closed to me.

After that, Mrs. Barren made up her mind she was going to get me into college. She went to Stockton and talked about me with Dr. Towlie Knowles at College of the Pacific, and got me a fifty dollar scholarship for my first semester. And that same spring— during Easter vacation—this wonderful woman begged and borrowed clothes from people, cut them down, and sewed a wardrobe for me. And she did that on her vacation.

Then she came home with me one day and talked with my father and got his permission for me to go to college.

I helped on the farm that summer in '33, and then went to college. Things I could major in were limited because counselors told me I wouldn't be able to find jobs in many fields. I was religious, and so I told them I would be a missionary. They agreed I could minor in that, but that I should major in social work. At that point, I really didn't know what I wanted except a college education. I was sure of that.

The college got me a job working in a home for my room and board. It was the Depression, remember, and tuition was high. But now and then there would be an anonymous gift for a worthy student. So, when my tuition was due, I would get a call from the dean's office that a gift had come which I could have. I was able to finish all but the last year of college this way.

All the time Mrs. Barren helped when she could. But she had two children of her own and her husband was sick, so things were hard on her. She came to see me every now and then. She'd find out I needed shoes and would buy me a pair. Another teacher, Miss Helen Householder, who had been my high school domestic science teacher, contributed ten dollars a month so that I would have spending money.

You know, I have always felt that if there is anything good in me, it's because women like these made it that way.

Another job at Pacific came as an NYA grant. I worked in the infirmary for forty cents an hour, dusting furniture and sweeping rooms. It was a doctor there who first discovered my arthritis when I was nineteen.

COP was a wonderful learning experience for me. And for the first time I became involved in student activities. During my sophomore year, I discovered interpretive dancing; and the class really made me feel welcome. I would wear my kimono and interpret Japanese dance for them. I think I contributed to their appreciation of Japanese culture.

There were many warm friends I made there, and my wonderful teachers helped to heal the wounds. . . .

BETTY COYLE IS A WRITER for national magazines and teaches article writing at American River College in Sacramento, California.

BETTY COYLE'S STORY

My economics teacher was an unemployed prizefighter, and the scuttlebutt was he was "punchy."

My father wanted me to go to business college but there was no money for tuition and no jobs after I finished, so when the Auburn, New York, collegiate center opened, I jumped at the chance to go.

I think the center was an excuse for the government to hire unemployed teachers, because there wasn't much in the way of curriculum. You took whatever they offered, like economics or geology. My econ 1 teacher was a not too bright unemployed prizefighter who happened to have a college education and a teaching certificate. Well, you know how young people are—the scuttlebutt was he was "punchy." Economics was not my idea of a fun course anyway, but this guy made it a real pain.

Anyway, I got an NYA grant for fifteen dollars a month, and that was just enough to keep me going. And I did go—swimming, roller skating, skiing, and dancing. Auburn is in the Finger Lakes region and the big bands—Dorsey and Goodman—all came to the Owasco Lake park pavillion.

The season opened on Decoration Day. I can still feel a thrill remembering the park opening. That meant summer had arrived and, since in upstate New York summer was short, you had to do a whole year of living in three months.

You'd meet kids downtown and they'd say, "Going to the lake tonight?" And the answer was usually "yes" about four nights a week. Of course, some of the kids made a career of it, and went six nights.

There was a beautiful pavillion on the lake. The dance floor shone like glass and in the center, one of those revolving mirror balls glittered from the ceiling. Facing the lake were windows and a porch lined with rocking chairs; the fellas would come out there pretending to watch the lake while we girls sat in the rocking chairs batting our eyes like crazy, trying to get asked.

It was a dime-a-dance deal—the boys paid, and we'd always look for a boy with a roll of tickets. The only time I bought tickets was if there was a really good band and I was desperate to dance. Then one of my girl friends would dance with me.

One time Ina Rae Hutton was there for a two-week stand and a bunch of us went horseback riding with some of her musicians after they finished—about 2:00 A.M. I remember we invited the bass player to come swimming with us the next afternoon and she said she couldn't because it would soften her finger tips and hurt her playing.

We lived to dance. And we danced hard. Once, about fourteen of us were doing the Big Apple in my living room . . . the vibrations started the piano rocking back and forth, and it literally walked across the room—scared my mother nearly to death.

"WE SOUTHERN DAMES—we so-called Southern belles—we were just 'patsy-setups' for later divorce and the sexual revolution," said Monette (the name she asked me to use) explaining: "My mother's dead now—I can't hurt her—but there's still family in New Orleans who would be shocked."

Now divorced from her third husband and a self-styled liberal feminist, "Monette" at sixty-two has spent most of her working life in public relations in a job which often took her to New York, Washington, and Hollywood.

"The girl that I was in 1932 never would have gone to Mississippi on a civil rights march," she said, "but the woman that I had grown into by 1963 would—and did.

"Those college years in the early thirties . . . what can I say? They were a fetal stage for women. We didn't see our own oppression; we didn't think of the blacks or of politics. We had no social consciousness.

"But how can I blame the girl I was then? I wasn't even allowed to breathe on my own. Between my mother, the South and its customs, and the weight of my family name—well, I had no 'me.'

"I was expected to be an example—I was constantly told to be a lady. I couldn't swear or be seen at the market without white gloves. So I grew up wanting to escape any way I could. Now this is not just my own personal feeling; I happen to know that other girls in the thirties felt the same way."

MONETTE'S STORY

There were the social butterflies, grinds, and the rest who didn't fit in anywhere. Any girl could make it who was halfway attractive . . . but if she wasn't, it was heartbreaks for that girl.

We were all "Deep South" girls at Southern Louisiana University during the early thirties. Nobody else sought out SLU as an educational institution—unless some "damn Yankee" girl trickled in because of her daddy's business or something.

SLU was not noted for its academic standing. A girl's only interest was *who*—not what she was. Of course, there were the same types in other schools . . . social butterflies, the grinds, and the rest of the girls who didn't fit in anywhere. Really, you could make it if you fit in any of these categories unless you weren't attractive. Then it was heartbreaks for that gal.

I broke the rules . . . always. My nickname was "Rebel." I was a brain, but I was a beauty, too, and popular, even though I was considered "aggressive"—and some boys didn't like that. But I could always use my attractiveness as a tool to get what I wanted.

You know they always show movies of the 1930s where the cheerleaders were popular; but that really wasn't true. The best girls wouldn't have considered being cheerleaders . . . they were just a little bit too athletic, too extroverted, and Southern boys were absolutely offended by such a girl.

By the early thirties we had really rebelled against the "flapper" image. We let our hair grow long, parted it in the middle, and wore it in a bun. Delores del Rio fashion. And we didn't use a lot of makeup like our older sisters. We wore none, except for lipstick: Louis Phillippe. An extra dark red lipstick, it came in a gold case I would have sold my soul for; it was so red it was almost black.

That was for formal occasions but for everyday I wore Tangee— it was almost as pale as butter in the tube but when you put it on it turned bright orange. God! We must have looked like hell.

And another rebellious thing we did . . . ha . . . and the girls today think they invented this. We wore no bras. I was considered a devil because of this.

You see, we were always trying to be different, but somehow we ended up in the same old thing. The normal fashion for dancing was a kind of Scarlett O'Hara dress—ruffles, crinoline, and all that. But deep in my closet I had a black satin-backed crepe, cut on the bias so that it was real revealing—whenever I walked it revealed every wiggle; course I made sure to walk with my hips sort of switching from side to side.

Outside of dances, the big thing was football games, and the custom was, if the fellas had money, they'd rent a studio apartment down in the Vieux Carré—the French Quarter. That was before the tourists came. Only poor folks and leftover families lived there then. By leftover families I mean people who had had money in the past but had lost it.

So several of the boys would rent a studio and we'd go over after football games on double or triple dates. Now don't get the idea that this was a group sex thing. It was just a place where we could do our drinking, necking, and petting; but there's a very distinct difference between that and going all the way.

You see, in one way we were wild but in another I would call us innocent. I really would. We were so ignorant! We didn't know anything about contraceptives—we called them rubbers—and we'd have giggling fits if somebody found one.

I remember boys could be so cruel then and they could accuse a girl of liking it. Really. If a girl got the reputation of liking sex, she automatically had to be a nymphomaniac, because good girls didn't like it. We were only supposed to like everything that led up to it.

The automobile was very important, the key to individuality and freedom; so much so that we gave names to our cars. My first car was a used Nash coupe—and I called it *My Blue Heaven* after the Gene Austin record. A friend printed the pet name *Hell Won't Have It* on the back of her car.

Every boy had to have a car, or access to one. Now this was in Huey Long's day so all the roads were narrow and dusty and in some instances even made of crushed shell—but to be free you had to use them. We thought nothing of driving 150 miles to go to a dance where Garber-Davis was playing—that was Jan Garber before he became famous. They'd hold dances anyplace which was big enough then—sometimes in a store—and they'd sprinkle cornmeal on the floor and we'd dance all night.

This was still during Prohibition so the car was important for buying liquor. Now if a girl was lucky enough to go with a medical student, he could steal straight alcohol, and then we'd all drink "dopes." Remember this was considerably before the "Pepsi generation"—and we called Cokes, "dopes." We'd just drive up to any Rexall drugstore in Meridian or Mobile and toot the horn for curb service. "We'll have four dopes," we'd say, and a boy would bring out four Cokes and we'd add the alcohol.

It was OK for a girl to drink white lightning, pure alcohol, or any booze—in fact, a girl was considered something if she could hold her liquor.

Every girl was crazy to get pinned. I wasn't because I wasn't that much in a hurry to get married, but I think we were all hunting husbands. But boys were important for a practical reason. A girl couldn't do anything or go anyplace by herself, so boys were absolutely essential.

I guess the high point of the whole four years was when I was named sweetheart of Sigma Chi. You were supposed to be picked because you were the prettiest and the most popular—and I was that —but I also had some influence. You see, it wasn't a democratic thing like beauty queen—it was who you knew.

And it just so happened that I knew the president of Sigma Chi at Alabama, and I got a beautifully engraved invitation to be their sweetheart. Well, that was the biggest thing . . . we were all dancing, dancing, dancing, and invitations to fraternity dances or balls were very much sought after. And they gave favors at these dances— really expensive ones—beautiful vanities and rings and slave brace- lets—and we girls kinda collected them like scalps or trophies, showing them off in our rooms.

Anyway, I went to Alabama and my dress was white chiffon— Southern virgins wore white. It had little pink flowers sort of tucked in between the tiers of tulle ruffles. Even my linen shoes were hand embroidered by French nuns.

We led off with the grand march—the one who leads it is the president with his chosen girl, and then two by two they walk into the ballroom while the band plays the "Sweetheart of Sigma Chi." We circled the room, and then when everybody was in, my date took me in his arms and swept me around the floor—that opened the dance. Now, that's romantic!

I might mention that I had a problem . . . I was flat-chested or thought I was, and I had Kotex stuffed in my brassiere that night.

That's the way I lived. I was brought up like Scarlett O'Hara before Margaret Mitchell ever thought of her.

I knew that there were black people—my family had once owned hundreds of slaves. I had a black gal as a nurse from the time I was able to walk—and a black cook, maid, and chauffeur. I felt closer to my nurse than to my own mother—I could talk things over with her. But I wasn't aware of black people as human beings—they just were there. They stepped off the sidewalk when they saw me com- ing, and they didn't look me in the eye.

I remember the fellas would steal a watermelon, cut it open, and pour booze into it, and then we'd get half-tight. The first thing the fellas would say was, "Let's go scare us some niggers." And they'd get into a car and throw firecrackers at black people they saw on the streets. It was awful—I see that—but I was protected then by my ignorance.

The whole question was so complex. My father was a doctor and a Klan member. I can remember when I was a little child he'd tell mother to get out his robes and things; he had to go down to the Quarter to "teach a nigger a lesson."

And all this time my mother instructed me to call Negroes "auntie" or "uncle." I got slapped in the face many times for being a smart aleck to our Negro servants.

"AFTER COLLEGE," she said, "I taught for two years, but I couldn't take it so I got into newspaper work which I enjoyed much more.

"After my children came, I quit, but when they grew up I went back to newspaper work until I retired in 1973."

BETTY FAHS'S STORY

If you didn't make the curfew, your roommate would slip down and unlock the door. But, heaven help you if you got caught!

My last year at the University of Wisconsin I lived in the Alpha Chi Omega house. It was a great year for me.

For a casual afternoon date we went to a place just off campus; honest to goodness, it was called the Malt Shop. On campus we had a student union which—being so close to Milwaukee—served beer.

My sorority house was right on the lake and had its own dock, so we did a lot of boating and sitting on the dock mingling with the fellas—that kind of stuff. Sunbathing wasn't too popular—it was too darn cold. In fact, I remember a snow blizzard we had in June.

Nobody had cars. One girl in my house did, and she would pile all of us in and we would slip and slide up and down the hills to class. Mostly I walked, or if I had a real formal date downtown at a hotel, my date called for me in a taxi.

Football games were a big thing. Wisconsin had a great team those days, and whenever I could afford it I would take off for football weekends in Chicago or Minneapolis. Wisconsin also had a good crew—and their boathouse was right on the lake near us. That meant we did a lot of boy watching . . . I'll say.

But the greatest thing for me was the friends I made. I'd always had five or six friends in high school, but in the sorority house I had more—maybe twenty girls whom I got to know very well. We had a big console phonograph in the date room downstairs, and I can still hear Tommy Dorsey's "Marie" and "Song of India" booming up the stairs. I stood three hours in line at a theater in Madison to see Dorsey one time. It was great, and we were jumping up and down—but no swooning or dancing in the aisles. That came later. I think we were a more sedate group—the class of '37. Our parents had really sacrificed to send us to college. Just a year or two later, the kids had loosened up and things were different—you know, swallowing goldfish and all that.

There was a lot of drinking going on. Plenty. We weren't supposed to have hard liquor on campus, but when a fraternity house had a party, somebody *always* spiked the punch.

My family had been cocktail drinkers, so I grew up with liquor around the house. It didn't seem like such a big thing to me, but some of the girls had really been sheltered. So when they got to college, well, there was some pretty wild drinking going on.

But the rules were strict, and most of us watched our reputations; at least, the girls I ran around with did. If you didn't make the night curfew your roommate would slip down and unlock the door. But if you got caught, you were in plenty of trouble—heaven help you then!

Not only would you be in trouble with the housemother, but the other girls in the sorority would chastise you at chapter meetings. You could get kicked out of the dorms, and your parents would be notified, and boy you'd sure get it then.

I remember a couple of girls who just disappeared from school and nobody really knew why or where they went; we just heard whispers. We didn't talk about sex. Even in our bull sessions it was taboo. We talked about who got drunk and passed out at a fraternity party—that kind of stuff—but not sex.

The big thing was *romance;* we talked more about dates, going steady, and the prom. We were pretty inhibited; I guess sex was like an iceberg—most of it hidden below the surface.

FOR FIVE YEARS AFTER COLLEGE, she worked as a bacteriologist, then later for twenty-five years as an expert in orthoptics—the science of straightening eyes.

In between these two professions she was a professional whistler, possessing a range of three and one-half octaves and a repertoire of the best known semiclassical music. Fred Lowery, the whistling virtuoso of the forties, told her: "Your high tones are perfect."

All this diversity comes in a very small package. Geneva Mangiaracine Hall at sixty years weighs eighty pounds, the "fattest" she's ever been.

"I don't really consider myself an unusual woman," she said. "My mother: now there was a fantastic woman. She was an obstetrician who immigrated from Italy in 1907. When the doctors in Boston had a difficult breech birth, they would call her. She never used instruments. She'd just reach in, turn the baby around, and pull it out. She had tiny, but extremely powerful hands. There wasn't anything she couldn't do if she wanted to, except maybe one: make a success of her marriage.

"My father left us when I was five. I didn't understand why until I grew older. I could *see* my mother then. She was a superior brain and very domineering. Well, you know what that does to a man. . . ."

GENEVA MANGIARACINE HALL'S STORY
I had a job making up the stock solutions for the chemistry lab. Eighteen years later they were still using my pH set.

In 1932 my identical twin and I both graduated from Girls' Latin School in Boston. After that we both applied for college admission at Simmons and at Radcliffe, and were accepted at both.

But after we were accepted, we weren't sure how we were going to get there. We favored Simmons and so we tried for a scholarship and won it; except they didn't want to show partiality so they split it between us.

Radcliffe had a great reputation. But we knew someone who went there and came out completely changed—really putting it on— and I didn't like highfalutin people.

That decided both of us on Simmons. But since we had only half a scholarship we had to go to work at once. I did some baby-sitting for the cousin of my chemistry professor. They had a son they treasured and had had a succession of sitters they weren't too happy with. These sitters had ransacked the drawers—gone snooping—so they really were suspicious. Years later, I found out they had put all kinds of little trick things on drawers to tell if I had opened them. Of course, at no time did I touch a thing, and they were quite happy with me.

They went out about three times a week and sometimes on weekends. They were very social and political so I had a lot of that kind of work. I tutored, too—in mathematics, trigonometry, calculus, physics, chemistry, French, German, English . . . just everything.

That first summer I was recommended to a Canada Dry plant to do bacteriology work for which I got $1.25 an hour—an unheard of salary for a student in those days. They assured me I could have a job every summer, but they closed the plant a few months later so I was just there the one summer.

Fortunately, when I was a sophomore I got the Whiting scholarship which paid my tuition—it was worth $250 a year at that time.

I must admit, I was lucky. I had the kind of mind where I could absorb everything from a lecture—put two and two together and come up with the right answer. The only time I got to study was during the trip home. I never lived on campus, but commuted every day, an hour each way on the streetcar. Sometimes, if I was working late at school, I wouldn't get home 'til midnight, and I'd have to leave by 6:00 the next morning. I had a job making up the stock solutions for the chemistry lab, and they had to be done by 7:00 A.M. I went back eighteen years later and I saw the pH set I'd made up was still in use.

Once, at a reunion, I told my anatomy professor that I still was upset about a B-plus she'd given me on a test. I told her that I'd worked every night that week, and when I got to the library the books were gone. She said, "If I'd known that, I'd have given you an A."

While I was at Simmons, my mother wasn't well and my grandmother who lived with us had gone blind—so I had a lot of work to do around our home. Sometimes, I don't know how I did it all—

except I was young, and I had one single purpose for living. I was determined to do something with my life. At first, I wanted to be a doctor—to be of some service to mankind while I was on this earth. But I soon found out that medicine was going to be impossible for me, the times just made it impossible. Bacteriology was a perfectly acceptable compromise for me. It was the best I could do, and I honestly loved it. I went to work at the antitoxin and vaccine lab for the state of Massachusetts right after I graduated.

At Simmons College they had what they called the Academy, which is comparable in grade level to Phi Beta Kappa, and it was unusual for a science student to make it at all, but I made it and in my junior year. I still haven't got over that. . . .

Remember, I was just a little squirt; nobody took me too seriously. I never had one date in all that time. I had only one thing on my mind. I was driven to prove myself by graduating from college.

CLARICE RODDA IS THE WIFE of a California state senator, active in community and educational work.

CLARICE RODDA'S STORY

My father made tremendous sacrifices for me to go to college. He was an Irish immigrant and, like most Europeans, he thought education was the answer.

I graduated from the University of California at Berkeley in '32. I'd spent five years preparing myself to teach, and so finding myself in the Depression was discouraging. Frankly though, I was probably better prepared to make do than some, because I had gotten so used to nothing.

I didn't come from an affluent family. My mother died when I was nine years old and my father was left with six children in Los Angeles. He was just a working man, an immigrant from Ireland, working for an oil company for the great salary of $125 a month. But like most Europeans he was willing to make tremendous sacrifices for us if we wanted to go to college; he thought education was the answer. All the time I was at Berkeley he sent me thirty dollars from his pay which was hard on him and not enough for me.

I had a maiden aunt who lived near me and she gave me a hand-out every now and then. She also got me little jobs that helped.

Three of us girls lived together in a small apartment near the campus. We didn't pay much, and we didn't get much; the place had no bedroom. We had a wall bed and a couch; two slept in the wall bed, and I slept on the couch.

I can remember on one occasion, it was the end of the month and we were having boys from out of town in for dinner. Well, the other two girls were as bad off as I was and we only had thirty cents among us. I decided to make waffles and apple pie for dinner. So I spent the money on apples and borrowed some eggs from the land-lady—fortunately we had some flour. We did things like that and tried to make everything go as far as possible. We rarely had money for anything like the theater or even a movie, and we didn't have many dates. Boys didn't have money either. All of us were poor, poor, poor.

If one of us did get lucky and had a date to go out, we got together and everybody chipped in something for that girl to wear. Most of the time, a really big party turned out to be making a batch of fudge or playing bridge.

This old couple ran the house where we lived, and they were very kind to us. We could bum things from them like beans or stew to tide us over until our checks came. Sometimes we would really get desperate and we'd hock things, like our beat-up old typewriter. We really needed it for term papers, but. . . . Our parents would have died if they had known about that.

Toward the end of the school—right before I got my degree—I realized I had to earn some money and there were no teaching jobs. So I started taking some classes in typing and shorthand. I didn't really want to, but I did it anyway.

SALLIE SUE SUTTON—A TEXAS COED

I went to Texas Woman's University at Denton and got my teaching certificate. I majored in chemistry. Twenty years later I could have really had fun with it but then no company would even look at me.

You know, I took physics and math. What a crazy lineup that was! I had started out to be a math major, but after I got one taste of college chemistry—they didn't teach it in high school in those days—well, I was hooked.

I didn't want to teach. I had some kind of crazy scheme that I would get a job with one of the oil companies in a lab somewhere. 'Course, I never got it. It's obvious; there weren't many jobs to be had and the men got them, naturally. They wouldn't even consider it when they saw my name—never even answered my applications—not with Sallie Sue on them. Now, if my parents had been smart enough to give me a name that could have been a boy's, I might have got an interview. But still I wouldn't have got the job.

Oh, I had a ball while I was in college though. I was the only girl in physics and one of two in chemistry, and had the whole class of boys to myself.

Even though I was going for my teaching certificate, I knew I'd never be a teacher. Why? Vanity . . . vanity. . . . I enjoyed kids, but once this nurse friend of mine and I took a trip between school years. We went to Michigan City, Indiana, to visit her family. At first it was a joke, we'd ask the boys "What do we do?" You know, after awhile that game became serious. "Come on, guess what do we do?" Half of them guessed she might be a nurse, but *all* of them guessed I was a teacher. Right then, I knew I'd never be one to get pegged like that!

One of my college classmates was Joan Blondell. Now, I went to school with Rosebud Blondell, but later she changed her name.

We used to have bull sessions with the other girls. She'd been out of school appearing on the stage. Her parents were in vaudeville, but they'd been operating a small store part of the time; you know, vaudeville died out because of the Depression. Well, in the middle of one semester, she got a chance to appear in the chorus on Broadway, and she left. Said she was coming back, but she kept on going up and never did.

CATHY LOGAN SPENT her four years learning to become an accountant. "I never used it," she said. "I wanted to get married, and I needed a job where I could transfer easily, so I got a secretarial job which I kept for an incredibly long time."

CATHY LOGAN'S STORY

The sorority house rules were very carefully written. Inside by
10:30 P.M., doors locked, lights off—but what the rules didn't say
was that the boys were supposed to be *outside*.

At the University of Nebraska, Tri Delta was one of the big six
sororities on campus. However the real reason I joined was the big
attraction toward living in a house on campus. They didn't have
dorms then, and girls had to room with approved families off campus. I think the boys could live anywhere.

The only drawback to sorority life came in my freshman year
when we were pledged: all of the pledges had to go to a study hall
in the evening which was terrible, because I could have managed
my own study time better.

But they wanted that. The big deal was that pledges had to make
good grades so they could be initiated.

The only other prohibition was smoking—absolutely none was
allowed. They were stricter than you have heard, I think. But it
didn't hurt us because, of course, we found a way of evading the
rule. Our house which faced north, had a sort of false front to help
cut the wind and we girls reasoned that it would be legal to smoke
there—that it really wasn't *in* the house.

Sororities had to have housemothers—although fraternities
didn't. I always thought it was good to have somebody you could
go to if you really needed an older person to talk to.

Of course, she saw to it that no boys ever got above the first floor.
Only one man was allowed above the sitting room, and that was
General Pershing who was actually a member of Tri Delta. And
even when he came, one of us had to run before him, yelling, "Man
on second, man on third."

We had a beautiful autographed picture of him over the mantel
which we always hid when a fraternity was coming—it wouldn't
have lasted a minute, you know.

The social part I loved was our Friday and Saturday dance
hours. Every sorority would entertain a fraternity—the whole membership would come for an hour of dancing between eight and nine
in the evening. It was just a device to get acquainted, but it sure
worked. I met really nice boys.

Sundays were quite a different situation. In Nebraska, they still had blue laws and you couldn't go to movies or anything. So we had endless all-day picnics and, believe me, the movies would have been better. Well, gosh, they were just big necking parties, being left to our own devices. I don't mean there was a lot of overt sex, but just about everything short of sex.

Actually, Tri Delta was very strict with its girls. We had to be inside by 10:30 on weekdays and 12:30 on weekends. The rules were very carefully written—inside by 10:30 P.M., doors locked, lights off—but what the rules forgot to mention was that the boys were supposed to be *outside*. And they weren't always, but we followed the rules the way they were written.

The clothes we wore to class didn't come in for much attention as I recall—although Tri Deltas had a campus dress code—hats and gloves to classes. Our house didn't want its girls to look weird, you know.

I didn't have an extensive wardrobe of school clothes, but I always had a bunch of beautiful formals. Now they *were* important.

NELL CADELL STILL HAS the mischievous spirit that almost got her expelled from Ohio Wesleyan forty-five years ago.

"They nicknamed me 'Battler,'" she told me, "and my husband still calls me that at certain times."

I was curious how a girl her size (she can't be more than 4'10") could earn such a nickname.

"It's really embarrassing now," she laughed. "I guess I got it from the freshman-sophomore woman's fight."

I couldn't help myself: "The what?" I asked.

NELL GOBBLEMEN CADELL'S STORY

All of a sudden we were fighting. Girls had their hair pulled out, faces scratched, and clothes torn off....

At the time of the fight, I was living in a campus dorm early in my sophomore year. You see, we had this tradition—all freshman women were supposed to wear beanies. The year before, I had worn mine with pride. But the '31 freshman class—including my sister—decided to ignore the rule.

Well, it was just overwhelming to us sophomore women, that these upstarts wouldn't wear beanies—we were incensed that they dared to rebel against the tradition, especially when we hadn't.

So the sophomore girls in my dorm had a meeting, and we decided to teach these freshman gals a lesson. We invited a bunch of them to dinner, and we asked them why they wouldn't wear the beanie. Well, they said hair styles had changed, and besides it was just too demeaning. All through dinner we were polite . . . but when it came time to leave, we told them something was wrong with the main entry. Actually we were luring them to the back where we had sophomore gals stationed with buckets of water and flour. We grabbed them in the dark and dunked their faces, first in the water, then in the flour. They left screaming mad and looking pretty ridiculous, of course.

Now, we sophomores were pretty satisfied with ourselves. We stupidly—very stupidly as it turned out—thought we'd taught them a lesson, and the next day they'd all show up with their beanies on. We never dreamed they'd congregate down at the corner, and try to do the same thing to us!

But when we came out, there they were, waiting for us with reinforcements—other freshmen women who had joined them. Naturally, we called all the sophomore girls out of the dorm, and then, all of a sudden, we were fighting. Girls had their hair pulled out, their faces scratched, and their clothes torn off, and all the time new girls kept coming to join both sides.

Well, I only weighed ninety-five pounds, and I thought I'd be more help directing the whole thing, so I climbed to this little balcony on the second floor of the dorm—with the cheerleader's bullhorn. I yelled encouragement to the sophomores and I warned my friends: "Hey, watch out, one of them is behind you!"

By this time the boys heard the commotion and were standing on the sidelines, egging both sides on, when the police came. Remember, it was a small town and there were only two poor, sad looking guys on motorcycles. They'd pull two girls apart and turn around to stop some others and the first ones would be at it again.

What can I say? It was just knock-down, drag-out, and nobody would give up until both sides were exhausted.

There was a terrible row about the thing—it even got on the radio—and when my mother heard my name in the broadcast, she took to bed with cold cloths. It was awful really—$3,500 worth of shrubbery was demolished—and this was a Methodist school!

I'd been very vocal and prominent during this whole thing, so they named me the ringleader, and I had to get up in chapel the next day and apologize publicly to the whole school.

I could have been expelled, but the dean of women was kindly and a friend of my family's so I was just put on probation along with the whole sophomore and freshman classes.

I was notorious—I had disgraced myself. Branch Ricky—you know he was with the St. Louis Cardinals—was a close friend of my father's. When he came to the campus during alumni week, he wouldn't speak to me.

So everything went down the drain. We sophomore girls were restricted to the dorms after dinner, and we weren't allowed to go to dances. Even the Junior Prom was out-of-bounds.

After about six weeks of that, we were bored and mad and feeling mistreated. We were especially mad at the upperclass women; we felt they hadn't supported us when we were fighting for the school's traditions.

We got even the night of the Junior Prom by putting Karo syrup all over the toilet seats in the bathrooms on their floors. Half of them were late to the prom because they had to change their dresses. Sure they knew we did it, but they couldn't prove it.

Anyway, the freshman girls, including my sister, never did wear those damned beanies.

Chapter Six

COLLEGE OF
HARD KNOCKS

"MY YOUNGER BROTHER thinks a Depression would be good for a lot of these young people," she said, shaking her head. "But I don't. I know what it's like to live on beans, and I know what it's like to do without what you really need. Mother made cornbread on top of the stove 'cause she couldn't afford to turn on the oven . . . all that stuff . . . I know what it's like."

NINA PARR'S STORY

I saved four dollars and sent it home so dad could come to Oklahoma City. I was so proud to give it to him.

We went flat broke in '31. My father was a small-town merchant in Wynnewood, Oklahoma, a town of about 2,200.

He had always been a successful man—owned three trucks. We had to sell our home to put money into the business. Mother begged him to save one pickup. She tried to get him to get out and save what he had left, but he wouldn't do it. He lost the grocery store, the trucks, a wholesale produce business—everything. He'd sure made a lot of money in his day, but I missed out on it since I was the youngest.

When hard times hit, it didn't seem to bother mother as much as it did my father. He was a Southerner from a very proud family, and he always said, "If your word's no good, you're no good." He always said, "My word is my bond."

Now there weren't any notes. They didn't sign notes in those days. But he paid out every penny he had and still owed more. He came home one day, and I heard him talking to my mother. He couldn't walk down the street and hold his head up, with the bills he owed. He said, "I just feel like going to the river and blowing my brains out."

You know this was scary for a young girl because a lot of men really did.

That same day I went to my bedroom, got dressed in my best clothes, crammed about half a dozen handkerchiefs in my purse, and hitchhiked to Oklahoma City. I called home that night with the news that I had a job with a doctor, earning ten dollars a week.

I found a room for five dollars a week and I could get a cup of coffee and a donut for a nickel—that was breakfast—then they'd fix up box lunches for fifteen cents. Lots of times I had dinner dates —every time I could . . . darn tootin' I did! I could have gotten into a lot of man trouble, you know, but things were more strict then. Thank God, I didn't.

I saved four dollars and sent it so dad could come to the city. He found a job there in a packinghouse at the stockyards. I was so proud to give him the money, and darned if he didn't have his pockets picked on the way.

Now, if anybody hasn't been through the Oklahoma Depression, they haven't been through the Depression because respectable people who had things went under. It was very degrading. My youngest brother lost his job with the Southern Pacific Railroads and came home and bootlegged. At one time there were so many bootleggers in Wynnewood they had to wear badges to keep from selling to each other.

'Bout that time, I got sick—no wonder I got sick—and my father lost his job so we both went back home.

My mother was the one who held the family together. My father said, "Oh, what in the world are we going to do?" He was so demoralized. But my mother, now, she took a wedding ring quilt she'd made to the banker's wife, and sold it to her for enough money to rent a big lot for a garden for a month and also buy some seed.

One day my father got a job with the city government. They

were Republicans at the time, and he was a very strong Democrat. When they asked him what he thought 'bout Roosevelt, he told them and lost his job. All in one morning!

But as far as making out goes, we made out. Like somebody'd have a cow and they'd share a pound of butter, and somebody'd have extra from the garden . . . there was sharing then without expecting anything in return.

SHE WORE A PLAIN BROWN, ankle length dress, completely without decoration. (Cherokees are not colorful, she told me.) She is short, of an average width—it's her hair that is not average—platinum white, thick, and caught in one long braid at the base of her neck.

For several years she has taught Indian studies at the University of California. "I am particularly interested in the mythological native American woman," she said, digging for a paper she's written on the subject. "Our legends tell us that a woman made the world, and she took clay and spittle and formed all the beings—birds, insects, man—and she put a cloak of knowledge about all—not just man—all.

"Women had prestige among Indians up and down the East Coast, of which the Cherokee is one tribe. Women held ownership of the burial hills; they chose candidates for tribal positions; and they held the power to impeach them.

"In my opinion you can judge a nation by how the women fare. Women in this country might fare better today if Indian custom had been followed instead of English common law. The European world didn't give their women a good position—they idolized them, like Mother Mary, but the women were chattels.

"The Iroquois from whom, by the way, the U.S. Constitution was taken, had a custom where the man went to live in his wife's house and took her name. The children of that marriage belonged to her. Women could be chiefs and could compete in sports. And the Iroquois woman's status was so high that if she beat a man at a game, no shame would come to him.

"In my own tribe, a Cherokee woman could be chief of war or peace."

In her classes on contemporary Indian literature, Sarah has several white students. "I hate to see my beautiful, white students carrying guilt," she said. "I would like to replace that guilt with knowledge.

"I am married to a white man and have been for thirty-four years—I see a little edge of pain arise in an expression on his face when he is confronted with the painful things the white man has done. . . . I see an edge of suffering in his face because he is white. That is why, for me, it is especially wonderful to see these Indian and white students dialoging, getting to things that people just don't talk about other places."

SARAH HUTCHINSON'S STORY

It was natural for me to be interested in medicine. We had an Indian medicine woman . . . but I found in the white man's world women were ruled out of medicine.

My grandmother is said to have been born on the Trail of Tears. My father is Cherokee . . . but his father had him put on the roll as one-sixteenth Indian. In those days the Indian was thought to have the mind of a child—he couldn't make contracts or conduct business—so my grandfather lied about his son's heritage.

I was born in 1920 in Claremore, Oklahoma, and I went to the public schools with my seven brothers and sisters. My father was a farmer, and my family always had a member on the tribal government.

The Cherokees were an unusual people . . . we had our newspaper and seminaries. The Bible was translated into Cherokee very early. Of course, there are two sides to that story. They did that to please the white man but they held on to their own Indian religion, and they kept a sacred fire alive for 3,000 years.

By 1934 I was in high school and working hard to graduate. A lot of Indians went to that high school . . . but no issue was made of it. They "painted us white." The Indian world knew who we were, and the white world knew who we were, and we just didn't get out of line. We dressed white and acted white and did everything we could to give up the Indian culture.

My father tried to teach us about our ways . . . not my mother . . . she was too frightened. You know she went to Carlisle Indian

School when Jim Thorpe was there, and she was punished for speaking Cherokee. I used to try to get her to teach my younger sisters and brothers, and she would not. "I would not want to see them punished," she would say.

Now, my grandmother lived with us, and she taught me many things. In an Indian family the grandmother is often the teacher. She taught me about the Green Corn Dance—which happens around the Fourth of July when the corn is knee high.

The myth about the oil-rich Indian with Cadillacs and diamonds is not true for the Cherokee. We were poor, and we did not wish for oil because to scar the earth is to abuse the mother. What is being rich? It is not being happy.

Oh, I think it happened to the Osages and the Creeks—and the oil money disrupted their culture—what was left of it. But the Cherokees had always gone in for education. We were the people who searched for knowledge. This is one of the characteristics that identifies us. So in the thirties I was trying to make it educationally. I wanted to go to medical school or law school—but there was no money, and the Depression . . . besides women didn't do those things.

It was very natural for me to be interested in medicine. We had an Indian medicine woman. But in the white man's world, women were ruled out of medicine. I used to go to see Dr. Malloy in Claremore. He had a ten-bed hospital, and I'd skip school to go there. After we returned from rounds he'd ask, "What do you want to learn today, Sarah?"

And I'd say, "The lady in the corner, what is wrong with her arm?"

He would take me to his library, pull a book off the shelf, and show me where it told about broken arms. I'd sit on the floor cross-legged and read until it was time to go home.

Then, I'd go to my uncle's courtroom—he was a district judge— and I would sit there and learn new words. I was fascinated with learning. You see, Indians never stop learning. They must continue. But I received very poor counseling in high school. They didn't really care. Number one, I was a woman; number two, I was an Indian. So my dad sold a horse so I could go to business college.

Even before I was old enough to go to college, I learned not to

care for gangs, to be one of the group—although I did have
friends. I was afraid I wouldn't live long enough to learn all the
things I wanted to.

I began learning at an early age. One of my earliest memories is
sitting under the kitchen table—'cause the tablecloth went clear
to the floor—and listening to all the grown-ups talk. And they'd
always say, ". . . in the days of the good old IT." And I'd run to my
grandmother Sarah and ask her what the "good old IT" was. And
she'd tell me it stood for Indian Territory. She told me that's when
we had our own land and our own government . . . to us, those
were good days.

Every year we would have the Dance of the Sacred Fire. It is so
religious that we don't talk about it. Indians don't talk about religion. Anything which is sacred need not have words put to it
because talking detracts from sacredness . . . but you learn at the
dances, you get the feeling of it . . . very deep. The Cherokees don't
use drums much, but the women lace turtle shells to their legs and
their movements make a hypnotic, rhythmic sound. There is
singing, wonderful singing. There is no drinking or rowdyness;
the sacredness overtakes the whole thing. Around the dance area are
the seven clan houses where the people of those clans sit. In the
center is the fire . . . it's built on a table of earth and the special fire-
keeper is always there as you dance around. There is no praying as
such. Indians pray without words, and they don't look down to
pray, they look up.

At the dances, I would meet my mother's cousin, Rita. She was a
hero in our family because she always got into trouble but managed
to get away with things. My mother and Rita went to the same
Indian schools; my mother would get punished but Rita wouldn't.
But Rita did not like to see my mother punished. Once late at night
she flattened herself behind a pillar, waiting for the matron who
punished my mother. Then Rita bit her in the buttocks and hung on
like a dog while the matron screamed. Rita is the heroine in the
family; I've heard that story a hundred times.

My father would not take government handouts during the Depression. He was mad at the government because of their broken
treaties. I remember my father . . . because of a bad snowstorm . . .
going out with his legs wrapped in gunnysacks to kill rabbits with a

stick. We ate them baked or fried as long as the fat lasted. Then it was gone, and finally the corn and flour, as well.

Father was a farmer. Bad weather, dust storms, and blizzards just ruined everything. So one day he took a gunnysack and left for town; he said he was going to bring back groceries but he had no money. I heard my mother ask him what would happen if the grocery man refused. And I heard my father answer, "If he refuses me, before I see my children starve, I will threaten to kill him." He was desperate. I can remember being frightened for him, watching him go into the horizon, growing smaller and smaller. But he came back with corn and flour, and he didn't kill anybody.

He could do that desperate thing; but at the same time he could tell the government agents, "Don't bring your food around here. It would make my chickens vomit!" He was so proud. He had seen what government handouts had done to Indians.

My father loved to tell stories; this is also a big part of our Indian culture. In the evening when the work was done and he felt like talking, he would retell the legends. But he could tease, too. I remember he told about this family—a family much like ours—with eight children who were hungry and the food was gone and a storm was on . . . they had nothing to eat but shoe soup. So they found the newest pair of shoes and they boiled them, carefully taking out the shoestrings because there were no nutrients in cotton fibers. They boiled the shoes and spooned out the shoe soup.

Now in Indian stories they leave spaces so the listener can fill in. I filled in that story: I got up and hid my new shoes—my only pair of shoes. Then I brought back my brother's shoes. How they laughed and teased, about how much I wanted to eat my *brother's* shoe soup.

A DETROIT GIRL

As a young woman I experienced almost everything a woman could experience during the 1930s. All hell broke loose!

My father committed suicide in 1930. He had worked his entire life and had retired owning a great deal of real estate, and suddenly it was worth nothing. I think he did it in a fit of fright: this thing about wanting to keep his good name. And, you know, there was no stigma attached to suicide then—it was in—many of his colleagues did it. His partner had jumped a week after the stock market crashed. Anyway, he was always contemplating suicide when things got rough. Even as a young man, my mother told me, he would talk about it. Suicide doesn't happen overnight.

I was twenty-one the week he died . . . that was a hell of a way to start adulthood.

So here I was with my mother, younger sister, and an aunt whose husband had walked out on her. Gorgeous, a gorgeous situation! Since I was the oldest, the decisions were left to me. My mother, you see, was a contradiction. She had escaped from a Russian ghetto, actually pulling herself out of there by learning the tailoring trade. She had been a member of the Communist Party so she wasn't exactly the kind of woman who had just gone from her mother's kitchen to her husband's kitchen. She was a woman who should have really done something, but my father had been very domineering—a fantastic man—but domineering. As a result, when she was left widowed all my mother could say was, "If only I was ten years younger." At forty-three, her life was over.

THE NEAT ROWS of corn and lettuce, the pole beans, and squash which fill the empty lot next to her home seemed strangely out of place in this neighborhood of $75,000 homes. "It's fulfilling to watch things grow," Edna Anderson explained, "but I confess, I want vegetables because this talk of another depression gets me so up-tight.

"I remember how my mother's kitchen garden carried us over the bad years in South Dakota.

"Have you ever baked fresh corn in a microwave oven?"

EDNA LINK ANDERSON'S STORY

I think if the Depression had not come, my father might have been more congenial with his children.

What I remember most is what the Depression did to the spirit of people. The tensions in my family, for instance, gave my mother a negative outlook—she always said life was just one disappointment after another.

She didn't really have much to look forward to because we didn't have anything, and during the thirties it looked like we never would.

My father was German and very strict. He lived by the rod, and *I mean he lived by the rod!* When we were at the table there was no conversation—much less laughter or joking. You sat down and ate —eating was a serious business to him.

I was a middle child—the third child—and I was the one that took the most guff from the rest of the family. You know the baby is protected, and the older ones have it all, so the middle one gets it. I think I really became aware of the strife—I felt it more each year as I was maturing.

In 1934 my father lost his job and went on WPA. This was such a tremendous blow to his ego that he developed asthma. At times it was so severe he could hardly breathe. It was a psychological thing, and it disappeared completely when he went back to work.

I remember standing in line with my father for relief food—to this day I can't look at navy beans and peanut butter. Taking charity was demeaning to him, and there were people who said snide things. This hurt my father deeply.

I think that if the Depression had not come, he might have been more congenial with his children. I don't know how many times I got whipped for hardly batting an eye. Toward the end of the thirties when I left to work in Washington, D.C., my father told me if he had his life to live over, he would treat his kids differently. That was one of the few times I ever felt close to him.

My mother? I think she accepted things as they came. She was busy, and I suppose that is an answer—she always had work to do.

I think because there was not much laughter in my home, I buried myself in things at high school. The band director handed me a trombone one day, and I tried for months to play it. I got the lead in the freshman play—I was the mysterious lady nobody knew 'til the end. But I kinda loused it up so I didn't get the lead the next year.

EVERYBODY TALKS about restoring faith in government and in our national leadership . . . but for Jane McMahon, I suspect, it may be forty years too late.

A bitterness born in the 1930s when her mother saw the poor cheated of relief goods; her brother kicking back part of his WPA earnings; and the rich around her growing visibly richer—all these memories continue to color her perception of government.

"The administrators skimmed the cream for themselves," she told me, "and we got the leavings. And we was supposed to be grateful to boot."

JANE McMAHON'S STORY

I remember my mother doing everything to keep us together. It took grasshoppers and sandstorms and no crops to make her give up.

My mother decided to try to keep our homestead when my father died in '32. They had filed on government land in southern Colorado four years before . . . mother said they had a pocketful of dreams . . . and she tried to hang on as long as she could.

There were five of us kids—I was the oldest girl and I had two older brothers, one twelve and one eleven.

After my father died, the sheep ranchers tried to move in on us. They'd bring their sheep in early in the morning and by the time we'd know it, those sheep would be all over the pasture. Now, we couldn't let 'em stay there because they'd eat the grass right down to the ground. We always kept a horse handy for just such emergencies and I'd ride out there with a dog, and get rid of them. They'd come right back the next day, so it was a constant battle.

But our biggest trouble was water. We didn't have the money to drill, so we'd take a wagon to the river and back it right into the water to fill up our barrels. We only had enough water for the house and stock—not for many baths.

The first winter after my father died was the worst; he had been too sick to plant a crop and we just plain ran out of food by February. My mother rode a horse through a blizzard to borrow some beans from a neighbor, and the man told her no. Then she went on to the next place—must have been, all told, five miles. He was considered a drunk and a no-good, but he gave her beans. He wouldn't sell them to her, neither, he gave them to her, which tells you something about his quality. My mother said that when that man went to the Pearly Gates, God wouldn't notice his breath.

I remember my mother doing everything to keep us together. It took a lot to make her give up. The summer the grasshoppers came, she took the younger kids down in the root cellar and fought the pests—tried to smoke them out. We'd put in a real good corn crop that year, and we were feeling good about it but the 'hoppers came and ate everything. And you know, they were so thick they were ankle deep. They were small—maybe one inch—when they came, but two days later when they left they had tripled in size—on our corn.

But that wasn't the worst of it, just the start. The winds came then, and there was nothing to stop them so they just ripped the topsoil up and sent it flyin'. I'd wake up in the morning and sand would be piled up so high that a horse could hide behind it.

Finally, in '37, there was nothing left, so we walked away. We just walked away from it; sold the animals and left.

By that time my oldest brother was on WPA . . . working on the roads. And he had to pay this guy—he was like a contractor—two dollars a week to work. And he had to buy his gasoline from the man's brother—oh, they had you tied up every which way.

My mother and I went into town and took housecleaning jobs—we worked for the top government commissioners. They had nice cars and good clothes, and my mother worked for a woman who had a basement full of things that should have been given to people. This woman'd get up every Sunday in church and make a little speech about the poor, poor people—and she had trunks full of stuff that belonged to them. That was stealin' as far as I was concerned. I never was religious but I knew right was right, and wrong was wrong.

SHE'S AN ANGEL, or as close to an angel as I'm likely to meet on this earth. And though she never had a baby of her own, thirty-one foster children and hundreds of hungry people called her mama.

Margaret Marks, who founded the Arms of Mercy Feeding program in Del Paso Heights, California, is an equal opportunity feeder. Every day, white, black, Mexican, male and female, old and young, some drunk, some dirty line up for her hot lunches. The price of admission? A hungry belly.

Although she is in constant pain from advanced arthritis, she refuses to wear the therapeutic steel brace her doctor prescribes. Instead she confounds him by working a straight thirteen-hour day. Why? "If I set down," she said, "I'll stiffen up and won't ever be able to feed God's people."

Despite all her problems, when "God's hungry people" line up each noon she feeds them, and that makes her happy. "I'm the happiest woman there is," she says—which is what you'd expect of an angel.

MARGARET MARKS'S STORY

Those were good days . . . there was *love* back then . . . I never saw discrimination . . . all I saw was love.

I didn't know no difference; it was no special hard time. My mama and me, we always worked hard.

In 1931 I quit school to help out, since mama was only making seven dollars a week to take care of me and my brother. She did day work—that's all we did back there in Louisiana—taking in washing, ironing, and day work.

I went once to pick cotton and I got a whippin' 'cause I stole off from school. Hid my books under a bush and went with the others. I just followed the kids. I always wanted to know something, always wanted to be doing something with somebody. Anyway, after the day was over, the man gave me thirty-three cents, even though I didn't know what I was doing. I picked the stalks and all. That was the only time I picked cotton.

My brother was older and he went on to Galveston. I quit school and went to work for Sam Puckett—worked for that one family ten years—Sam and Jessie Puckett. I took care of their little Sammy for them; he was my first baby.

They were rich oil people, and they took care of me. They even had a clothing store. And she would take me down there and we'd visit all the "up" people. Mama and me, we didn't live good, you know, but we were with the best of white people. We were treated real good—my family.

My mama never had no trouble with her kids; we were in church from sunup to sundown. Everybody in Lake Charles knew us and liked us. Mama was working for the Charleston Hotel, day working. We had a pretty good living; we had a few chickens and a pig.

I lived the way I wanted. Every summer we went to Colorado Springs and Denver because Mrs. Puckett was a TB patient. That's where I learned to drink goat milk, and you know, if we'd get to a hotel that was prejudiced—you know, discriminatin'—they wouldn't stay there.

I can't get used to discrimination. I've never lived it. I slept right in their house and did just what I wanted to do. All the white people thought a lot of my family.

But I was raised strict. I was twenty-six years old before I ever knew what a man was. Like when they did decide to let me start having company, I was on one side of the room, the boy was on the other side, and grandma was in between.

Every Sunday, rain or shine, we went to the New Sunlight Baptist Church. Nellie Lutcher, she was our pianist since she was seven years old. That whole Lutcher family is nothing but musicians.

Every Sunday was church and we didn't go to no picture shows on Sunday or nothing. My mama was *awful* strict . . . not kinda strict . . . *awful* strict. She knew where I was every minute and I appreciated it. And I was crazy about my grandma, too. I was the onliest girl and I was like "Miss Ann" in the family. She gave to me as far as she could. She gave me a little white fur coat; it wasn't new clothes, but, my goodness. . . .

Now, Mrs. Puckett and them, they would give us clothes: the seconds out of the store every year, but no white fur coats.

The Pucketts they were crazy about my grandma too. They kept her in Granger pipe tobacco, and they helped bury her.

Those days was good days in one way—there was *love* back then. That's the reason when people talk about discrimination, I say I never saw it. All I could ever see was love. We all got along, and I never in my life gone to no white people's back door.

I didn't have to. Whoever you are, you have to be trusted . . . then they don't tell you to go to no back door.

A PHILADELPHIA GIRL

My father had a big ice and coal business with a fleet of trucks in '34, when the bottom fell out for him. He came home one night— oh, I'll never forget it—he just ran away from everybody. It hit him so hard that he ordered my mother and all us girls to the third floor. He wouldn't let us come down . . . and he kept my only brother on the second floor with him. It was the only night in my life I ever remember my mother and father not sleeping together.

The next morning . . . everything was fine. He sent me to the store for candy for all us kids. That was his way of saying he was sorry.

TUBERCULOSIS is not the "white plague" today that it was during the Depression decade. And its modern victims are rarely taken to state sanitariums, like Ila Gilson in 1931.

"I've had no other problems with it," she told me. "I was one of the lucky ones. Completely cured."

The nine months she spent in the Texas State Sanitarium at St. Angelo are chronicled in a scrapbook she still keeps. It is filled with pictures of smiling young women, both patients and nurses, indistinguishable from each other except for the nurses' white uniforms. I asked why the sick looked so healthy.

"TB's hard to tell except in the final stages. See her?" she asked. pointing to a pretty young girl with a short bob. "Now she died a few months after this picture was taken. She knew she was going to die, but she was always so gay. This is her poem—"Be Optimistic." I clipped it out of the hospital paper and put it next to her picture. See, she dedicated it to Dr. Hoskins—she was crazy about him. Do you want to hear it?

If Dr. Hoskins says you'll die
    before another year rolls by,

Don't curl up and begin to cry—
Be optimistic.
When one lung he says you ain't got,
    and the other one is halfway shot,
Don't wait to be planted in the family plot—
Be optimistic.

ILA GILSON'S STORY

We laughed and joked a lot. We couldn't risk losing our sense
of humor.

I was living in Abilene—not Kansas—Texas . . . that's about
halfway between Fort Worth and El Paso. I'd had diphtheria twice
and that's what ran into TB. My doctor found out because I kept
having a temperature and losing weight—so he applied at the state
sanitarium for me. You know, it didn't cost anything and I got the
best of care.

I had to wait three months to get in, and then I got this letter I
keep here in my scrapbook: "This is to notify you of a vacancy at
the state TB sanitarium. Please come at once and write or wire me.
It is impossible to hold a vacancy indefinitely with more than one
hundred ladies on our waiting list. (Signed:) Dr. McNight."

It was a community in itself—about 5,000 counting employees
and patients—just a little community.

The first thing they did was put me on complete bed rest for
three months in the "in" building. Complete bed rest means
eight hours every day in bed plus all night. I had my meals served
in my room. There was more than one "in" building—they had
a couple of buildings where the real sick ones were—they never did
get up.

That was really a most wonderful institution. If there was a married couple with active TB, then their children were put in the pre-
sanitarium and sent to school. Of course, there were some young
children that had it, but it was almost always fatal to them.

Now, while I was on three months bed rest, I wasn't allowed to
read. We called that kind of rest "chasing"—chasing the bug. And
if you broke any of the rules about being up, or ran a fever or some-

thing, the doctors would "flatten you"—put you in bed and not let you get up.

I know this sounds funny—but it was kind of fun. Things were not all that great at home then, and I met people and made a lot of close friends.

After the "in" building, I was moved to the "up" building—and I wasn't in bed for a straight eight hours during the day. I'd go to bed about nine o'clock in the morning and stay until noon. I'd go to the dining hall for lunch and about one o'clock I'd go back to bed and stay 'til four o'clock. The rest of the time I was up. I could talk or read or stroll around the grounds. Of course, how much you could do depended on what your doctor let you do.

After a few months, I improved enough so that I could go to the "out" building. There we got to do about anything we wanted, within limits. On Thursdays they had lectures and shows and you could go to the recreation hall. Us girls had lots of good times together . . . you see, they separated the men from the women. There was a joke around that they put saltpeter in all the food; I don't know whether they did or not, but it *did* taste kinda funny.

The rumor was that a man with TB is extra passionate or something. So when they had shows, they had them one day for men and one day for women. But there were ways to get around it—when we were in the "out" building, we had store privileges and we used to meet men there.

My best girl friend had to have surgery. They clipped a nerve on her neck that went down to the base of the lung; that immobilizes the lung so that it can rest. Some of the patients even had a rib removed so that the lung would collapse, but they were usually pretty bad.

It was a great place—a haven for "lungers." I was diagnosed as only "moderately advanced" so it wasn't too hard on me. Sometimes we slept in a screened-in porch, and we'd take hot water bottles and lots of wool blankets. Every now and then they'd come around and take our picture for the "Chaser." That was the hospital's monthly paper for lungers.

Seems like everybody had a sense of humor—we laughed a lot and our nurses and doctors were really the best. They thought some of the names we made up were great, and they'd use them—like we called the car that took us for X rays, the bug wagon. I guess we couldn't lose our sense of humor—it would have made everything worse.

I was lucky—like I said—I got out of there after nine months, completely cured. But you can understand, nobody back in my hometown knew where I'd been. I didn't dare tell anybody I'd been in a sanitarium because they'd have avoided me like the plague.

After I left, I wrote to some of my special friends back at the hospital. One got worse and went back to the "in" building. She died later. Sometimes that happened. You'd look like you were getting well, then something would happen.

A GIRL IN THE OZARKS

My dad died in '35, and my mom had died the year before. They were both older, see, because I was the last of twelve children. So I went to live with first one older sister and then another. That's when I made up my mind not to get married—and I was fifteen and they were putting all kinds of pressure on me to get married.

But I saw what it did to them. All those women would just sweat over those wood stoves that put out a terrific amount of heat, and they'd cook those big meals every day. On the farm, you had big meals even in the Depression because you grew it all.

I thought my sisters and those other women were real stupid. For instance, they would do all this cooking and then there were two tables: the first table went to the men and boys, and the second table to the women and girls. Women got the leftovers. I resented that very much. If I'd been grown, I'd have accepted it; but I was just a kid and I could see that it wasn't right. I remember sitting there thinking, "We just have the necks and wings. If it was me, I'd have some nice pieces stashed up there in the warming oven for me to eat later."

It was just amazing to me how those men could figure that they should have the best and whatever was left was good enough for us. And all the women accepted that!

Like for instance, one of my sisters was scrounging for necessities for her kids and I heard her ask her husband for a little money, and he said he didn't have any. Later on, she was scrubbing on a washboard out in the yard and up to the top floated a twenty dollar bill out of his overalls. Now in those days, that was a fortune. She didn't even know where he got it.

So, I told her, "Take it!"—but she wouldn't do it.

If that had been me, I would have taken it. I would have stuck it down in my bra and he could have whistled for it, and I would have had that money as a nest egg when me and my kids was hungry.

"A FEW OF THEM MARRIED LEMONS and, consequently, they ended up not in such good shape themselves," Hope Moat told me. She was talking about her high school girl friends back in Cincinnati who mistreated her when her family lost their money in the 1930s. "I tell my husband that my mortal sin is not being able to forget or forgive them."

HOPE MOAT'S STORY

They would be walking past on the way to school . . . and they would make fun of me. You know the way kids can be cruel.

I always said, my name is Hope, I have Faith, and I accept Charity —only in the thirties it was no joke. We did have to accept charity: we called it relief, WPA, church baskets, anything we could get.

Let me tell you, we were well-to-do when it started. We lived in one of the best areas, had cars, and took trips. My dad owned the Buick automobile agency. But people started going over to Ford in 1931 and that took care of the luxury car business. We lost our shirt just trying to hang on. Everything went—house, cars, savings, and business.

So we rented an apartment and my dad did whatever he could. He shoveled snow on bridges for WPA one winter and did anything to bring in a few sheckles. My mother never worked; she had chronic bronchitis and coughed all the time.

Finally, some decisions had to be made. My parents just couldn't keep the family together. My mom and little brother went to live on my grandparents' farm, my father looked for work wherever he could find it, and I went into one of my high school teacher's homes as a live-in maid.

Now this family was pretty nice to me. The surroundings were pleasant, and I understood I had to take care of myself because my parents were under. But that family worked my tail off for my room and meals. I did everything for them for two years.

I had had a lot of friends. I sang for weddings and parties all over town, and I was popular, I thought. But when we lost our money, some of the girls began treating me very badly. They would be walking past the teacher's house on the way to school, and maybe I'd be out on the front porch washing the windows or something. They would make fun of me, the way some young kids can; that's the way they were cruel to me. And when I'd get a solo part in the school play or something they'd be angry and say things that hurt me deeply.

Actually, I think that hurt me far more than being without my family. It was just a terrible time for me.

On weekends and holidays, I'd go traipsin' up to grandma's and we'd all be together, the whole family; and everybody played an instrument and we sang. We just got closer as a family during that time and, believe me, I understood that they wanted me with them. If I hadn't known that, I might have got into trouble. I knew one girl who thought her parents didn't love her anymore, and she just looked for love anywhere she could find it—and mistook anything that was dished out for love. She got into trouble with the boys—pregnant, you know.

My mother would call me often when we couldn't be together. She knew I got pretty discouraged. "Don't say I can't, say I'll try," she'd tell me . . . it was kind of our family creed those years.

A SOUTHERN BLACK GIRL

The only crimes I can remember during the Depression are things that white people did. I remember once a fourteen-year-old Negro boy was shot by a white and my daddy brought home a gun. He thought there was going to be a riot.

My brother Sam worked downtown driving a truck. This one Christmas Eve he was coming home from work and some white boys—for no reason at all—tossed a firecracker and tore up the leg on my brother's pants.

White boys don't need a reason: that's their fun. Then they got in a car and started chasing Sam, and they cut up his face. They left him for dead, but he got up and rang a doorbell. It was a white neighborhood, and they never even came to the door.

Somehow, he got home and just then I came walking in from shopping with my mama. She just fell over on the bed when she saw him. I called the doctor and when he came, I held the flashlight while he worked on him. There were just tubs of blood all over the living room. And you know what was bothering Sam all through this? He kept saying, "Now, they'll think I'm a roughneck . . . now I'll look like what they think I am." And it really bothered him a lot, the scars on his face.

They were trash, you understand. They were trashy, ignorant, white sons-of-bitches. They didn't have anything to do with real people, and that's how I felt.

The police came but they never did do anything; and Sam's boss came but he wouldn't put himself on the line or all his customers would think he must be a "nigger-lover."

BONNIE HARRON AND HER DAUGHTER run a successful pottery business marketing the Happy Mushroom, a popular gift item throughout the country.

Bonnie writes short stories about "loners."

BONNIE HARRON'S STORY
I used to look out the window at all the apartment houses and imagine there was a lonely little girl behind every window.

My father lost his job with Bethlehem Steel in Chicago early in the thirties and like so many other families, we headed for California, to Concord in the San Francisco area.

For a couple of years my father's new job was secure—secure enough so that he bought a new house. But when they cut him to two days at the mill it wasn't enough to keep up the mortgage.

I remember that my father became very ill and went to the doctor, and he finally became completely paralyzed. My mother always blamed the doctor for trying out a new theory.

Now, she couldn't pay for his hospitalization. So the only thing she could do was divorce him and place him in a charity hospital. It tore her up to do that, but by this time he didn't recognize her or me so it wasn't like he knew what was happening.

My father had been an Olympic swimmer—even taught Johnny Weismuller in his early Florida days. All we had left of him was his medals which my mother felt obliged to keep—for sentimental reasons, I guess. We always lugged around this steamer trunk full of worthless trophies with the gilt peeling off.

I guess it was about '33 when we moved back to Chicago, my mother expecting to go back to work as a commercial artist at a calendar company where she'd worked before. I realize now my mother was naive at times, because she assumed this job would be waiting for her. The company wasn't even there.

Having a small child—I must have been about eight at the time —was always a problem for her, and to my mother's discredit she always let me know that I was what the want ads called "an encumbrance." It made me feel awful guilty, but it also made me want to be awful good.

During the next four or five years she worked all over Illinois, Wisconsin, and Michigan, and I went to more than twenty grammar schools. You know, somehow I was always in transit when they were teaching long division, and I didn't learn it until I got to high school.

But I was a good kid—a damn good kid. I had a sense of responsibility that told me I had to be good because my mother expected it.

I had a very supportive fantasy life. I could always imagine myself in quite nice situations. But I was alone a good bit of the time, and like most lonely kids I read a lot. I was very conscious of loneliness when I was young; I used to look out the window at all the apartment houses and imagine there was a lonely little girl behind every window. I remember one time when we heard my father died, someone said, "Oh, now you must take good care of your mother." And I wondered to myself, "Who is going to take care of me?"

Mother worked for a plastic surgeon once and I used to play in the kitchen while she worked upstairs. There was a Negro maid there who probably didn't get paid much, and in her resentment she'd take things out of the drain and off the floor and throw them in the soup pot. When I told my mother, she said, "Well, we'll just go down the street to a restaurant and eat."

But mother was defiant in her own way, too. She had an aquamarine ring and another ring with three rather large diamonds in it. Now, lots of times they were in hock, but when they weren't she'd be doing housework for people, scrubbing their dirty floors and flashing these impressive rings under their noses.

A GIRL FROM LONG ISLAND

We lived in East Northport, Long Island, and my father had a restaurant. He could have made it through the Depression if he'd put beer in, but he wouldn't so he lost everything.

In 1933 my father left. He just disappeared and we didn't know for about two years where he was. I was the only girl and the apple of my father's eye, but my mother never talked about him; she wouldn't discuss him with me.

They turned off everything—water, electricity, everything—until we were forced to go on relief. It was a disgrace then, you know, and all my friends knew, and I just withdrew; I couldn't face anybody.

I stayed in bed under the covers and read books—fifteen to twenty books a week. There may have been 5,000 books in our city library, and I'm not exaggerating when I say I read them all.

About this time I came under the influence of a neighbor woman. She was a hunchback, and she had many distorted ideas about life and people. But I was looking at the world with such a sour attitude that for a time we became friends. Maybe we needed each other. She told me about her abortion and her fights with her drunken husband, and it seems my whole life became negative. I just eroded with self-pity for almost five years.

"THIS IS PROBABLY the most enjoyable day I've had in months," Leah Parnes told me enthusiastically. "I'm thirty-five years younger today!"

She is a woman who, in her own words, loves life—a woman with opinions about the way life should be lived. "There is one word that separates the young women of the 1930s from those of the 1970s," she said, "and that one word is *restraint*.

"I don't believe in ungovernable urges. I had as much life and vibrancy as girls today, but I knew that unless I restrained myself I could never be happy.

"I came from a *ballabotisha* home—that's a Yiddish word, hard to translate—it means practicing respectability, doing the socially acceptable thing. There aren't many *ballabotisha* homes today, unfortunately."

She went on: "The best thing that ever happens to a woman is finding a good man. I thought that at eighteen, and I still feel the same."

A natural humorist and singer, she has entertained and raised funds for Jewish groups for forty years. "Perhaps you would like to see my clippings later—but first a piece of cake?"

"No, thank you."

"Then a piece without icing?"

"No," I said, pleading a diet.

"Well then a small fruit?"

LEAH PARNES'S STORY

A fella taking a girl out in the thirties would try things, but if a girl came from a respectable home she was expected to reject his advances. . . .

By 1930 I was eighteen and that was a marriageable age. A girl thought primarily of where she was going to attach herself and find an eligible husband who would make a living. It was a time when I went out and got socially oriented.

Women who were working at that time were confined to factories or shops, or if they were really intelligent, they went to college. Most of us were looking for husbands, and it was a big city. New York City was *the* city of the whole world. There was no better place to live and grow up.

I was born on 127th Street and St. Nicholas Avenue . . . it wasn't

Harlem nor was it the East Side as it is today. The cream of Manhattan lived there. My mother had a tailor shop there and worked from morning 'til night, seven days a week. As a child, I helped by delivering suits to the hoi polloi, but I always had the feeling that whatever I was taking was costing my mother her health. Young people had a conscience in those days toward their parents; we pitched in and did our bit. My mother never said to me, "Leah, you have to go out and work." I automatically helped; there was never any question.

So I had been working at this and that for years when I realized that I had to get married; otherwise there was a terrible stigma on a girl. If you reached the age of twenty in the 1930s and you weren't married, well then, you were an outcast.

After I got out of high school, I went to Woods Business School on 125th Street—it was a commercial business college—and on my way to school I met a young man in the subway. In those days you weren't afraid to say "hello" to somebody. Since I had met him three times in one day, I thought it was fate, so I said, "hello."

He was attending business school just across the street from my college. So we began to travel together, and we became very much acquainted.

He was Russian-born and had enrolled in the business school to improve his English. Well, as time went on we became very much enamored of each other—and he gave me a beautiful lavaliere. But he took ill and died the following week . . . a terrible experience for me.

By that time I was almost nineteen years old, and that's when I met Morris, my husband. I met him at a club; it was called the Matrimonial Club. Several people started it as a way to make money. You paid your dues, and these people eventually made off with them. But I didn't know that at first. I went for the social functions and dances. I would sing for the club members and put on a show for them. Attractiveness was vital, but if your personality was such you didn't have to be beautiful. A little extra talent, that made you stand out . . . then you became popular.

That's how I met my husband. He walked in with my girl friend's boyfriend, and I looked up and said to myself: "That's the man I'm going to marry." When we talked, I found out his mother's name was Esther and my mother's name was Esther, his father's name was Morris and my father's name was Morris; and we were both the babies of our families. I thought this must be fate.

To get back to the Matrimonial Club: If a couple met at the club and married, they were given $500. Now that was a great sum, so naturally people were interested. But during the time my husband and I were keeping company, the organization went bankrupt and was investigated by the police. They said the organization had set up phony marriages and had been milking the funds. It was just one of many frauds in those days. People were poor and everybody was scheming to make money, so they'd dupe the public.

Those clubs were not really unusual—we didn't have places where we could go to meet. A young lady couldn't go anywhere unescorted, and when I was growing up I was instilled with a sense of respectability. We had to do the right thing. If you wanted to be a good girl, you could be one. A fella that took a girl out in the thirties would try things, but if a girl came from a respectable home she was expected to reject his advances . . . and of course no girl made advances to men.

Morality was well-defined. Women didn't sit by themselves at restaurant tables. They never, never went into bars. And they never went all the way.

The result of any of these indiscretions was ostracism by her immediate family, her friends, and her temple group. Every girl knew right from wrong. Our behavior was governed by the Ten Commandments and all the unwritten laws as well.

The only thing my mother worried about with my three brothers was that they might get a girl from a good home "involved"— pregnant she meant. That would have meant marriage—an arranged wedding—and immediately, too.

So there was always this fear—boys and girls went together sometimes for four or five years and sexually didn't go beyond a certain point until marriage . . . and I think that was the way it was for millions of us.

We all accepted this. I knew that boys were wary of girls who were loose in their morals. I knew of cases where a girl would "get loose" out of love for the boy—and she was dropped, like that . . . like a hot potato!

HELEN KIRSCH IS AN INVALID, spending her days in a wheelchair recuperating from a heart attack. The day we talked, she sat behind a card table in her living room, taking a few hours away from the writing of her Portuguese-Spanish family's history.

HELEN KIRSCH'S STORY

During the hard times, after we lost our ranch, our whole family went out to pick fruit. My father'd get the job and the whole family would begin to pick about four o'clock in the morning.

My family was dairy ranching near Planada, California, on the west side of the San Joaquin Valley during the thirties until the Bank of Italy foreclosed. The bottom dropped out of the price of milk and we had to mortgage all our cattle and equipment. The bankers were hard-boiled in those days; they just didn't give the ranchers a chance.

There was a big influx of people from the South . . . especially Oklahoma, at that time. I've read *Grapes of Wrath* since and I didn't recognize any of that. We accepted them into our community, and my father hired them if they were willing to work and weren't lazy. See, where I lived there were mostly European immigrants and a few Mexicans. Now, if a body was lazy the rest of the people didn't have any use for them, but if they'd work then we were willing to help them. They managed all right—poorly perhaps, but they managed.

Now if they were lazy and just wanted to be taken care of, we'd send them packing. Old-country people just wouldn't put up with them.

It wasn't a bad way to grow up. We always had horses to ride, and we could go swimming anytime we wanted to. We had a creek on our property, and we swam in irrigation ditches— they had cement on the sides and sand on the bottom, but they were deep.

During the hard times, after we lost our ranch, our whole family went out to pick fruit. My father'd get the job and we'd all begin about four o'clock in the morning because it would get too hot to work about ten o'clock, and then we'd all go back in the evening.

We picked grapes, and I remember we got one cent a tray—if I hurried, I could make a dollar a day.

I didn't mind the grapes as much as the figs. I hate figs to this day. We got ten cents for a 100-pound lug—but you had to crawl on the ground all day. That's right; they smoothed the ground underneath the fig trees, and then the figs ripened and fell down and you crawled along and picked them up. It was either crawl or stoop, and stooping all day can break your back.

That summer in '33, the summer before I was a senior in high school, I worked in figs every day, seven days a week, all summer. I made twelve dollars for school clothes. I really had to keep at it, too, because if I took too many rests I wouldn't get my box full by the end of the day. See, I didn't drag the lug; I filled a bucket and then carried it to the box. But I had to keep my eye on it while I was picking because there were a lot of people working, and some of them stole.

GENA HEDGER

I just adored the ground my father walked on, but he ran off when I was ten, so it was just my mom and me from then on. We fought. We were too much alike, but we had lots of fun and did lots of things, too. You know, people that don't get along still can have fun together. Oh, I guess I was a spoiled brat, but after my father left, I was the man of the house for a long time. I felt like I was responsible for *her*.

But my mother was a natural businesswoman; she could sell you your own shoe strings if you weren't careful. She worked and saved and pretty soon owned a lot of property. I grew up working in my mom's variety store in Enterprize, Oregon, until she finally went broke in the early thirties. The taxes just wiped her out—wiped out everything we'd worked so hard for.

A few years later, some friends of mine asked me over to play a new game called Monopoly. I cried the first time I played. That was exactly the way my mother lost her property, so I hated Monopoly. I said, "That's no game—no game of fun—that's real life."

WHEN I WAS GROWING UP FEMALE in the thirties and forties my mother considered bare feet nudity. Young girls, she taught me, come in two varieties—nice and otherwise. Mary Damon, as a young woman, had been otherwise.

From 1933 until World War II she prostituted herself in several Midwest cities, escaping into war plants when the streets got to be too tough for an aging hooker.

The famous madam of San Francisco's Tenderloin district, Sally Stanford, said that most of the girls who turned up on her steps during the desperate 1930s were unfit for the work. She gave them a piece of change and sent them on their way. "It's certainly a helluva note," she observes in her book *Lady of the House,** "when the need for affection drives an unattractive girl to try a racket for which she is entirely unsuited in order to get a little intimate attention from men."

MARY DAMON'S STORY

This cowboy started following me. Funny how men can tell which girl to follow . . . and I went with him and stayed the night.

My father was a dairyman, and I bottled the milk and washed the bottles. There were between twenty and thirty milkers so I had a big job. From the time I was five years old, I bottled all the milk that supported the family—the eight of us.

I hated that work, running the separator and pasteurizing the bottles. My father was always promising me he'd teach one of my sisters but somehow it always fell to me.

During the Depression there was a lot of throatcutting among dairymen. By '33 the price was down to four cents a quart. Mom was always mad about it and dad was off to meetings in town all the time; I got more fed up every day.

My two aunts came down from Oklahoma City for a visit that summer. They wore pretty dresses and nail polish, and I thought they were real brassy. I told them I'd give anything in the world to

* Stanford, Sally, *Lady of the House,* New York, G. P. Putnam's Sons, 1966.

get away from home and live in the city, and have a job, and maybe get married. . . .

'Course, I'd got to be twenty-two years old and I would have married anybody. But you know, with my homely face, I didn't have a chance with the boys. I know my dad thought I'd just stay on the farm with him forever. That's why I think he didn't want to teach bottling to my younger sisters.

But I'd managed somehow to save some money—$10.37 exactly —and a few days after my aunts left, I did too. I went to Oklahoma City and got a job the first day doing housework. I became a live-in servant. I considered my employers wealthy. They had liquor up in their top cabinet and could afford to mix drinks for people when they came in. Of course, they paid me very little—three dollars a week—but it was enough. I bought some Hoovers: they were kind of a wraparound dress and they were cheap—that's why they called them Hoovers.

I had every Thursday afternoon and evening off, and I'd ride the streetcar downtown and go in some cool drugstore and order an ice cream soda . . . which maybe I'd had only a couple of times in my whole life. Imagine having money to spend as I pleased. I thought I was in the lap of luxury. I was fed, I had a place to live, money in my pocket, and not one damn milk bottle to wash.

I'll have to be honest and tell you I was so happy to get away from home—just to an outrageous extent. I can't understand people who don't want to get away from home. Oh, I don't mind returning for a visit, as long as I'm sure I got money to leave again.

I know I exchanged one kind of housework for another, but I got paid—money, money, money!

I guess the first time I met a man who liked me was when I went to the state fair that fall. Now the state fair was an OK place to go because it was considered to be a very educational thing to do. I remember just walking around watching all the girls with their boyfriends, when this cowboy—his name was Whitey—started following me. Funny, how men can tell which girl to follow . . . but they can. And I went with him and stayed the night.

The next morning when I got back to the house, this lady was waiting for me. I told her it was so late that I didn't want to disturb her so I stayed in a hotel—in those days you could get a room for fifty cents. But, of course, she sacked me on the spot. Oh, she didn't get common or anything. She didn't shout or make accusations but she had an expression on her face—as if she thought I was a bad girl and maybe she didn't want a bad girl touching her babies.

I went back and stayed with Whitey and went on to the next town with him after the fair closed. I don't know whether I loved him that much, since I don't yet know what love is. I just knew I liked being with a man.

There was never any question about getting married. The subject never came up. In about a month, he wanted to send me home but I didn't want to go home. Men, when they take you and use you, don't want any other man to have the same chance—they want you to go back in your little shell. They don't want to feel responsible for what they know is going to happen, for making a tramp out of you. They just always want to send you home.

And anyway he probably figured I'd have no luck if the best I could do for loving was let somebody pick me up at the state fair.

I don't regret it. I guess I thought I was living, and living that way is better than not living at all. But I didn't go home. I went back to Oklahoma City after I promised him I wouldn't run the streets, but that's what I did, and for a hell of a long time after that.

EVELYN GASSLER had a pot of hot, strong coffee brewing when I got to her house. She served it in glazed ceramic mugs, eyeing my tape recorder warily. I explained how harmless it was—that she couldn't possibly sound as nasal as I did. She smiled, a short woman who had an air of shyness about her.

"See the school over there," she said, pointing out her kitchen window. "I graduated from high school there last June.

"When I was a young girl in Alabama and had to go to school, I never liked it, but now that I'm a grandmother, I'm thinking of going to college . . . maybe take accounting. I've discovered I have a natural aptitude.

"You see, I don't just like accounting, I really love it. Figures. It's figures and the balancing. When you do it right and it all balances, that's just the greatest feeling."

EVELYN GASSLER'S STORY

The rollin' store was a big truck with a long body and on the inside it had all kinds of groceries and dry goods . . . anything under the sun you could imagine.

I was only four in 1930, but I remember it . . . I remember it because I got a little brother. Now, my mama sent me over to my uncle's house just a little piece away to stay while she had her baby.

When I came back, I heard the baby crying and said, "What's that?" She said she didn't know; it must be a car or a mouse. But I kept listening, and I could hear the noise coming from her bed . . . and it was coming from beside her in the bed. I said, "Mama, where did you get that baby?" and she said, "off of the rollin' store."

The rollin' store was a big van sort of thing and it had all kinds of groceries and dry goods and anything under the sun you could imagine. It was an old truck with a long body, and the insides were shelves stocked with cans of stuff. There was an aisle in between and the bolts of material and oil cloth and kerosene were piled 'round. On the outside, the man had cages hanging for chickens he bought, and he'd go on down the road. If somebody didn't have a chicken, they'd buy one from him or trade something for one.

No money changed hands on the rollin' store, since nobody had any money to spend. My mother traded her eggs and hens and fryers, butter and things, for things we couldn't raise. Now, I remember he paid my mama ten cents worth of stuff for a dozen eggs.

One week, my mean brother . . . well, he swiped two eggs and ran down and met that rollin' store and bought some candy. He wanted some candy that bad! Now, my mama wouldn't buy any 'cause she figured we didn't need it. With the two eggs, he bought ten of those little kisses, and there was eight of us so everyone of us got one.

Anyway, the week after my baby brother was born, I ran out to meet the rollin' store man and I said, "I want to see the rest of them babies you got in there." 'Course he didn't know what I was talking about. My mother probably gave him a wink or a nod or something. So he said, "Well, we're fresh out this week. I gave your mother the last one a week ago."

And, you know, I didn't suspect anything. Oh, heavens no. I

didn't know what pregnant was. Mama had her last baby when I was twelve years old, and I never knew until I came home from school and there was a baby again . . . I never knew.

In fact, when my older sister got married, she wanted me to come stay with her until after her first baby came. I asked her, "How's it gonna come out?" And she said, "I don't know, but it is." You know when I found out how it did, I couldn't believe it.

When I was ten and I had my first menstrual period, I had no idea what was wrong. I thought it was something terrible, and I hid it for days until my mother found out. I was using hankies, anything I could find. And finally my mother found one that I hadn't buried, and she sent my older sister in to talk to me but she never said a word herself.

By 1939 our cotton farm just couldn't make our livin' anymore. Daddy didn't have any money; he was wiped out. He had to go to Mobile to find a job and so he sold the dog. Isn't that terrible? Took our pet dog to town and sold him for twenty dollars.

SHE WORKED AS A DOMESTIC ten years to earn her tuition for nursing school. Today Frances Ridgway is the head nurse at a university medical school hospital.

She walked miles to school in head-high snowdrifts and later lived and worked away from her family, determined to finish high school. Today, she sends her daughter to an expensive private school.

"Everything has changed in my life," she said, "I have a nice home, a good job . . . I can't even believe my salary . . . and the family went to Hawaii last year. But still the memory of that small town where everybody looked down on me because I was poor . . . still that memory causes me a feeling of uneasiness. So until today I have tried to never think about the past."

FRANCES RIDGWAY'S STORY

I washed and cleaned . . . the dirty work, you know. I started to school with six dollars . . . but I used to make a nickel for each book report I'd write for the boys on the football team.

The Depression caused my family to change their way of living. There were six of us kids and in order to feed us all, my parents traded their town home for an eighty-acre farm. There was no electricity there, no running water, and no flush toilet. And the house was back off the road a half a mile.

But my father thought at least we could eat, living on a farm. And we did, even if it was only beans. My mother would put up 600 or 700 quarts of beans every year.

When I reached twelve years old, I wanted to go to high school; but back in northern Michigan they didn't encourage farm girls to get much of an education. Now, I really insisted that my parents let me go live with this family who paid me two dollars a week to take care of the house and kids.

I did that kind of work for the better part of four years. Sometimes I stayed at home, but when I did I'd have to walk almost four miles to get to the place where the school bus stopped.

I'll tell you, I washed and I cleaned and did all the dirty work, you know. Anyway, when I started that first year of high school, I had six dollars saved, and that was enough to buy all my supplies until Christmas. I supplemented my income in another way, by writing all the book reports for the boys on the football team at a nickel apiece. And you know for a nickel you could get a big, thick pad of paper.

During my senior year I got an NYA grant of six dollars a month for helping the teachers correct papers. I thought that was wonderful.

But on the whole, it was hard. I was so very poor. I had one skirt I made out of an old coat in home economics class. And I wore NRA pants. You know, my family got food supplements, and they'd come in sacks that had NRA stamped on them. My mother'd dye them a dark seal brown, but the NRA was still there. My brothers used to always call my NRA pants, "Nuts Running America." I forget . . . I think it meant National Recovery Act.

Anyway, I had no clothes and no money but I finished at the top of my class and I competed for a scholarship and won. It was to Wellesley, a big Eastern college for women. Well, of course, that was out of the question. I didn't even have the money to get there, let alone all the extras I'd need.

But I had a goal for myself. Ever since I was twelve years old there was one major goal in my life . . . one thing . . . and that was to never be poor again. I wasn't especially attractive, and I was poor. I couldn't do anything about the one, but I made up my mind I wasn't always going to be poor.

AN OZARKS GIRL

Reading was the thing I wanted most to do when I was in my teens. The only book we had in our house was the Bible . . . never a magazine . . . couldn't afford a newspaper, ever, that I remember.

Oh, we heard about what was going on by word of mouth. Everybody was still talking about Lindy, and we heard about the gangsters like Dillinger. But, Chicago was on the other side of the world so it had nothing to do with us. I was never afraid of people . . . just God. He was the only one I was scared of.

So the outside world didn't really mean much to me. Like I said, newspapers weren't something you had delivered to your house; they were something you papered the wall with. Every spring, my aunt and uncle would come from town and bring all their old newspapers to us, and then my mama wallpapered our house with them.

Most of my reading was done by standing on my head reading a newspaper pasted on the wall.

Every evening of the world, my mama read the Bible to us in front of the fire. While she was reading, our bodies were in constant motion, turning from front to back, trying to keep warm.

After Bible reading, we'd all make up stories, and they were always about scary things.

There was a bond between my mother and the women she knew . . . nobody was dressed better than the other. I don't even think they thought about it. And no woman thought of herself as sexy. If she did, she kept it a secret; she would have been considered a low-type person if she had ever admitted to any human being that she was sexy or that she had sexual feelings of any kind. If there were any sexy women around my part of the country at that time, I didn't know it.

No, the thing that held the women together was drudgery and their hatred of sex and having babies. I think that was their bond.

I have overheard women friends of my mother, and I heard my mother make remarks often enough about sex, such as referring to husbands as dirty old men. "I would rather see a snake coming toward me than a dirty old man," I heard my mother say.

And for my mother, the terror of her life until the day she died was that one of her girls would have another baby. She had three daughters and every time we were pregnant she was terrified. It was never a joyous occasion for her. She had four children, all of them alone or with a midwife, and to her, having a baby was literally jumping into the jaws of death. That's the way she talked about it.

Sex and drudgery . . . drudgery and sex . . . that's what held them together. Their whole lives were just one monotonous round. Washing, baking, and sewing; canning, gardening, and . . . she sewed all her kids' clothes by hand. By hand! She could make the tiniest little stitches all straight in a row. When she got her first sewing machine for seven dollars she was so scared that I would break the needle. Since she couldn't have bought another, she wouldn't let me come near it. I remember resenting that woman terribly because she wouldn't let me use that sewing machine.

SHE DOESN'T WANT ME TO USE her last name. Even after so many years, Ellen was more than a bit uneasy about her experiences on the road. I sensed that she was leaving much of her story untold, but when I probed she withdrew. At one point, remembered frustration brought tears; at another, her face hardened as she recounted being hustled over a county line in the middle of the night.

There was some hint of the youthful rebel remaining. "Remember a few years ago," she said, "when the kids were throwing bombs?

"Of course I was horrified, but some part of me understood. Sometimes I'd think—if we young people in the thirties had banded together, we'd have thrown bombs, too. But we didn't. We were like sheep."

ELLEN'S STORY

I was arrested thirty-one times for vagrancy before I got to Chicago.
There were days I was pretty hungry . . . and I slept in all kinds
of places.

I couldn't find a job, and I voted for Franklin Roosevelt. I don't
know what I thought he was going to do for me, but by the summer
of '34 there still wasn't a job for me, and I was getting to the point
I had to get away from home. It was just too much. I felt really
suicidal some of the time: hopeless, and worse, useless. I don't think
I would have done anything to myself, but I was reacting violently
to my situation.

The only way I could get away was to hitchhike. That upset my
mother a lot, but there were a lot of young people hitchhiking then,
although more boys and men than girls. She took me out on the main
highway north, crying all the way, and gave me her last two dollars.

I was gone four months. I got clear to Chicago and I was arrested
thirty-one times for vagrancy and put in all sorts of places to get me
out of sight. Some of the cops, of course, just picked me up and
dumped me on the edge of town. I said, "I'm just looking for a job."
But they told me they had their own unemployed so they didn't need
me. There were days I was pretty hungry and I'd just ask for food
or ask to work for food—and I slept in all kinds of places.

So when I got to Chicago, the police picked me up again and took
me to a place where they put prostitutes that wanted to kinda
straighten up . . . and I was there for a week. I was locked in a room
and fed; they brought me a tray of stuff twice a day.

Of course, I was no prostitute but I had no visible means of
support, and they didn't know what else to do with me so they put
me in with them.

After one week, they took me to Traveler's Aid and told them
they wanted me shipped back to Florida. I argued that I didn't want
to go back, but they didn't listen. It didn't matter what I said, you
know; they just wanted me out of Chicago.

So I filled out an aid application for the caseworker at Traveler's
Aid. She nearly fell over when she saw I was a Radcliffe graduate.
She said, "uh huh," disbelieving at first, but then after she talked to
me she decided I was what I said I was.

So she threw me the keys to her apartment and tore up the application for aid. She lived up on Rush Street with her brother, and they fed me and I applied for a job at Marshall Field and got it.

I spent the rest of the summer working in the French dress section and there wasn't a hell of a lot going on in that department, so after a while I got restless. And for another reason: I know they meant well, but this woman and her brother thought I had some kind of psychological thing about hitchhiking and they kept trying to get me to go to a psychiatrist.

One day while they were at work, I just left them a note and hit the road. I got as far as Washington, D.C., and—by gosh, I was arrested again and this time they put me up in the YWCA. They didn't have facilities for women, and you know, they could see I was a nice girl who could carry on an intelligent conversation. They didn't know what to do with nice girls.

Somebody at the Y told Melvina Lindsey about me. She was a famous columnist at the time on the *Washington Post,* and she came out and interviewed me. She wanted to know the scoop about conditions on the road, and she thought I had made some good observations. I told her I'd tell her if she wouldn't syndicate the article in Florida, and she promised.

After that, they put me on a Pickwick bus with a big, blue charity ticket which meant that I couldn't get off except to go to the bathroom and eat and always when the driver was there . . . so I couldn't get away you know.

When I got home, I was too embarrassed to call my mother so I walked in unexpectedly and she and my sister were reading a full-page spread in the Sunday paper about everything that had happened to me.

Talk about being mad! But it had an unexpected benefit for me. I was immediately offered opportunities to speak about my experiences all over the country, and I did, taking the line that young people looking for work were treated as criminals.

Anyway, I made enough money from my lecture tour to buy a motorcycle. I was still restless. I can't explain it now, but it seemed that I wanted to get away from where I was or who I was, I don't know. Anyway, I bought an old Harley Davidson, a secondhand police motorcycle with a sidecar. This boy I knew taught me how to ride and I started out. On one trip I went up to Radcliffe; I still had friends there and they were all amused at my antics. I think they had decided by that time that I was kinda nuts.

I was gone for six months, and everywhere I went I got a lot of personal publicity. I went over 13,000 miles as far north as Portland, Maine, and as far west as Boulder Dam and Los Angeles. When I got to Milwaukee they gave me the key to the city and made a plaster cast of my motorcycle. Milwaukee, you see, is where they make Harley Davidsons. They went all over it and measured it with a micrometer. They said they'd never seen one with so many miles as that one had on it.

I guess that last trip cured me because I took a job with the state government—when I got home from the motorcycle tour everybody wanted to hire me. After that I traveled in very conventional ways.

EVELYN JOHNSON IS STILL TALL and thin. In her early sixties now, she's also ill. According to her, she's had ". . . three and a half strokes," in the past few years.

"Men have no respect for women these days," she said, comparing the seventies with the thirties. "They're in your house not five minutes and they want to know where the bedroom is."

EVELYN JOHNSON'S STORY

One of the men was friendly . . . he just thought I was a scared boy. Whenever I'd speak to him, I'd try to make my voice sound about three times as low as it was.

I was living on the East Coast when the Depression hit. I had just graduated from high school and my father was working for the government in naval aviation. Well, we were transferred around just like servicemen—from Pensacola to Norfolk and back again, and to all the small navy towns in between.

My mother had passed away and I was trying to get a job. In those days you didn't go ahead and become a stenographer just by graduating from high school; you had to take a business course outside of school.

So, not being trained to do anything, I worked as a waitress to save for business school. I gave every penny of my tips to my father and I asked him to keep it 'til I had enough for the course.

After several months, I said to him one night while he was reading the paper, "Well, daddy, don't you think I've got about enough money saved?" And he said, "What money?"

He had been going out with a woman about thirty years younger than he was, and I came to find out he had spent all my money on her.

In those days, you didn't speak back to your father. And when I got mad, he said, "If you're trying to call me a thief, get out of my house. Never put your foot over my threshold again."

And there I was, out in the middle of the street at night with no place to stay and not a cent to my name. I went to my boss at the restaurant, and he was a kind old gentleman; he put me up for the night at his house.

The next morning, I told him I had to get out of town. I had always heard good things about California so I wanted to go there. He advised me to think about it real good. "Don't take a step you'll be sorry for," he said. But I'd made up my mind, and so he said, "Well, then, come on with me."

He took me to a hardware store and bought me some secondhand overalls and a wool shirt . . . bought me an old hat that didn't halfway fit and took me to the railroad yards. You see, I was trying to disguise myself as a boy so I could ride the freight trains.

Let me tell you, I didn't know much. When I got put out of the house, I had no idea of what life was about. In those days your mother explained it to the girls, and your father explained it to the boys. My father hadn't told me anything so I didn't know what the heck to expect. But this old gentleman, well, he'd worked for the railroad before he got into the restaurant business and he told me what to do to get by.

I pushed my hair up under the hat and pulled it way down on my face. I was tall and real skinny so I looked just like a young boy. Anyway, he shoved a twenty dollar bill in my hand, and told me to use it for eating purposes.

Took me six days to get to California. It was in October, and it got pretty cold on the cars so I managed to buy a Levi jacket off a man. That's how I kept from freezing to death.

There were lots of men in the cars. I always held my head down and had that hat pulled down. I was so scared I couldn't see straight.

One of the men was friendly; he just thought I was a scared boy. And whenever I'd speak to him, I'd try to make my voice sound about three times as low as it was. Sometimes, he'd get off the freight and go get me a couple of sandwiches and coffee. But believe me, I was so scared I'd practically heave up the sandwiches after I'd eaten.

So you know when mother nature called I always waited until the train stopped, then I'd go hide somewhere. I was in good health and I could do that.

If it was a long, through train, they'd just put the cars on a side track, leave them there for hours and then another engine would come and hook on to us and we'd be going again.

Most of the men on the car weren't really hoboes or bums; they were married men trying to get to California to find a job. See, they just thought I was some boy skipping out on school . . . and in those days, I could climb a freight just as fast and good as anybody you ever seen in your life.

They were good men. If one had tried to pile on me, the others would have protected me. But I was glad to be off there. I still had some money, so I got a bath and cleaned up and had a waitress job two hours after I got to California.

A TEXAS GIRL

I got an abortion when I was eighteen, and it's a wonder I didn't die. I ended up hemorrhaging and had to go to the hospital for surgery.

My mother helped me—not so much because she loved me—but to save her good name. I paid for it later, because she always reminded me I was a tramp and I'd ruined myself.

I was so dumb. I didn't know anything, but the boy ran around and hunted up the midwife—a dreadful quack who just butchered me on a kitchen table.

That was only after the ergot had failed. You see, we believed in those days that ergot or some medicine that had ergot in it would abort you, but of course it didn't.

I guess I was lucky I didn't die; but for a few weeks I remember wishing I would.

"THE THING I MISSED MOST of all was piano lessons," Jayne Hobbs told me. "I always felt that if my mother had lived she would have seen to it that I got them.

"I used to envy the other girls their clothes, but if they could play the piano, then I really hated them."

Today she owns a piano and plays, according to her own evaluation, acceptably well. "It's been the joy of my life," she said. "All my children have taken lessons."

Jayne thinks mothers made the difference in surviving the thirties: "They scrounged and remade, and they could somehow manage to eke out whatever their kids needed."

JAYNE HAWKINS HOBBS'S STORY

I accidentally found a good trick. . . . I said, "Please, ma'am, could I have a drink of water?" . . . and she says, "Here's a nickel."

When my mother died, my father was left with four children. To be fair to the man, I guess he made the best provisions for us that he could, but it's quite clear to me he just didn't know how to take care of us without mother.

Anyway, he took us to St. Louis to live with this German family, and he made a business deal with them for our keep. Somehow he bought a special recipe for coconut macaroons . . . and they *were* delicious cookies.

All day while we were in school, the Mrs. would be making these cookies and then she would meet us after school with a trunk load. They sold for fifteen cents a dozen which was quite expensive then, so she only took us to the nicer neighborhoods. Anyway, she would put these packages of cookies in our baskets and drop us off on a block and then come back about an hour later and pick us up.

A lot of the people thought the cookies were too high, so we carried little cut-up samples around to prove how good they were . . . only sometimes I'd get hungry and eat them. I'd go down the streets and up on their porches and knock on the doors. Sometimes I'd sell my basketful fast, and sometimes I wouldn't do so good, until I found the trick.

You see, when we weren't in school we worked during the daytime and one summer day I accidentally found this good trick— I went up to the door and this woman was almost hostile when I asked her if she would buy my cookies. Well, I had been out so long and it was hot and I really needed a glass of water. So I said, "Please, ma'am, could I have a drink of water?" And I could see she didn't want to be bothered, but she went in and got me a glass and just as I said, "Thank you, ma'am," and turned away, she said: "Just a minute. I don't want your cookies, but here's a nickel." See, she had a good heart but she was gruff.

So after that, I used that trick because all we got was six cents profit on a dozen, so a nickel—and still having the bag to sell somewhere else—was eleven cents profit. And sometimes they'd even give me a dime.

But you know, I found out fast that I couldn't pull that trick too often because I had no bathroom to go to. I only did it when I thought I wasn't going to make a sale. I actually learned to judge where I could use it and where I couldn't. And I did that for two years, almost every day. Maybe we'd each sell twelve packages and there were four of us working, so you can see we were making our own way all right.

I don't know how my sixth-grade teacher found out, but I remember she started to tell it out in school. She must have seen the horrified look come over my face because she only said: "I am so proud of someone in this room. I found out that a lot of you kids go out and play after school but this one child goes out and sells cookies to help out her family."

Now, I could have died of embarrassment—because you know I wanted to be like every other kid in the class—but after that I was a little prouder of myself.

I earned my keep from the time I was ten. And I never stopped as young as I was, and I never found any excuse not to work like a lot of kids. My father had a favorite expression: "Root-hog or die," he'd say. That meant if I didn't work, I didn't eat; so I worked.

PART THREE
WOMAN'S WORK

A BRIEF TEN YEARS after their first vote was counted in 1920, 11 million American working women held jobs in offices, factories, and retail stores, making up almost one-fourth of the country's total labor force.

But this soaring progress for women in industry came crashing down with the stock market in 1929. During the next few years their wages steadily declined until women office workers in New York City who had previously earned forty-five dollars a week were taking home only sixteen dollars. A mid-thirties survey of factory girls in Chicago showed they averaged twenty-five cents an hour—one in four making a low ten cents an hour. In the North, maids toiled a month for ten dollars, while in the South women cooked for other families just for the privilege of taking leftovers home to their children. And black women in Alabama, working twelve-hour, six-day weeks in steamy hot laundries made a pitiful $5.85.

The needs of the unemployed and underemployed helped to develop social work into the growth profession of the 1930s. And social work was uniquely fitted to women's traditional nurturing skills, drawing thousands of college graduates into its ranks.

No one knows how many women were unemployed during the thirties. Separate records for women were not kept. But we do know that there were 12 million, or almost one-third of the total labor force out of work by 1932. If the old percentages held true, 3 million of the unemployed were women.

Unskilled workers were the first to bear the full effects of the Depression, but professional women weren't far behind. "I was one who found myself caught with family responsibilities," wrote a teacher in 1936. "Though I possessed unquestionable credentials, I was unable to get into the public school system which was glutted with applications. I was finally given an adult education WPA appointment which helped me preserve my morale and self-respect."

WPA (Works Progress Administration) helped many women survive during the thirties with jobs in social services, libraries, and other traditional areas of women's work. And in 1935, when the NYA (National Youth Administration) began, younger women were put to work in their communities—sewing, lettering signs, and running children's playgrounds.

But while it took another world war to bring women into formerly all-male occupations, women of the thirties found they had power in the union movement.

It was a decade of labor turmoil and labor advance. Union pressures helped bring shorter working hours, higher wages, social security, and the beginning of fringe benefits. And women were everywhere on the picket lines, raising their voices in every song from the "Internationale" to:

> "Barbara Hutton has the dough, *parlez-vous,*
> Where she gets it, sure we know, *parlez-vous,*
> We slave at Woolworth's five and dime,
> The pay we get is sure a crime,
> Hinkey dinkey, *parlez-vous.*"

Their song didn't thrill Tin Pan Alley but 110 striking Detroit dime-store girls in 1937 made their point in six days of hoarse singing. They forced Woolworth's to grant them a raise—appropriately enough—five cents an hour.

Some union women of the thirties looked beyond wages and benefits to call for far-reaching reforms. In her popular book, *Women Who Work,* published in 1934, Grace Hutchins denounced the "double slavery" of both work and housekeeping, saying it would only end when women demanded maternity leave and day nurseries. These victories, she urged, "could be won when women, together, organize and strike."

These victories were not to come in the thirties nor has the entire battle been decided yet. But such rhetoric helped shape women's attitudes in those near-revolutionary days when most were making do with whatever job they could get.

For actresses during the thirties, radio provided employment and a showcase for their talents never equaled before or since. There was drama, music (high brow and low), and glorious comedy.

Radio gave listeners friends they could count on. Afternoons, after school, kids could be uplifted by Little Orphan Annie or Jack Armstrong. And what scrimping housewife would not feel better knowing that Ma Perkins was coping with her same problems over in Rushville Center? The moon "came over the mountain" when Kate Smith came over the air every week. And Mary Livingston, likewise, could be regularly depended upon to say, "Oh, Jack!" in her exasperated, nasal voice. Jane Ace, that Mrs. of Malapropisms, delighted husband Goodman and everyone else with such expressions as "ragged individualist" and "Congress is still in season."

Some of the dancing during the thirties was done to music provided by professional women musicians. For if Benny Goodman was the "king of swing," then Ina Rae Hutton was its queen. The former child vaudeville star and vocalist led a flashy, all-girl aggregation before she was out of her teens. By 1940, *Metronome* magazine voted hers one of the top big bands.

During the 1930s women's hands held many of the tools of recovery. Although most were not highly paid or recognized, it was obvious that "woman's work" was no longer only in the home.

Chapter Seven

THOSE WHO COPED CREATIVELY

JEAN GATES HALL WAS MOVING the morning I arrived at her 1940s-vintage stucco, set back from a quiet hospital street. Stacks of canvas paintings, framed pastels, and watercolors nearly hid the few pieces of over-stuffed and over-used furniture waiting for the moving van. Two tabbies stalked us along the small entry hall and into the kitchen.

"This is the new place I'm building," she said, showing me black and white contact proofs of a house outlined by rafters and bare boards. "It's just beautiful. See, here is the deck. It's going to be ten by thirty feet, jutting right into those tall pines.

"I suppose it's a cliché dream these days, getting away to the country. But I've been planning it for years."

Jean retired in 1974 after fifteen years as an art teacher in a Sacramento, California, junior high school, a late-blooming career made possible by a master's degree she didn't finish until she was forty-eight.

Married in the waning days of the Depression and divorced after the war, Jean raised a daughter on the low wages of one certain kind of high prestige job. "The kind," she explained with a wince of bitterness, "that an under-educated woman with ability builds for somebody with a degree to take over at higher wages." Realizing she'd never gain security without a diploma, she returned to school.

But on this morning—her career behind her—Jean and I sat drinking coffee at her kitchen table. "I've been thinking about those days, ever since you called," she said, straightening a mound of handwritten notes with long, tapered fingers—the kind my mother termed *artistic*.

"What are you calling your book?" she asked.

"Making Do."

"Well, I wouldn't. I'd call it, 'Accepting Fate.' "

JEAN GATES HALL'S STORY

Walt Disney laughed and said, "You know what would happen if we had one of our pretty girls working with the men."

I'd have to begin back a little earlier than 1930. For me, the Depression started when I was sixteen. That must have been in 1927.

I was living in Hollywood with my mother and twin brother, and both us kids had to quit school to go to work. We had two older brothers, but one *wouldn't* help and one absolutely couldn't, so the job of supporting mother fell mainly on us younger ones.

That was a tough period of life for me. I had to get some kind of job. But I was so shy . . . so shy it was painful for me to apply for work. I remember, after seeing an ad for a soda jerk, walking up and down in front of the drugstore, trying to get up the nerve to go in. When I finally did, the woman told me she'd just hired someone not five minutes before.

I went home and told my mother the job was filled. I didn't dare tell her that I'd missed out because I was scared.

During that time I started a correspondence course in art which my twin brother—he was such a good guy—paid for. I finished this course over a period of four years, which gave me art training I hadn't had. It turned out to be good experience because by the time I finished I had a portfolio of art samples to show around.

Now you wouldn't remember, but in the early thirties they had large, pastel drawings of Ann Harding and other actresses in front of theaters advertising each show. They were hand-drawn by local artists who could quickly produce a pastel which would be slapped up every week or so—whenever the shows changed.

I knew I could do this. So I made some beautiful samples which

I carried around, except there were no jobs. By this time the Depression was really on.

But the theater owners complimented my work; one suggested that I try the cartoon studios.

So I began making the rounds of the studios, going back day after day, week after week.

I'd been out of steady work for a year. Oh, I'd done some baby-sitting, and filled in as a waitress. We were living frugally on my brother's pay as a messenger boy for Universal. His sixteen dollars a week was our food and rent money.

Hollywood Boulevard didn't have any glamour in those days. I remember the apple sellers during my job-hunting walks. They looked so old and desperate. They upset me because I felt that I would end up with an apple crate: that it would just come to that.

When the first dime store opened—it was a Woolworth's—they advertised to apply at eight o'clock in the morning. That's when I arrived, but I was still pretty naive. I was the tail end of a mob of people. It even made the front page; 500 people had applied for twenty-five jobs.

I felt terrible, very depressed. We had to have some more money. Our food supply was always low. I can remember mother asking, as I worked on a cartoon for my portfolio: "What do you want for lunch, Jean?" I'd say ". . . a bacon and tomato sandwich." You know, she made it with *one strip* of bacon on it. When she came back and it was all gone, she'd always ask, "Would you like another sandwich, dear?" I did want another but I thought, "better watch the bacon" and refused. We didn't go hungry, but we lived lean.

You wouldn't remember Doris Kenyon. She was a working actress, and she was my cousin. She lived in another world, you know. She was never a star, but she did get some good second roles. She was in *Ones Who Could Care* with Rudolph Valentino; and with Ramon Navarro when he did those lovely Hawaiian scenes.

She didn't help us financially because, well, mother was terribly proud and wouldn't ask. And we never let her know how down we were. But she would send us her cast-off clothes—boxes of them—in a chauffeur-driven car.

They were things she might have worn just once during a picture or to a party. Usually they had makeup all over them.

Once there was this beautiful dress with smocking and tiny accordian pleats all around. It was rose silk and I dearly loved it. It fit me perfectly. But when it came back from the cleaners, we had to scrape up three dollars to pay for it. I just cried my eyes out because I knew when it got dirty again, I'd have to throw it away.

Finally, I got a job at Charles Mintz's—one of several small cartoon studios around then. Every major studio had its own shop—there was one at Warner's, Universal, and of course, Disney—but I went to work at Mintz's first. There were about twelve young women there. We worked for fifteen dollars a week. My job was to fill in color on the celluloid. We worked all day, and there were no coffee breaks although we stood and stretched sometimes.

But we really resented that we had no place to eat our lunch except at our desks. Naturally, we all brought lunch because we couldn't afford to eat out. We wanted a room, a small room some place. We knew there were extra rooms stacked with supplies. So we asked several times for one, but nothing ever came of it. One day all twelve of us took our lunch bags and sat along the curb on Hollywood Boulevard, right in front of the Charles Mintz studio. We ate our lunch with our feet in the gutter.

Oh, that was unfeminine. It took a lot of guts. Remember, we wore dresses in those days, not pants.

I won't say I was totally responsible for the rebellion, but I encouraged the rest to stand up—or in this case sit down for our rights.

It was a strike of a sort and, of course, the men at the corner drugstore came out to gawk. Charles Mintz himself came out, and he was so embarrassed he pulled his hat down over his eyes and walked off.

Well, word got out that the troublemakers would be disciplined, but twenty-four hours later they cleared a small room and put in a couple of chairs and a little cot. It was a narrow space, but it was *our* lunchroom.

Most of the women hadn't been eager to join us, but when we won our spot they all crowded in. I felt triumphant. We sure got our point across.

The only way you could get a raise in those days was to look for another job. Studios were doing well. Disney was growing, but not in the big time yet. None ever gave raises until you threatened to leave for a better job.

So when I'd hear via the grapevine that maybe they needed an inker over at Harmonizing Studios or Universal, I'd go over during my lunch break. And during my vacations, I'd really pound the streets. Then I'd come back and say, "Well, they've offered me eighteen dollars over at Harmonizing," and if they couldn't meet that I'd change jobs. I worked at Harmonizing, Universal, and Disney after I left Mintz. In seven years, I bargained my salary up to twenty-seven dollars a week. Not one studio ever gave me a raise voluntarily.

The last two and a half years I worked as a cartoonist at Disney. Toward the end, during 1937 and '38 I was working on *Snow White*. This was a big gamble for Disney—a feature-length cartoon. We were all excited about it.

I was still an inker, but I was one of the head inkers. I traced all the art work on celluloid that the animators drew on paper. After I inked, the painters colored the celluloid on the reverse side.

I didn't want to be an inker the rest of my life so at night I went to Chouinard, one of the finest commercial and fine arts schools in Los Angeles. My teacher, Phil Paradise, who headed the fine arts department and was an exhibiting painter, encouraged me.

My hope was that maybe I could be an illustrator and I was doing really well, especially in pastels and watercolors. Mr. Paradise was so impressed with my work that he entered a pastel of mine in an art show and it won first prize.

About that time Chouinard offered me a scholarship which was one of the few they ever gave. I was so excited, but the scholarship only paid for tuition and materials.

I still had to support mother so I turned to my older brother for help. He was twenty years older than I, and he was sending his daughter to Bryn Mawr. He had that kind of money. But he didn't understand me at all, even after I wrote him a very blunt letter, as one adult to another, about his responsibilities to mother. He had no understanding that I wanted to make a life career as an artist. He wrote back, "No, you'll have to make do some other way."

I went to my mother. "Mother, couldn't we move to a smaller place," I begged. We were paying thirty-five dollars a month and I thought we could get a place for twenty dollars. My twin brother was willing. He thought it would be great fun to live in a kind of garret while I painted. But mother simply . . . couldn't. Her pride wouldn't let her do this for me. She wouldn't apply for relief even though we were eligible.

Mother didn't understand any better than my older brother. I showed her the painting that won first prize and she said, "That's very nice, dear. You'll find a way."

But there was no way. No way I could get any money so that I could take that scholarship. Mr. Paradise was simply shocked.

I remember as I walked to the Disney Studio, standing on a hilltop where grass was blowing. I thought, "Oh, my God, there's Van Gogh's grasses," and I wanted to paint so bad but I had to work. It did something to me. It got to my inner self.

After that I wanted desperately to get out of inking at Disney and into the background department where I could do watercolor and air-brush work. I had the talent and training for it.

But there were only men in that department. And, only men were animators. That was the highest paying job. The only women working at Disney were either in the office or were inkers.

One day I went to the gas station across the street during noon hour and telephoned Walt Disney himself. You could reach him by phone in those days. I gave him a fictitious name and told him I had three years of art school and plenty of watercolor work. I said I'd like to show him samples and apply for a background job. He was very pleasant but he said, "We only hire men in that department. Our women work in the inking department. Why don't you come in and apply for that job?" But when I insisted I'd still like to try for the watercolorist's job, he laughed, "You know what would happen if we had one of our pretty girls working with the men."

I knew what he meant. He was afraid that the men couldn't work with us around. But I came right back with, "Oh no, Mr. Disney, I wouldn't be a problem." It was no use. He'd already hung up.

A short while later, I began talking union with about a dozen other Disney people. We met secretly at each other's houses. We didn't want anyone to know what we were doing. We could have been fired for just talking about it, let alone trying to organize.

They did form a union and even had a strike, but by that time I'd left Disney. I got married and moved to San Francisco. Late in 1938, I applied for WPA and I got on the artist's project for one year. I got eighty dollars a month and food stamps. My husband and I lived in a little artist's studio.

It was the most wonderful year of my life. I was what they called an *easel artist*. I went on cable cars all over San Francisco and I could paint whatever I wanted, whenever I wanted. Once a week my boss would choose three works. These works were hung in public buildings. They were called WPA art works. I could have the ones he didn't want, so the harder I worked the more I could keep for myself.

Eventually I had enough left over for a show at the Paul Elder Gallery where the great Alfred Frankenstein gave me a good review. That *was* a thrill. I even sold one watercolor for twenty dollars.

I was still on WPA when I entered a national contest sponsored by the Corcoran Art Gallery in Washington, D.C. There were thousands of entries from all over the country, and they were to pick seventy-five works. I sent three, and two of them were selected for the show. They sold for thirty dollars each. That was big money and a feather in my cap. I thought I was really on my way.

But shortly after, my husband got a job and I had to go off WPA. Then I got pregnant.

JINNY FROM OHIO

I was fresh out of college in June, 1939. There were no jobs to be had, so my friend Cynthia and I decided to go into the commercial swimming pool business.

We had absolutely no experience in the business world . . . and only ten dollars between us. But we did have a lot of ambition and even more nerve. The pool we rented in our hometown of Wooster, Ohio, was located across the road from the fairgrounds on the edge of town. We paid the owners our ten dollars as a deposit to take it off their hands for the summer.

The pool was kind of isolated . . . we were within screaming distance of no one, so we hired Cynthia's sixteen-year-old brother to give us protection in exchange for unlimited swimming privileges. Cynthia and I then took up residence in a room above the combined snack bar and ticket booth.

The water for the pool was obtained from an underground river by means of a well and was pumped into the pool through a two-inch pipe.

It took two months to fill it . . . and a lot of electricity to run the pump.

Now, the electric company required a ten-dollar deposit before they'd turn on the electricity, and neither of us had it, but we knew someone who did . . . the owners of the pool. So we had the nerve to borrow our deposit back, temporarily, and pay it to the electric company.

On our best day that summer we took in fifteen dollars gross. On our worst . . . nothing. It rained. But everything was going swell until my friend Cynthia fell in love with a boy named Clark . . . and out of love with the pool.

By this time I was getting tired of the whole deal myself. There were some irritations that went with being a businesswoman. The bathroom was in the basement, you see, with the toilet in one corner and no walls in between. We reached it by means of a trapdoor . . . which got to be pretty old stuff after a while.

THE HANDS THAT MARCELLED, curled, and crimped thousands of heads during the Depression years are swollen with arthritis today. Unknowing, I reached for her hand, sending a shock wave of pain through her.

RUBY BRADY'S STORY

In one shop the manager got mad at me because I wouldn't talk a customer into a ten-dollar permanent. I was supposed to work on her vanity. . . .

I graduated from Hammond's Beauty College on March 16, 1936, the night before the Johnstown, Pennsylvania, flood. I'd wanted to be a mortician, but my mother wouldn't let me. I always liked doctoring and nursing, and I was interested in the human body. But what I knew definitely was that I didn't want to finish high school with no trade and end up cleaning other people's dirty toilets or washing their babies' butts. I'd had enough of that.

Anyway, the night I graduated I stayed in town with a girl friend, and the next day we saw the manhole covers bouncing around on the street—it had been raining and raining. Pretty soon the water came in to the first floor and we moved what we could to the second floor. We acted kind of crazy, singing "River Stay 'Way from My Door" . . . you know, young girls are silly.

We all finally ended up on the third floor, watching the rats swimming by, squeaking and squeaking. The next day the water receded, but it had messed up everything. Down in shantytown where all the foreign people lived, they'd been wiped out.

The water had come up seventeen feet and when it went down, everything stunk from dead animals and mildew. My girl friend's family had to throw all their furniture out, and they just took hoses in their house to clean out the mud and stuff. You know it must have been bad with $40 million damage in a town of something like 10,000 people.

Anyway, as I said, I had just graduated after six months at beauty college. I got a job shampooing until I could pass my state board exam in cosmetology. Then I went back to Hammond's as an instructor. I'd teach during the week and work in a shop on weekends.

We gave Croqunole permanents then. We clamped them into the machine—it always reminded me of a milking machine. We mapped the hair into inch squares—we had different wraps for the curliness you wanted—and then we steamed the curl in. I've heard all kinds of things women tell about how long they stayed under the machine, but the longest was fifteen minutes. It just seemed like hours. Sometimes the solution would run and since it was hot, you could get burned.

We gave a lot of manicures, too. And a lot of bleaches. Everybody wanted to be a blond like Jean Harlow. They were so messy, I got to the point I wouldn't do them. They were such a dead, dull color in those days.

I remember one shop where the manager got mad at me because

I wouldn't talk a woman into a ten-dollar permanent. I was supposed to work on her vanity, but this woman's husband was out of work and I couldn't be that greedy. And I was always getting in trouble for giving too many curls in the one-dollar permanent: I was only supposed to give them fourteen.

In those days, we got paid mostly on commission, usually 15 percent of what we sold. If I had a good week I'd make fifty dollars. But money wasn't my goal. I liked making women feel good about themselves . . . having their husbands look at them and think how nice they looked. It was also pride on my part because they liked my work. A quarter was a huge tip in those days.

I remember we wore white uniforms, white shoes, and white caps, just like nurses. The white symbolized cleanliness, and we did sterilize our equipment. We had to be very careful that we didn't transmit things. . . .

Most of the women who came to me were older, married women —younger women couldn't afford to have their hair done every week so they just came in for permanents once a year or when they got married.

Everybody wanted Betty Boop pin curls; we didn't use rollers then. There were two ways of doing pin curls: a sculptured curl which you wrapped around the finger for a smoother line and a tighter curl—like a spit curl—which lasted longer. Women wanted that bandbox look—none of this natural stuff. They wanted everybody to know they'd just come out of the beauty parlor. At night, they'd put crimpers in their waves to keep them in—God, I remember waking up with those metal edges digging into my scalp.

My customers sometimes talked about family problems, but not much; people kept their problems at home those days. When they didn't, I figured they had to get it off their chests so I just let 'em go, then I'd forget it.

I used to make my own wave set because I didn't like the white film the commercial stuff caused. I made it out of flaxseed. See, you boil flaxseed until it gets thick like egg white. The only trouble is you can't let it get too old or it turns sour on you.

I got a job dressing hair for the funeral parlor in town. Nobody else wanted it: lots of people are afraid of the dead. I always said I liked it because my customers never complained.

But the truth is, I got $5 for each one and I only had to do the top and sides. It took just fifteen minutes, and I made a lot of extra money that way. Only thing was, I couldn't eat afterward.

HER CAREER IN ADVERTISING, newspaper reporting, and public relations work took Marie Girard from New York City in the thirties to the Nuremberg trials in Germany after World War II.

Today she lives in a California retirement village, rescuing stray dogs and cats and finding homes for them.

MARIE GIRARD'S STORY

I had a chance to write Jell-O commercials for the Jack Benny show. They paid twenty-five dollars a commercial and that was top money.

I had these friends—a young married couple I had met in Los Angeles—and she was from New York City and very homesick. She wanted to go home to mama, and they were going to drive. They asked me if I wanted to go along. I said sure. So I scraped up a little money and started out with them.

We went to her mother's apartment, and there wasn't any room there because people were sleeping all over the floor. It didn't take me long to realize it was a Communist cell, and my two friends were Young Communist League organizers. Well, they'd sung some song as we traveled and all that, but they didn't say anything too much. I guess they figured I was one of them. I don't know.

Anyway, I just said, "I'll go on now." Of course they wanted to know where I was going. I didn't know. I just knew I had to get out of that apartment. So I left in the pouring rain with eighty cents in my pocket, walking with my suitcase along Madison Avenue, thinking—"What now, Marie!" But I was so entranced with the city, I could hardly realize I was getting soaked from the rain.

What I'm going to tell you will seem silly, but I took that last eighty cents and went to see *Jumbo,* the Billy Rose show. It had been running a long time and was tremendously popular. I was dying to see it. My God, when I think I took my last penny to go to the theater. . . .

That night I stayed in a Salvation Army residence for women

called the Evangeline Home on 13th Street. It cost seven dollars a week and I got two meals a day—they let me stay free until I could get work. The home really attracted high level women. There were loads of interesting people—name people from radio and magazines—living there because it was a good, cheap place to live.

I remember I thought everybody knew Ernest Hemingway but me. A lot of them had come back from Paris when the Depression started, and they all talked about him.

Remember, they used to call them the "lost generation"—the expatriates who lived in Paris during the twenties. I didn't buy that. Mine was the lost generation . . . the class of '32. I took all kinds of jobs the next few months to stay alive, in a laundry, three stories *down*, sticking sheets into one of those mangle things. That paid better than a lot of jobs because the heat was so awful. Another time, I worked at Orbach's as a strike-breaker, only I was so dumb about things that I didn't know I was a strike-breaker until the rocks started coming through the window at me.

Then I worked at the Dartmouth Club, and I had to sneak in 'cause it was so . . . there was a rule that no woman could ever step over the threshold or be in the building. They thought, I guess, there was something poisonous about women. But they got so hard up they had to have some kind of clerical work done. So I worked there for three days in a closet. If I hadn't been so mad it might have been funny. I had to go to the back and knock, and they looked all around before they let me in. Then they took me to this windowless cubicle of a room and shut the door; even brought me lunch on a tray. I never saw anybody, never talked to anybody, just because I was a woman.

For a while, I had to get a job every few days to keep eating and paying my rent. Fortunately there were lots of envelopes to address and lick in New York in those days.

But I finally got into an advertising agency in an office right next to the Chrysler Building. It was just a menial job at first, but I was interested and I worked myself up in three years.

It wasn't a big agency—the big agencies had car accounts—that's how you could tell whether they were big or not. But the Don Harold Agency where I worked was well-known. Harold was both a writer and a cartoonist and I worked up to the point where I was his "girl Friday," and I also did copywriting and reviewing. I had a chance to write Jell-O commercials for the Jack Benny show. They paid me twenty-five dollars a commercial, and that was top money.

I got to go to a lot of plays and stuff—Don wouldn't have time or he wouldn't want to go, so he'd give me the tickets and I'd review movies, radio shows, and plays. That way I kept entertained, for free.

I never did make enough money to get out of the Evangeline Home in all those three years, but I saw a lot of exciting people come and go. Some of them were on the staff of a magazine called *The New York Woman* which was, I guess, one of the first efforts at a liberated woman's magazine. It was slick and very handsome and it lasted just about three issues. I guess it was about thirty years too early, but you know, some of us were trying even then.

IN SPITE OF HER fictionalized reporting as a young cub on a small Texas newspaper, Carol Hayes went on to journalism school and traditional assignments on other Southern newspapers.

Today she free lances magazine feature articles, "all carefully researched and factual," she assured me, laughing.

CAROL LU HAYES'S STORY

I'd go to school two-thirds of the morning and then dash over to the newspaper office, work like hell 'til 12:30, turn my copy in, then dash back to school.

My father was in the farm machinery business in San Benito, Texas, which is twenty miles up the line from Brownsville. He had left a much bigger company to go into business for himself, and they tried to squeeze him out by undercutting him. So his business wasn't good. I can remember he was always worried at tax time, and sometimes my mother would wander around—just off in space somewhere—worrying about money.

But we owned our own home, and we had a Mexican maid so we were pretty far from destitute. Still there wasn't a lot of cash around.

Once the man from the gas company stopped me on my way to school and asked me when we were going to pay our gas bill. I went home and told my mother, and she was just mortified. After that, I always crossed the street when I saw that man coming, and later on when his son was killed in the war . . . I know it's awful to say . . . but I couldn't make myself feel sorry for him.

Anyway, when the local newspaper editor saw my column in the high school paper and liked it, he offered me a job as woman's editor of the local daily—for five dollars a week.

I'd go to school two-thirds of the morning and then dash over to the newspaper office, work like hell 'til 12:30, turn in my copy, and dash back to school.

San Benito was a social town. I ran news of people coming and going, all the bridge parties, and high school graduations. There wasn't a lot of money around so the hostesses in San Benito had to be ingenious. Some of these ladies would pay back all their social obligations by giving three parties in one day. They would get the house cleaned, order the flowers and refreshments, and then have a formal morning coffee, an afternoon tea, and a late supper—took care of everyone they owed in one day.

Weddings were the biggest news, though. I had to describe in detail what every woman wore, and they had to be listed in order, according to the town's social hierarchy. The wedding party came first, then the woman who presided at the punch bowl, then the woman at the guest book, and then the guests in order of their importance in town. Later on, I worked for a North Carolina newspaper, and there I had to list everybody's grandparents. But we didn't do that in Texas.

Age was important then and carried some status. The outstanding older lady at the party usually poured the tea from the silver service. Now that same silver service appeared at all the parties because it was borrowed around. Sometimes, I'd be describing it three times on one page.

We used a lot of adjectives in those days . . . everyone's party and decor was wonderful, beautiful, marvelous, or charming.

After a while that can get a little boring, and I always needed items to fill up my columns. One day I was just sitting there with extra space, and I made up a woman. I called her Mrs. J. C. Eddern and I said she had gone over to Brownsville for the weekend. Later, Mrs. Eddern entertained small groups—nothing ostentatious, just quiet, informal gatherings of out-of-town people. Well, you know I wasn't working for *The New York Times* where complete accuracy is demanded. And San Benito was a big enough town that there could be some people living in apartments that everybody didn't know.

It worked fine until the woman from the Retail Credit Union called and wanted to know where Mrs. Eddern lived. I got a little scared then—I was just fifteen, after all—but I described her for the RCU woman and everything.

The next week, I dropped in a notice that the many friends of Mrs. J. C. Eddern were saddened to hear she had moved to San Antonio.

Chapter Eight

THOSE WHO LENT A HELPING HAND

HER INTELLECTUAL VIGOR and self-assurance have prevailed in spite of barriers she encountered—first as a young woman entering medical school during the twenties and, later, as a science teacher and social worker during the early thirties.

"I've watched women in time of economic distress," Lillian Cantor Dawson told me, "and I've seen women pay a double price —professionally and as human beings. Maybe that's why our survival instinct is so great.

"I tell my young liberated sisters, 'Watch out during recessionary times!' They think they're new in the field. But forty years ago women were fighting for the same things."

Lillian Dawson thinks poor women pay an especially terrible price during hard times. "If you grew up in coal and steel communities as I did," she said, "you saw the toll these industries took on the men. But the final price? It was paid by their women. I used to see them walking uphill to the mine shaft, carrying their husbands' lunch buckets . . . wearing shawls and heavy coats, trudging through the snow and ice, always with two or three kids behind them.

"And I've seen them standing there when something went wrong, waiting at the mine opening, crushing garlic because they believed garlic would heal their men's bruises, standing with terror in their eyes, waiting for their men to come up alive or. . . .

"I have seen women like this even though the mode of their life was ghastly. Amongst the Poles and Slavs it was their men's style to get drunk when things got too bad. That excused them for beating their wives. The wives took it because they felt their husbands were so miserable!

"My mother and I did charity work together—we'd hear the shouts in the back alleys, and we'd know some woman was getting it bad. And the children would run out into the street.

"I remember hearing one of the girls say, 'If any man ever beats me, that will be the last he'll ever see of me.' Well, that's OK to say, but there were only two other professions open for a poor woman . . . prostitute and servant."

Lillian Dawson had a positive experience with her own parents whom she characterizes as two people who communicated. "We knew that papa was number one with mama," she said, "and mama was number one with papa. We were very secure children."

After dropping out of medical school because of poor health, she received a master's degree in education; and the summer of 1930 found her finishing her first year of science teaching in a Pittsburgh, Pennsylvania, high school.

LILLIAN CANTOR DAWSON'S STORY

Working women paid a heavy price during the Depression, and many of them actually stood between the coming generation and death.

I had just finished my first year teaching when the Depression hit hard in Pittsburgh. Women were laid off so that men could be put in their place. There I was . . . after a very short career. I was out, and I had spent my life preparing to teach. Even though my salary was helping my family, it didn't matter. This was one of the things that women had to accept at that time.

However, during my school years I had taken about twelve credits with Dr. Marian Hathaway who was one of the first people to give social work a professional standing. Anyway, we had met socially once and she'd said to me, "If ever you change your goals, will you come into social work? I think you're a natural." So, when I lost my teaching job I went right to her: "Well, here I am without a job." She asked me if I would consider a position with the temporary emergency relief group of Allegheny County; of course, everybody thought it was going to be temporary then.

The first thing I knew I was made supervisor of aid to the aged, blind, and children. I went into the neighborhoods—remember it was when John L. Lewis was trying to organize the coal miners. I found the children didn't have enough to eat, and many out-of-work mining families were coming in from outlying areas, resulting in terrible overcrowding.

Personally, I don't think John L. Lewis used the best methods, but they were certainly effective. During the middle of winter in '30, the miners decided to march . . . yes, and the women and children marched with them, and they all sat down in silence on the steps of city hall.

The police couldn't get rid of them because they were hungry and they desperately wanted some kind of help. The mayor—I can't remember his name because I've tried for years to block the whole thing from my mind—was not a thinking or feeling man. He ordered the firemen to turn hoses on those people to get them moving. I saw mothers throw their bodies around their children when the water hit, and it was so cold—nine degrees above zero that day—that those women froze in a few minutes. It was one of the blackest days in the history of Pittsburgh.

No, the women didn't die that day; they got pneumonia and died later. Their orphaned children were taken into Catholic homes. But it did get headlines in the newspaper, and Lewis won that battle.

I saw it all. I was downtown, like many social workers, trying to pull strings, trying to get somebody to take these people in out of the terrible cold. We couldn't budge the bureaucrats. You know, when a man has a political job he isn't going to buck a Carnegie or a Sloan.

I saw many families around that city living in hovels with no coal, no heat. Young children went along the train tracks picking up bits of coal that had dropped from trains. If they were caught they were arrested or smacked very thoroughly. Those women, the mothers, tried in every way to keep their children alive. We tried to help them, but relief in those days was not organized to take care of all of them.

The number of professional women and blue-collar women who had been ousted out of jobs impressed me. Some of them were family breadwinners. It didn't matter as long as a man was available for a job. Remember, we're talking about a male-oriented society. When I was a young high school girl and marched for women's suffrage, we had eggs and tomatoes and stuff thrown at us. The underlying attitude really hadn't changed much by 1930. Teachers were let out right and left. Nurses were getting thirty dollars a month. Women in labs with degrees in pathology got fifteen dollars a month. Working women paid a heavy price during the Depression, and many of them actually stood between the coming generations and death.

I worked for nine months in those conditions, and then I needed a vacation. I was very young and dedicated. I stopped sleeping, and I wouldn't allow myself a day of sickness. I told myself, "All right, so if you give in and get sick, who's going to take your caseload?" But after awhile, this took its toll, and I needed to get away for a few weeks.

I went to New York City and visited relatives, but about the tenth day of my vacation somebody told me Workman's Circle needed a director. I went to see the executive secretary and he hired me on the spot. It meant leaving my family in Pittsburgh which I didn't care to do, but at that time I was very ambitious. So with fifteen assistants, I started the social service bureau of the Workman's Circle.

The Circle had been organized since 1920 for the needle trade —for garment workers in New York City who were chiefly Jewish and from Poland. They had literally been in a slave situation so they banded together into the kind of union they called Workman's Circle. They probably had the best social medicine that there ever was in this country—for nine dollars a month a whole family was covered from birth to death. They were known worldwide for their treatment of TB and had a famous sanitarium. TB is what happens when ten or twelve people sleep in one room. This was a way of life then: one greenhorn moved in with another until there were thirty people in three rooms, and when one had TB it went to the others.

Included in this medical coverage was a psychiatric clinic which must have been one of the first in the country. Day after day, I saw droves of women coming in with problems. Most of these women were working in the needle trades with their husbands . . . many were doing piece work in their homes when they could get it. One of the first benefits these women received at the Circle was that they began to space their children better, except for the very orthodox who felt about contraceptives the way Catholics did. At any rate, the women would come, walking from the Bronx to Brooklyn, walking six to ten miles to be able to talk about their problems.

Many of these women carried double loads. Their husbands weren't working steady, and their children were crying because they weren't fed well enough. It was just a massive problem. We tried to feed them and we tried to have fairs in order to get clothes for them. These beautiful women would take clothing twenty sizes too big and somehow make it fit their children so they could go to school.

One time the women came to me and said: "We have an insurance policy. Can you get it cashed for us?" And I said: "But you've had it so many years. You don't want to lose it." But they convinced me their children needed clothing and food more than they needed the policy.

I went to the Metropolitan Insurance Company—these were policies you paid ten cents a week for—and the policy was not supposed to have any turn-in value. At first I talked with assistants, but I couldn't get anywhere until I insisted on seeing the top man. I told him about the women; I painted as true a picture as I could. He finally agreed, and I got a cash surrender value for those policies. Now for these women, that was their nest egg; they had saved for it a penny at a time.

When WPA came in, they had a project in which they said taxi companies could hire men three afternoons a week at fifteen dollars if those men were certified by a social agency. That meant I had to fight for recognition as a social agency. And I did, and we *were* recognized. I placed 300 doctors as taxi cab drivers . . . 300 *medical* doctors. Nobody realizes what the Depression meant in large urban centers. These men pleaded for a chance to earn that pittance. It meant that they at least could bring some milk or bread into the house.

There are a hundred stories like that; but I don't think men could have done what they did if they hadn't been backed by their women. The women carried such a load. I came to believe in those years that the female of the species is entrusted with the perpetuation of life at her own expense. Perhaps nature compensates for this burden in a way: women develop the strength to survive anything.

LILLIAN KREUCHER'S FRONT DOOR, with its four panes of colored glass, is as much in vogue as her quilting hobby.

"Here's a full-size, 192-block quilt," she said, holding up a many-colored creation stuffed with old stockings. "You take a piece of material and sew it together on three sides, making a kind of pocket. Then you roll up your stocking like you're ready to put it on and stick it in the pocket, leaving it all kind of fluffylike.

"Sew up the fourth side with double thread, make as many squares as you need, and that's how you can have something outta nothing."

Her friends save their material scraps and old nylons for her, and she rummages in secondhand stores for the rest. Each quilt costs less than five dollars to make, and she is triumphantly proud of her achievements. Pinned to her living room wall are faded snapshots of a dozen quilts long since given away.

LILLIAN KREUCHER'S STORY

The chief operator told me: "You young girls got to learn what work is." They paid me five dollars for fourteen-hour days, seven days a week.

When my dad left us, I moved with my mom and grandma to Charter Oak, Iowa. We had to go on relief—got ten dollars a month for groceries and six dresses a year . . . for all three of us.

My grandmother was eighty-five then and let me tell you she could eat three healthy meals a day. Weighed about 145 pounds . . . so when she lost her sight, my mom couldn't haul her around anymore and she had to go live with my Aunt Doris on her farm. After that, grandma just went downhill because Aunt Doris didn't cook as good as my mom.

Finally I got a job at the Kansas Light and Telephone Company in town. The chief operator interviewed me. She says: "Now I want to know, do you have to take a day—one day a month off—to be sick? We can't have that."

And I said, "No ma'am. I'm not ever sick."

She says: "You young girls, you got to learn what work is. You can't always be takin' off."

I got the job. The pay was five dollars for seven days a week, fourteen hours a day. I worked the night shift—you see there were only two of us—and I worked from 7:00 P.M. until 7:00 A.M. and then I came back to relieve the chief operator for two hours at noon.

Now I was her relief, see, but I didn't have one. I worked there four years without a day off. Once I wanted to go to my high school alumni banquet and she was real unhappy about that.

They didn't mind if I slept at night, after the records and paper work were brought up to snuff. I had a cot in there and a buzzer system that woke me up if a call came in.

We had six long distance lines. We could dial some of the smaller towns around but the rest of them farther up, like Omaha or Chicago, would have to be belled through the county seat. We aso had a postal telegraph. The railroad depot had the Western Union but they closed at 2:00 A.M., so anything after that I'd have to phone out to Omaha.

In a small town—Charter Oak was about 800 people—well, a small town switchboard was the emergency center. Those people depended on their operator so you couldn't let yourself get flustered. If you did you were out of luck, see, and your patrons would get upset and then the whole system fell apart. When somebody called in yelling: "There's a fire!"—you had to find out where and do something quick. It was my duty to ring the fire bell, and then the volunteer firemen called me to find out where it was.

We were the town timekeeper, too. At noon, it was my job to blow the noon whistle, and that usually meant most people knocked off for lunch.

Once there was a flood. I had a call from the county seat of Crawford County that the river was flooding. I alerted the town council and also those people who lived down on the river.

I was responsible for about 500 phones—all the ones in town and out in the rural areas, too. It was a big job.

You know, people got to know me and they'd depend on me for the darndest things. "What can I do about my husband," one woman was always calling me to talk late at night. "I know my husband is foolin' around with so-and-so. . . ." They'd just want me to give them answers to their problems. And then their kid would get sick, and they'd call: "How did Doc tell Mrs. Petty to fix that mustard plaster?"

There was a woman living along the hall in the same building. I used to go to high school with her boy and she was nosy as all get out. She'd hang around the switchboard, and she'd listen. Then she'd get around to saying, "What was wrong with Mrs. Parker?" I'd say: "Oh, I don't know, I didn't pay much attention." Now that would surely make her mad.

Oh, I couldn't chat with everybody. You had to draw the line. 'Cause some people would report you if you visited too much and I was pretty strict, too. I kept the rules as good as the chief operator.

This Catholic priest in town could tell the dirtiest stories, and he was always telling me, "Now, about 10:00 P.M. I'm going to call over to the next parish, and I'll have a joke for you afterward, so you just come in on the line."

I'm a Lutheran and I never heard a priest tell dirty stories, you know. But his were real classics. One time he called, and he wasn't in a joking mood. His new car had disappeared and he told me to call out the sheriff. Well, you know, they found it at the bottom of the hill. He'd forgot to set the hand brake.

But generally—like I said—an operator can't do a lot of gossiping. I knew everything that was going on, all the hanky-panky and who was carrying on with whose wife. Yeah, and we had our hurly-burly girls, too. But I kept my mouth shut.

Wednesdays and Saturdays were the biggest days in town 'cause that's when all the farmers came in to their frozen meat lockers. They'd play a little pool and drink some beer and maybe go to the movin' picture show. About 9:00 P.M. my board would just light up with wives calling for their husbands, wanting them to come on home.

Lots of weeks one or the other would leave me a piece of meat at the telephone office. 'Course, Christmas was the big time for a telephone operator. The townspeople appreciated the service I did, knowing I was there all night if they needed me, so they just brought me a load of things. I never bought a slip the whole time I worked there.

But after four years, I began to think of quitting. Lots of times I'd be sitting at the breakfast table too sleepy to eat . . . with my eyes propped wide open. I never did get enough sleep because I'd just get to bed every morning then mom would wake me up to go on noon relief.

When I went in to quit in '39, the chief operator offered me a ten-dollar raise, but I turned her down. Clerks in grocery stores were making fifteen dollars a week and teachers were getting ninety dollars a month . . . they were living well. And of course everybody back there had a fur coat. The first hundred dollars a girl made went for a fur coat then. It was a matter of prestige. When a girl started working, you know, that's what she got or everybody wondered what kind of stupid job she had.

HELEN GRANT'S STORY

During the early thirties, I was working in the YWCA in Honolulu, and although Hawaii felt the Depression it wasn't nearly as severe as it was on the mainland—partly because of the Hawaiian economy, I suppose, which was based on pineapple, sugar, and tourism. Although tourism fell off, the fleet was always there.

By 1935 I was beginning to feel a little isolated. I could drive around the whole circumference of Oahu in three hours. So when a job opened in San Francisco, I took it.

The Depression was in full swing when I got home, and it certainly had an impact on our programs. I worked with classes which were a spin-off of WPA: the Y became a great center for education. The government provided the money for the instructors and we provided the facility. Just hundreds of people crowded in every night, all trying to learn skills against the time they might have a chance for a job. And we had lots of classes in vegetable gardening so people could grow their own food.

The YWCA residences in San Francisco and Oakland were filled with young women whose wages were pretty low. The whole idea of the residence was to serve the needs of the low-income, young girl migrating into a strange city situation. At that time, I think the minimum wage was only sixty cents an hour, but the Y was battling always for better minimum wages and working standards for women.

I don't know where people get this business about strict regulations at YWCA residences. Even back in the thirties, we didn't have a curfew. If there was one, it was somewhere about 2:00 A.M., which isn't too restrictive. And, well, the whole attitude of young people about it was very different then. They respected rules, and their parents certainly *expected* them to. When nice girls left home to work in the thirties their mothers said, "Stay at the YWCA." The whole life-style for a young woman at that time made it entirely unacceptable for her to go into a strange city and get herself an apartment. It just wasn't done.

"I'M REALLY BOTHERED about the mythology that's developing about the 1930s," Eleanor Fait said, sipping the last of a cup of tea. "It's developing faster than any truths about those years. I hope you're after reality . . . sometimes I think reality can be more entertaining, even sensational.

"My point is, we weren't all escaping. Our lives weren't sterile. Women of the thirties are certainly not entitled to the pity of younger women, as we were not passive under-achievers."

Tall, maybe six-foot, and wearing a wine-colored pantsuit, Eleanor Fait is a striking woman. And, undoubtedly, no under-achiever herself. Serving in the military during World War II, she later went to Europe for the United Nations to work with displaced persons. Since 1957 she has become a recognized authority on older worker employment and associated problems of aging. California's former governor Ronald Reagan appointed her to the California Commission on Aging.

ELEANOR FAIT'S STORY

Sure you heard about cheaters who hid things when the caseworker came, but believe me . . . believe me . . . there wasn't any of that. Those people had nothing . . . they were starving before they asked for help.

I graduated from Mills College in 1930, and came out right into it. My father died two months before. We were well-off people, but the Bank of America, it was the Bank of Italy then, took everything. They took four ranches . . . everything but our home in Woodland. The year I graduated, we didn't have enough money for Christmas dinner.

When the Depression started, they gave no credit at all—zip, like that, they foreclosed. There's a statistic somewhere that the Bank of Italy owned one-third of California in the early thirties.

I hadn't been trained for work. I was a science major in botany and bacteriology, and I had expected to go on and get higher degrees. Instead, I was faced with how I was going to eat and my mother and younger brother were in the same situation. We all had to get out and scurry around, and we didn't do very well at it.

Well, I was twenty-two and I had a great mental block which took several years to overcome. It was an absolute refusal to recognize the fact that we were poor, and that we were probably going to go on being poor. For years I thought maybe if I just flapped around, it would all straighten out and go back to the way it had always been—with the ranches and everything.

And, too, when I graduated from college, there was no recognition among us that there was a depression. We didn't realize what was happening.

I had to cut loose from any connection with my college friends—I couldn't manage it any longer, what with the clothes and the luncheons.

My first job—after I finally figured out that I had to get one—was from a San Francisco private employment agency. They got me a job selling books on commission, and I was to pay all my expenses. Imagine that! That's how green I was.

So I was assigned the country east of Delhi, down in the San Joaquin Valley—all that desolate land—with farmers scratching around to keep from starving.

I was selling *Volume Library,* and I learned the patter and went through the training—which was all quite an ordeal for me—and I went out there to those run-down farms.The farm women literally had not seen anybody to talk with for months. They were so glad to have somebody come to the door that they were nice about the books and listened to my spiel with great interest. I'd think, "Oh boy, maybe I've got a sale." But, of course, I didn't. They'd say: "Now, we'd love to have them, but. . . ." That went on for three weeks until I saw I wasn't going to sell anything, so I came dragging back home to Woodland.

After that, I did whatever I could—typing, baby-sitting. We still lived in a nice house, but we couldn't heat it and our meals were awful skimpy.

Early the next year, that was '31, I was offered a job in a settlement house. I hadn't had any experience or training but I suppose my educational background helped. For fifty dollars a month, I started my career in social work. The people were a big mix of Orientals, Mexicans, Greeks, Negroes, Armenians—all living in real poverty. The center was operated by the Episcopal church and in order to get the job I had to become a domestic missionary . . . that was the classification. I had to join the Episcopal church and be baptized before they would hire me. I was so desperate, after the books and all, that I would just have done anything.

I worked hard and I stayed for a year. I guess we were considered a kind of outpost because we'd get mission barrels full of clothes from the East . . . just incredible boxes of the most awful kinds of stuff. It was up to me to paw through them and try to find something decent to give to the people.

We started a food program with just any bulk food we could get our hands on. I went around to merchants and asked them for food they couldn't sell—some of it was moldy. People think they can give the worst stuff to the poor.

I started a great many classes for youngsters—they'd be considered old hat now, but they were somewhat innovative then.

One class was called the Polite Club and it was just how to use silverware and that sort of thing—training they didn't get in their homes.

My favorite project was a Girl Scout troup. It was such a big thing for those little girls. I had a long distance battle with Girl Scout headquarters about uniforms. I told them it was absolutely impossible for these girls to buy uniforms. Couldn't headquarters settle for white middies and skirts, any skirts? And finally, after much writing and phoning, I got permission.

I did all the teaching and preliminary work. They sent me a troop handbook and the girls worked on the Scout code and the

other things they were supposed to learn. Finally, we were assigned
a troop number and a district—and they sent a woman up from
San Francisco. The big day came . . . all the girls were clean and
spruced up. They were so excited.

Well, when the district organizer came she took one look at
my crew and said, "Why, you can't be a girl scout troop. Look at
the colors you've got." She meant the little girls—not the skirts.
It took me a long time to forgive the Girl Scouts for that.

But my girls never knew. I went right on pretending we were a
troop and using the handbook.

Nevertheless, I got pretty discouraged because of that, and when
Associated Charities in San Francisco offered me a job, I took it.

I got there just when it collapsed—I mean it just ran out of money
so the city took it over, and then the San Francisco city treasury collapsed and it was taken over by the state of California, and the next
year by the federal government.

The worst thing was that my caseloads kept getting bigger until
I had 800 poor families. Eight hundred! They were starving or
they wouldn't have been able to qualify.

My first district was out by the Panhandle area near Golden
Gate Park, the thin end where it's only two blocks wide, and
Stanyan Street. And sometimes I had the Haight-Ashbury district
which was just a family neighborhood at that time.

Of course, in '32 and '33 the times were the worst. More and
more of my classmates from Mills showed up as caseworkers, so I
figured other people were having the same trouble I was.

I was working south of Market Street one day. Negro families
were beginning to move in then, and I was checking houses. You
know, I was sent out to see if people had one crust of bread too
many, to see if they could get along for another day or two without
another relief check. Anyway, that day I found two little Negro
children by themselves with the front door standing wide open.
One was about two and the other about three years old. "Where's
your mama?" I asked. They didn't know. I checked with the neighbors and evidently mama had just taken off because the kids had
been alone for two days. What else could I do? I picked them up and
took them back to my office which was in the old Lincoln School. I
had these kids at my desk and my supervisor—the so-called profes-

sionals had taken over by this time—gave me hell. "You know you're not supposed to get involved," she yelled.

I didn't know where to take these kids. It was dark and they were tired and scared—so I took them to my boardinghouse. When the landlady saw me coming in with them she evicted me on the spot —bag and baggage.

At first I didn't know what to do—then I thought: the Episcopal church owes me something, at least they owe me taking care of these little kids. They took them all right. I don't know what happened to them. I had five million other things happen like that. . . .

And there were old women. They made a lasting impression on me. I was young and when you're young you don't identify with old women—but I never could forget them. It was hard for me to believe that women could get to be old and sick and still have so little, living in those horrid little hotels—tiny rooms with no heat and nothing to eat except what we authorized. And there were hundreds and thousands of them like that.

There was one old lady who had been a binder for a book manufacturer, and I sat and talked with her occasionally—not about her allowance—but about her life. Sometimes we'd have coffee. I wasn't supposed to use up her supplies, but I did a few times anyway. I could see it meant a lot more to her than the coffee. So this one day —out of the blue—she gave me a beautiful leather briefcase that she had made for me—and I was just bowled over. It had my name on it and everything. Well, the last thing a caseworker was supposed to do in this world was take anything from a client, but I did, I took it; I wasn't going to hurt that old woman's feelings for anything. But I couldn't get over how she did it, how she must have sacrificed on the eighteen dollars a month we gave her.

Sure you heard even then about cheaters who hid things when the caseworker came, but believe me . . . believe me . . . there wasn't any of that. Those people had nothing, and remember, it was the height of degradation to take relief. It was a tremendous stigma, and so they were starving if they came for help.

I got so I couldn't stand it anymore. It made me sick all the time, and I quit and went home to Woodland. I kept thinking what the hell's going on anyway: this isn't the way I thought the world was going to be.

Chapter Nine

THOSE WHO TOILED

HER EXPERIENCES AS A LABORER in an Ohio shoe factory gave her an appreciation for education. "I went back to high school when I was 26 years old," she told me, "and I graduated from college when I was thirty-three."

She retired after teaching high school for twenty years and is now working on a master's degree in English literature. "I keep thinking I need more education," she said, "or I'm afraid I might end up back in that factory."

JUANITA'S STORY

I made more money than I dreamed possible—twenty-five cents an hour working on a conveyor belt, ironing leather shoes.

My mother named me Juanita—you know, after the song. I always hated that name. It was so fancy and I wasn't.

I dropped out of school in the beginning of '33. I didn't have any money or proper clothes. That was my freshman year in high school and let me tell you, I had a pretty grand wardrobe. My mother had bought a spool of thread for a nickel and three yards of fabric at ten cents a yard. I don't know how she did it, but she managed to get a dress and blouse out of that three yards. A neighbor woman gave me an old coat, and my mother made a brown skirt from the back of it.

I remember exactly what was in my closet. I had a brown skirt and a red blouse and a red cotton dress. Another woman gave me an old lady's coat with a moth-eaten fur collar and, oh yes, a pair of high heel shoes. I was only a skinny kid of fourteen. I must have looked rather strange in that getup.

Talk about making do. I invented it.

We didn't have anything, not even enough to eat. My father was trying to get on WPA, but that didn't come along 'til later. I knew I had to get a job right then. What else? I lied. Told 'em I was sixteen and got hired in a shoe factory at Fort Smith, Ohio, just across the river from Kentucky.

I started out making a lot of money, more money than I had ever dreamed possible—twenty-five cents an hour working on a conveyor belt, ironing leather shoes.

You see when the shoes were formed on the last, they would get all wrinkled and I had to take a long, tubular iron and press around the leather to get it nice and smooth.

I took ten dollars a week home to my parents. Did that for four years. They always gave me back enough to buy stockings. My dad insisted on that. He didn't want me to go bare-legged around men.

My parents wouldn't let me live in town even though it was twenty-two miles to work every morning and twenty-two miles back to Greenup, Kentucky, every night.

I took the ferryboat across the river, and rode horseback or on a wagon the rest of the way. I bummed it. Some nights I caught a ride in a car and would get home fast. Sometimes I had to walk. In winter I wore rubber boots to my knees. Lots of nights it took me three or four hours, just depending on what kind of ride I got.

That was the nightmare time of my life. I ironed leathers until my hands blistered and my back ached. After two years, I moved on to the cleaning room for more pay—forty cents an hour. I brushed suede shoes with wire brushes to remove glue and pen marks or whatever else got on them during their journey from the cutting room through the lasting room.

At any rate, I spoiled the few dresses I owned.

I hated that shoe factory. I remember cryin' in the bathtub one night as I watched soapsuds run blue, green, and brown across my stomach where I had held the shoes.

JOANNA FROM IDAHO

To get tuition money for teacher's college I worked on my brother-in-law's farm during summer vacations. At first, he had me helping my older sister in the house, cooking for sixteen hired hands.

You work like crazy for sixteen men. They come in, gobble up their meal, and there's nothing left but a table full of dirty dishes and sticky pans. Then you start digging the vegetables or making a cake—just starting the process all over again for the next meal. I was sick of scraping pans. I told my sister's husband that working in the house was too confining. So he says, kind of smart: "Well, then, Missy, think you can handle man's work outside?" And I said back, just as smart, "Yes, I do."

So after that I threw sacks on the harvester, loaded wheat, and drove the tractor. But what I loved most was working with horses. After a day in the fields I looked forward to taking them back to the barn. Just for fun, I'd line up eight horses side by side, and I'd take 'em on a dead run for about three miles with me balanced on two of their backs. I stood tall, bouncing along, my toes hooked under their collars, and everybody'd stop work to watch me.

I worked three summers for my brother-in-law. He got so he told everybody I was worth any two men he ever hired.

"LUPE RENALDO IS THE WOMAN you *must* talk to," said the enthusiastic male voice. I had telephoned the senior citizens' housing office in a southern California county, asking the name of a Mexican-American woman who might remember the Great Depression.

"Yes, ma'am, I talk to you," Lupe agreed when I called. "I got a story to tell."

And she did. When we met she had a badly bruised and swollen leg, the result of a shoving match with a sixty-six-year-old Anglo woman. Lupe had accused her of trying to lure away Joe, her third husband, since gone.

"I was drinking a little too much," she admitted apologetically. "And I got mad. This woman pretends to be my friend before my eyes, then try to steal my husband."

Nervously smoking, Lupe described an adolescence that made

Cinderella sound like a carefree teen. Motherless, she had remained behind in Mexico as a child servant when her father migrated illegally to California's Imperial Valley. Two years later in 1924, her father returned and spirited her north. She was to live with the epitome of malevolent stepmothers who tried to sell her into prostitution at fourteen.

"I ran away and they put me in a juvenile house in Bakersfield," Lupe recalled. "Finally a Mexican couple promise to adopt me but they put me in the fields to work. I pick 550 pounds of cotton every day and put it in a long bag tied to my body which I drag along behind me. When I'm nineteen my foster parents arrange for me to marry with a man twenty-four years older than me."

Lupe is short with dark hair and moist black eyes. Spindly arms and legs hang from a thick, round trunk. At sixty-four, there is no vestige of youthful good looks if, indeed, there ever were any.

The two-room apartment displays no sign of Catholicism—no madonnas or pictures of Christ. It is next to bare, containing only a bed, sofa, coffee table, and television set.

On the coffee table is a vase of dusty, pink, crepe-paper roses.

LUPE RENALDO'S STORY

If you don't drink, you don't work.

My daughter was born in 1930. That's when the Depression started, you know.

We lived with my husband's six brothers. He was not the oldest, and they took advantage of him. Didn't give him any wages. I went through hell, you see, because two months after we marry I still didn't have no shoes.

I say, "Pete, why can't you buy me shoes?" And he say, "Why don't you go ask my brothers?" I knew then that I marry an underdog.

The brothers lost their farm in 1933 and we move to Indio and rent another farm. We find an old house with a big kitchen and wood stove. We couldn't get any eggs or meat. We eat beans and sweet potatoes, always sweet potatoes. I used to scrub them and put them in the oven every day.

We have to start all over again, planting onions, okra, potatoes, and beans. We don't have chickens and that house never seen a steak.

I never forget that I am so tired when I get up at three o'clock in the morning. You know, my husband and my brother-in-laws, they never were no gentlemen with wives, like in this country.

I wake up with a kerosene lantern, start chopping wood, and carry those big load, drop 'em in a box by the stove, and start filling the stove with wood. Then I peel potatoes and put on a big pot of beans.

After I clean up from breakfast I go to the fields and come back before noon to cook for them. In the evening I was all tired, all sun-burned. I used to have a lot of nosebleeds, you know, because of the sun; it get so hot—124° in summer in Indio.

All those years we picked the crops and bring into Los Angeles to the market. My brother-in-laws used to get home with the money, but my husband never got any. We was just working for them for nothing.

My little girl was seven years old. She had never gone to school yet. It was very far. So I told my husband—I says, "You know I would like to have my divorce." I approach him very nice and sweet only thinkin' about my daughter. I say, "This is the only precious thing that I ever have in my life and I want her to have a little more school than what I had." You know I only went to third grade in Mexico. Not a day to school in this country.

So my husband he say all right; he give me divorce then he take me to Los Angeles. That was in 1937. They were having Depression in Los Angeles. I started right away looking for work but I didn't speak English and I had no experiences in no factories or anything since I was just used to the fields. So I end up working in this lousy Mexican bar.

All it was was drinking and smoking and all that. I was brought up different—poor but with teachings of right. You know my first thought was to put my little girl in Catholic school, and they say they would charge me $2.50.

I made a dollar a day for eight hours. I opened bottles and serve the beer, and the first day I was working, the owner she was listen-ing to me and she was watching me. When one customer offers to buy me a beer, I say, "No."

"Lupe, don't you drink?" she ask.

I says, "No, ma'am."

"I'm sorry," she says, "If you don't drink, you don't have any work."

I begged her *please* don't just fire me for that. I already make arrangements to place my little girl in a good Catholic school. And she says, "Well, start drinking, Lupe. Every customer who pays ten cents for your beer is another dime in the register."

It was a lousy place to work, because you see I still have that moral in me that I'm supposed to be respected. But anyway it was a job.

LEONA HUFFMAN'S STORY

My husband was a dentist in Boise, Idaho. One day in '32 he just went fishing . . . and he fished for the rest of the bad times. He got tired of putting money in people's mouths without getting paid for it. No one could get a job because factories closed down. Even the newspapers quit, if you can imagine that.

I needed a new dress, and I couldn't buy it because the dress shops weren't open; the manufacturers in the East had closed down. I finally made one out of old scraps.

So at twenty-eight, with two little girls, I just had to go to work. I took a job as a salesclerk in the J. C. Penney Company, and worked throughout the Depression. I never quit after that. Kept working in one store or another until I retired in 1967.

In the thirties there was no union, but you didn't think about it. Any woman lucky enough to have a job, better not complain about conditions. I went to work at eight o'clock in the morning and worked until six o'clock, six days a week. Then I'd have to go back after supper for two hours to do my stock work. Oh, we never got paid anything different for it. Besides working long hours, if there was some special holiday like Easter, where they were going to have extra stock, I'd have to go in Sunday and work three or four hours. I never got an extra penny.

There was a mood then: you just lived from one day to the next, always wondering what was going to happen next. You just kept thinking, "Well, the government ought to do something."

My Aunt Kate is fifty-nine now. But I remember her best in the early forties when she was on top of my world. She may not have had the blondest, smoothest pageboy and the slickest, blackest seal coat in Fairmont, West Virginia, but to me she did. Every girl should have an Aunt Kate, and I hope they do.

The Christmas I was overwhelmed by a biography of Madame Curie, Kate bought me a $10.95 chemistry set which must have set her back a half-week's pay. It had a magnificent, three-door cabinet, a Bunsen burner, glass vials, and tiny, metal scoops for all kinds of exotic chemical creations.

On the cover of the enclosed booklet a boy about my age lifted a test tube as if for a toast, gazing heavenward. Great historical inventions rose from his head in a dreamlike balloon.

That winter I started the Butcher Elementary Scientist's Club and charged my sixth-grade classmates a penny to come after school and watch me experiment.

When Kate married a tall soldier and moved away, I lost my dearest friend and was forced into an early maturity.

Today she lives a few blocks from my house. Her hair is white and she wouldn't dream of wearing an endangered species. One hot California afternoon we talked about the thirties and how young women made do.

KATE PEMBERTON'S STORY

It made you lie. I got a lot of jobs by faking—saying I could do things I couldn't. If they had asked me if I could sing grand opera, I would have said yes.

I was sixteen on Wednesday, and on Friday I was graduated from Fairview High School. It was May of '32. The mines were shut down, and when the coal mines are down in West Virginia nothing is moving. They had been down during the twenties, and there had been a lot of violence. One night when I was ten, I remember mom and I were coming home on the interurban, and I asked her what all those searchlights were for. She told me it was a strike. That same night Brenda, a schoolmate of mine, was in bed when a bullet came through the window and killed her.

I think the Depression must have lasted twenty years in West Virginia.

There were no jobs for sixteen-year-old girls in Fairview. Nobody in that town had a steady job except the mailman, and he made thirty-two dollars a month. We all thought he was rich.

So I started doing odd jobs . . . anything I could find. I cleaned house and canned tomatoes. The very first job I had was washing jars because I only weighed ninety-five pounds and my tiny hand could get all the way into a jar.

I worked for a quarter here and thirty cents there.

Finally, people in Fairview didn't even have a quarter to pay me so I started hitching rides into Fairmont about ten miles away. Arlie Stiles used to work in the car barn, and he'd give me a ride in if I got out on the road early enough. I had to bum. It cost fifty cents round trip on the streetcar, and that was out of the question.

I took an English course at Fairmont High that fall and I'd meet teachers who needed their windows washed or whatever. And I washed dishes downtown in Dave's Restaurant when I got the chance, or cleaned tables.

Pop was in his early sixties and only picking up a carpentry job here and there. So what I earned during the day usually went on the table that night. A quarter could feed a whole family. You could buy a can of Campbell's pork and beans, add water and catsup and a little molasses and have a meal for five.

All the time I felt overwhelmed and anxious; maybe dread is a better word. I always kind of dreaded how I was going to get to class. And, of course, there was a certain amount of humiliation because I wasn't paying my own way. I knew I wasn't the only one, but that doesn't help when you're sixteen.

The first big money I made was for addressing envelopes at Fairmont Wallplaster. That lasted two weeks and I got a dollar and a half a day.

After that job which was around Christmas of '34, I didn't work for almost a year. Every day I dressed and hitchiked into Fairmont and made the rounds. There were always people with twenty years experience standing in the same line I was. Well, I tried to dress the best I could and act as if I was perfectly calm. And you always tried to sell skills you didn't have. I never said I couldn't do it.

It made you lie. I got a lot of small jobs by faking and saying I could do things I couldn't do. If they had asked me if I could sing grand opera, I would have stepped right up and said yes.

There were no minimum wages and no employment offices trying to help you find work. I mean, if you got a job, you got it by going and knocking on doors.

I was always tired. It would be early when I'd leave home— usually with no money for lunch—and dark by the time I got back, pretty worn out and hungry. Discouraged, most of all.

Finally the NYA came along, which was like a WPA for young people. And in the summer of '36 I worked setting up a town library above my Uncle Don's Texaco garage. But the funds ran out before I finished and they just came and took the books away and shut the project down. Then I worked the playground at the grade school for four months. This was NYA, too. We were paid every two weeks and I got six dollars every payday.

About that time the CCC camps opened and nearly every boy in Fairview signed up. Of course, it was worthwhile, and they took a burden off their families which was a help. But there was nothing comparable for girls. They had an NYA sewing program, I remember. But I never learned to handle a needle.

CCC took a load off the job market but only for older men. At that time, women weren't competing for the same jobs. So it didn't help us any.

By 1938 I'd been out of school for six years without a steady job. When I heard they were moving a Westinghouse lamp plant down from New Jersey to Fairmont, I was so excited I got sick. The day they started hiring I was in that line at 5 A.M.

Guess what the first requirement was? You had to be five feet six inches tall. That let me out. I was only five feet one inch and I couldn't fake *that.*

But they soon changed the rule since there weren't ten girls in Fairmont that tall. You know five feet four inches was tall for a woman then. We hadn't had our spinach!

Six months later I got the call and was hired by Westinghouse. Worked there for the next six years. They paid forty cents an hour to start.

After the government got behind the unions, we all joined the

United Electrical Workers, CIO. Westinghouse tried to keep us from going union—said they'd take good care of us. But we found out the girls up north had a union and were making a dollar an hour while we only made forty cents. What Westinghouse said after that wasn't very convincing.

The whole plant was predominantly female except for the supervisors. When our local was formed there was only a handful of men, but the women elected all men officers. It never occurred to us that we shouldn't. But there was a gradual change. Our second set of officers had one woman. The third time we elected all women officers and I became business agent.

Well, that was unheard of for a woman because that meant I was chief union negotiator at Westinghouse. And that just didn't happen. It made the papers, and they got me out to WMMN to talk about it on radio because it was such a big deal.

I was considered very aggressive by some of the other women. But it seemed natural to me, because my father had backed the suffragettes, and he always said Eleanor should have been president because she was smarter than Franklin. And when he was elected mayor of Fairview—on the Socialist ticket, mind you—he appointed Edna Yates as water commissioner. You know the sky fell. A man had always had that job.

Because of my pop, I grew up with a feeling that it was great being a woman.

We sure didn't call ourselves women's libbers, but there *was* a change in the late thirties, especially among union women. We started considering ourselves capable of exerting authority.

VERA BOSANKO'S STORY

It was 1930 when they closed down the oil fields in Texas. Just stacked the rigs and shut down. My husband lost everything—even his insurance.

'Bout that time Mr. Godwin died. He was my father-in-law so we had all these cattle to look after. Couldn't sell 'em. Weren't worth anything. I kinda cooked for my husband and the boys. Milked the cows and had a garden. I canned everythin' that wasn't movin'.

Picked berries that growed out in the wild there. And we had a pecan orchard. Didn't make anything off it, but we had us some real sweet pies.

All of a sudden my husband was killed by a beef. The hired hands, they was going to hang a slaughtered steer up in a tree when one of them let the pulley slip. It hurt my husband inside. He got bad sick, took to hemorrhaging and. . . .

I was pregnant with Jimmy Lou, my youngest girl, so I took the other four children and went over to my aunt's. I was only twenty-four, but I didn't want to live with nobody, nobody at all. I wrote to my cousin up in this small town of St. Jo, Texas, and he let us come up and stay in a little two-room house he had. I raised a beautiful garden. That helped me out. And I washed for milk; washed clothes for a party that had a milk cow. But I finally had to go on WPA. You could sign up and then you got these little slips of paper. With these you could buy all the groceries except tobacco and liquor and such things.

Shortly, WPA put me to work in the canning plants. Summer of '34 it was. Then this caseworker from out of Fort Worth came up and told me they needed a real nice lady to take a library job at the high school. This paid forty-two dollars a month. But about every few months they'd come in and say they just didn't have no more money for this project. I'd go on home, and there'd come a telegram in the evening mail telling me to go back to work the next day 'cause they got a bit more money.

That went on for about six years. Well, it was kind of scary. I never knowed where the job was going. Maybe that's the reason why I turned whiteheaded when I was a young age.

"I DON'T WANT TO WORK," Nico Rodriguez said. "I'm tired now, I'm old, but they keep calling me. Not so many young womens want to clean a house today for any lady."

For forty years, she worked in other women's homes—the one place where she could escape the life of a migrant field worker—the one work which would ensure her children the education she knew they must have.

A deep anger helped her stand up to government officials, employers, and even her own family. It was an anger born in the barrios of Texas towns and nourished by limited options. Talking about the thirties brings her to frustrated tears: "I have to fight," she says.

NICO RODRIGUEZ'S STORY

WPA told me I cannot work because I lose my citizenship when I marry my husband. I say, "Then explain it to me how my kids gonna eat? How I'm gonna feed them?"

I'm born in San Angelo, Texas, and raised in Brownwood. I work in the field, picking cotton, cutting wood, shearing sheep. My brother used to shear the stomach of the sheep, tie him up, and I finish, because we were six girls and my father have only three boys. The boys, soon as they grown up they leave—fly and go—and so it was six girls and my father. I am oldest girl. You name it—I did it.

Almost nineteen, I get married. I marry because I was working too hard. I get mad. I'm not going to work like a man the rest of my life, I says to my father. I am gonna marry the first one that asks me. So here comes one, and I see him.

I got married on Sunday by the Catholic church and I went to work on Monday, and up to this day I haven't rest! I can tell you that much. I get married on Sunday and on Monday I'm chopping cotton.

I am strong and healthy. The first doctor I see in my life was when my first baby come. I am so embarrassed. But I never have headache, never have backache, and I used to work from dawn 'til dark.

Five babies come—two boys and three girls, and when they are so big, I try to get work with WPA. My husband can't find work because of Depression.

They won't let me work on WPA. I have to fight. The place where I went to put my application, they tell me that I cannot work because I'm not citizen. I say, "How come I not citizen? I born and raised here and my father and mother. What else do you want?"

The lady call a man who say, "But you lost your citizenship when you married your husband. He is a citizen of Mexico."

I ask him, "You mean I get job only if I divorce him? What am I to be, and what are my kids to be? Give me paper to explain it to the judge why I divorce this man, because he is not citizen."

And the man says: "I can't do that."

I am mad and I say back to him: "Then explain it to me how my kids gonna eat? How I'm gonna feed them?"

So he said he'd think about it. "No time to think about it," I told him. "I want answer quick, because I'm not gonna let my kids starve to death."

Then—two, three days later—they send me a card to report to work. He wrote to Dallas or something, and they send papers for me to sign. I go to work in the sewing room and get thirty dollars a month, and I make so many pants that they give me a raise to forty dollars a month.

When that WPA stop, we go back to the fields until I press my foot down. I tell my husband, "This is it. No more field work. We have to educate the kids. We have to stay in one place and think about them now. . . .

We have big fight, but I win. I told him if he wanted to go on the field, to go. I stay with the kids.

And that's when I start to work in the houses, you know. I have to do housework, have to do whatever come in. They pay one dollar a day, practically nothing . . . but it is enough. And I settled down on the town and since my oldest son go to school, I don't go back to the fields ever. I know my kids need the education.

My husband used to say it cost too much, but I didn't pay any attention to him. I say, "The door is open. You can walk out and walk in whenever you want, but *I am not going to the fields.*"

Every lady seems to like me—except one. I mean she wasn't nasty or anything, but I didn't like it the way she act. She says, "Well, Nico, I want you to clean the whole house, iron and wash and do the windows and clean the cupboards and put in new paper. . . ." I just look at her and I say, "You a woman . . . I a woman. Do you think you could do all that in eight hours?"

Afterward, that woman help me lots of ways. She give me some clothes for the kids and if she had things she didn't use, she give them to me.

I was real lucky, thanks to God. That's one thing I don't have to say, that I was so poor I had to go on welfare . . . never had to sign for no kind of help.

A TYPING TEACHER

I worked for this business school-employment agency on commission. It was a good way to make money, because here were these raggy-taggy looking women standing in line, and I would say, "You really should brush up on your business skills so just enroll in our school. . . ."

When a teaching position opened up in the school, I really wanted it but I had to learn the Wiese-Koover typing system. Now, I couldn't type very well myself but I was a good teacher. So before I went for my instruction, I bound up my finger so they couldn't tell what kind of typist I was. You don't have to know *how* to do something, you just have to know how to teach it. The woman whose job I took could type 100 words per minute but she couldn't teach worth a damn.

The manager of the agency school insisted that the teachers not see each other socially. She was a fast-talker type and she said, "I don't want you teachers to congregate—ever—here or at home or anyplace."

Naturally, the first thing I did was call on one of the girls and who should show up but the manager. She was the grandmotherly type, I guess. She would invite me to dinner and pay for it, and then make me dance with her.

There wasn't anything going on; she wasn't physical. I think she just wanted to have fun and didn't know how to have it. She had a family somewhere, but they kept away from her. There was never a pass or anything. . . .

Still I felt terrible, but what could I do? I had a well-paying job. And that was the sad thing about the Depression. You see, you stood a lot of things. I stood still while one of my bosses patted me all over and hugged me, while he told me about his Boy Scout sons and his nice, motherly wife. When he wanted to put his arms around me, he did. And I just stood like a stick and took it, instead of kicking him a good one.

I had to eat. You can put up with a lot to go on eating.

"I GUESS YOU KNOW what you're doing," she told me, not sounding all that sure, "but it's hard to imagine anyone who is interested in the thirties anymore.

"Oh, maybe those 'old folks' who live in retirement villages, and are a little bit 'emotionally retarded.' I find it difficult to talk with people eternally stuck on the subject of 'when I was young.' The past is only interesting because it explains how I got here."

Despite her anti-nostalgia stance, Peggy Paladino has a lively memory of the days when she was a young working girl in Indianapolis, Indiana. "I was a trained legal secretary and I got seven dollars a week for my first job," she recalled. "My daughters keep telling me to be quiet about it, because it embarrasses them to hear me admit I got paid such a stupid salary.

"But I didn't get it because I was inefficient or dumb; that's just the kind of salary women were paid."

MARGARET O'DONNELL PALADINO'S STORY

As bad as some of them were, I hung on to my little jobs like they were life rafts . . . worked overtime, never complained, got there early, went without lunch, did extra jobs . . . anything to keep the axe from falling.

When my grandfather died in 1936, my whole world fell apart. The family just did not hold together. I was sent—not asked if I wanted to go—to business college that fall, and from then on I was strictly on my own. There was no more money or help. My family had lived in the town for years, then suddenly we were scattered all over the state.

I had my business school expenses and the rent for three months. After that I took care of myself. I never asked for a penny, and I wouldn't even take a job in a business that had formerly had dealings with my grandfather. I didn't want people to think I was helpless.

All of this must have been quite a blow for my mother and grandmother but, at the time, I'm afraid I was just a self-centered young person. I didn't think anyone else could possibly be in the spot I was in. Later, I helped my mother pay off a note—she had borrowed some money to go to business school herself. How I ever did that on the salary I made, I'll never know.

One thing I do remember distinctly is sloshing through snow looking for a job. I wore those funny old galoshes then, and each morning I would take the bus and make the rounds of the employment agencies.

They charged fees and would send me out on these horrid jobs that no girl in her right mind would take. But if you refused, they got really nasty about it. Finally, I got a job from some "floating information." That's the way we got most of our jobs in those days. Somebody would know somebody who knew somebody quitting. So I'd be right there when the boss started looking for a new girl.

My first job was for seven dollars a week as a legal secretary working for three attorneys. I remember after I paid carfare, rent, and food I had a nickel left over each week. Of course, I was looking for a better job from the first day I was there. The only way I could do that was to hunt on my lunch hour or write resumés and then try to follow them up the next week.

Looking for a job wasn't always pleasant in more ways than one. It didn't take me long to observe that women usually came off second best. You'd answer an ad and some man would chase you around the desk. Once, one of them grabbed me in an elevator. I applied for a job in the John Mansville Roofing Company, and the boss wouldn't hire anyone but brunettes. At another interview, the man didn't like the way I *sat*.

I had a girl friend—her boss made her drink orange juice and get weighed every morning—weird stuff like that. But we had our own grapevine, and word got around after awhile.

But as bad as some of them were, we hung on to our little jobs like they were life rafts. I did not spout obscenities at the boss or go on strike. I did everything possible to keep the axe from falling . . . worked overtime, never complained, got there early, went without lunch, did extra jobs . . . anything to keep the paycheck coming.

In '38, my sister and I got a great little apartment together for thirty-five dollars a month. It was furnished and carpeted and even had a fireplace. The landlord would slip our mail under the door for us, and the mail came twice a day.

There were lots of tearooms, lunch places, and drugstores and they all had good, cheap food. I never spent more than a dime for breakfast—I'd get coffee and a big, fat bun and they would toast it and put butter on it for me. Lunch would cost me maybe fifteen cents and I'd get a sandwich and a piece of pie for that.

I used to wonder if I was going to go on *forever* making less than ten dollars a week. I never had any money left over for savings or fun or the future. I worked five and a half days then, and during the week, I saw very little sunlight. Especially in the winter, it was dark and snowy and cold when I got up, and after working all day, it was dark and snowy and cold when I got home. I once went with a boy for five months before I saw him in the daylight. His name was Bob, and he was studying to be a doctor.

In '39, I think it was, I was sort of between office jobs, so I applied at RC Cola for this inspection position. I had to sit on a stiff chair in front of a magnifying glass with a light behind it and inspect the bottles for dead mice, cracks, sticks, and dirt. Bottles moved down the conveyor belt between the light and the magnifying glass. It had an hypnotic effect on me . . . the foreman was always shaking me, "Peggy, are you *awake?*" I'd be in a trance, you see—that light and the rhythmic click of the bottles, and the steam and heat in there.

When they found out I could type they had me sending out post-cards for some kind of contest. But if there was a jam on the line, we'd all jump in and help when the boss said so. I put bottles into six-pack cartons, then those cartons into bigger boxes. If we got any overtime, I sure don't remember it. We got no breaks, no benefits . . . unless we married the boss's son—no insurance. Nothing! In fact, if we were late to work they docked our pay, and if it happened too often we didn't have a job. There were mornings when I'd wake up late and think, "Oh, for corn's sake, I missed the stupid bus." Then I'd call a cab. They came right away; in those days they were cheap and fast. Just like in the movies, I'd say, "Driver, please step on it," and he would: taking shortcuts and swooping around cars . . . .

A PENNSYLVANIA TEACHER'S STORY

Allegheny College was a liberal arts college with a very high percentage of people going on for graduate work. They limited the enrollment of women, so I was lucky to get in. They'd allow one woman for every two-and-a-half men. I guess they wanted to keep the percentage of women low to keep from downgrading the college. That's laughable—but true.

When I graduated in 1930, I got a job in a small town near Pittsburgh teaching English and dramatics in the high school. Of course, if you taught in those days you had to be single. I remember we had a little lecture at the very first teachers' meeting. We were told that they expected us to spend our weekends in town—at least three out of four—and it was "suggested" we go to church.

I smoked then, and that was the worst thing a teacher could do. I remember my roommate and I would wait 'til after dinner and then we'd go into the bathroom, and open the skylight. We didn't dare smoke out in the open, even in our own apartment! It would have meant instant dismissal, if caught. I doubt if I smoked a pack of cigarettes a week, so I don't know why I bothered. Except I remember thinking at the time that I had a right to do what I wanted in my own home—it was just sort of a gesture of independence.

I didn't date much even though a couple of fellas liked me, but I was pretty chubby in those days. One year I took off 72 pounds just by cutting out the fat in my diet and doing a lot of exercise. I went to one of those places in Pittsburgh where you lie on rollers. You wouldn't believe this one place, where you came in, undressed, and put on a pair of longjohns. They fastened some electric rollers across your stomach and up and down your back. They also had me roll on barrels. That cost me ten dollars a month.

Even after I lost weight, I was always too bosomy for those days —you know the style was sort of flat-chested. Once my homeroom gave me a sweater for Christmas. One of the kids' fathers told me he heard the boys talking and they thought I had the best figure in school, only they didn't say "figure."

SHE IS, BY HER OWN DESCRIPTION, a very private person. She insists her picture not be taken (although I assured her I had no intention of doing so), and that the pseudonym Enid Wilson be used. "I've always liked the name Enid," she told me, explaining her choice.

We never met face-to-face. She mailed me the number of a public telephone, located in a hotel lobby in downtown San Francisco. Her instructions were to call her at 2:00 P.M., Tuesday, February 18. "It's warm in there," she wrote, "and I won't be overheard."

I was curious if such spy-story intrigue meant a confession of dire proportions. It didn't.

"I don't really want to talk about the thirties," she admitted but agreeing to, nonetheless. "If my set-up were happier today, I could sit back and talk about those days. But in the last couple of years my world has collapsed.

"I owned a restaurant—worked all my life for it—and taxes wiped me out. Now I'm back down to nothing again. So I just sit in my room—and I hear people talk about the happy times in the thirties—but I can't remember them."

She hasn't married, and I think something hateful happened between her and her family after her father's death. But she didn't say so—precisely. Perhaps I only read things which weren't there . . . or perhaps it was the tired, sad voice of a woman who wants to be left alone.

ENID WILSON'S STORY

We had inspection before every meal. The maitre d' lined us up and we stood in a row with our hands out in front of us so he could see our nails.

My family had lived in Bucks County, Pennsylvania, since the 1700s. We were Quakers and got our land grant from William Penn.

We had a beautiful farm with a seven-bedroom house. You could call us landed gentry, I suppose. We had every amenity.

I wanted to be a teacher more than anything, and I was encouraged to pursue an academic career. In those days, teachers boosted you up to think that you could conquer the world, that when you were through school everything was going to be yours. When I finished and found out differently, well, it made me bitter.

My family lost its first big batch of money when father invested in Florida property during the twenties. We had a relative in real estate there who convinced us to do so. Anyway the land was under water and worthless. When the crash came in '29, my father lost the rest; everything went: the money, the farm, everything.

I remember waking up one morning. Everybody was screaming. I couldn't understand what was going on. I got up and looked out my window; mother was running and my sister was yelling, "Dad is hanging in the barn!"

We were left more or less penniless.

There was no possible way I could go on to college, so I answered a want ad for waitresses in the Catskills. After that I got to travel. I'd work the Catskills in the summer and Florida in the winter.

But in that first place, I was so green and scared. I roomed with four other girls that I'd never seen before. It was a funny little dormitory room with a leak in the roof . . . somehow when you're young those things don't mean so much.

I started work in the dining room of this resort hotel and they were very, very strict. If I dropped a glass or a spoon, the maitre d' would make me stay to sweep the floor after work. In those days, part of the training was punishment . . . you were punished for any little thing you did wrong. In between customers, we shelled peas and diced vegetables in a side hall until a buzzer rang for us to serve a party.

And we worked as many hours as was necessary, seven days a week.

In Florida, we served breakfast, lunch, and dinner. If they were having a big banquet or something after dinner, we stayed until one or two in the morning. Then back up about 6:00 A.M. to reset our tables.

We bought our own uniforms and they had to be spotless. Absolutely not a wrinkle in them, and we'd have inspection before every meal. The maitre d' lined us up, and we stood in a row with our hands in front of us so he could see our nails. And there had better not be a wrinkle in back or a spot anywhere. We would all circle 'round, like a chorus line. Complete decorum was demanded of us —we were to work silently and quickly—but with grace and style, much style.

In those days, only French service was used in the very good rooms. You'd bring everything to the table on one heavy tray: four dinner plates, the meat and vegetables in a beautiful silver dish. Then you put it on your tray stand and served from the side with fork and spoon, always with a napkin under your hand, so that your fingertips never touched so much as the rim of the plate. Cups and saucers were placed just so. You didn't bang them down, you put them down quietly with the handle pushed to the right. It had to be just the angle so the customer could pick it up without turning it the slightest. And then I poured coffee with a napkin under my hand. Everything was done beautifully.

At first I resented all the pomp. I had been brought up in the democratic Quaker way and taught that everybody should wait on themselves. After awhile, I got into the spirit of the thing. I don't know why but I enjoyed doing things with style.

And the people, my customers, were so wonderful then. They were elegant and classy. They not only expected the finest service, but they knew enough to be appreciative. John D. Rockefeller—the old John D.—was one of my customers when I was at Daytona Beach. He was a very friendly, jolly man, and he teased me about the way I pronounced words. I had some silly little colloquialisms I hadn't outgrown yet.

Tipping was very rigid in those places. They more or less had a code, just like people who travel by ship to Europe, and they knew just how much to tip. If it was a party of two, and they stayed a week, the tip was usually five dollars . . . that was for three meals a day.

I never made more than fifty dollars a month in wages, but during a season I made much more than that in tips.

During the off-seasons, I'd go to New York City and get a job. For five dollars or ten dollars, the employment agencies would get you a little drugstore job or a counter job in a Greek restaurant. After dining room service, it was a bit hard to get used to. The customer would give you the order, and you'd yell at the top of your voice at the cook.

I worked at the Gateway Restaurant at Grand Central Station, and I'd catch the train down to Atlantic City on Friday night and get a job on the Boardwalk, just for the weekend. Several of us would go, and we sort of figured we would meet dates where we worked. But it didn't seem to work out that way for me. I'd always meet men—all my life I met men—in bars and places, and they'd always have the wrong idea. But there was no other place to meet them.

Some of my customers were famous people. Once Orson Welles sent me with a note over to Robert Taylor's table. I was so scared; you know, that's big stuff when you're twenty-five. And I served Jan Pierce, the opera star; sometimes he'd sing while he waited for his dinner. Sometimes people don't turn out to be what you think they are. For instance, Lowell Thomas had always been one of my idols. When I was a kid growing up, I'd listen to all those wonderful broadcasts from Katmandu and other far away places. But I found him to be very demanding and overbearing in person. That was disappointing.

Once I had a date with Gene Kelly when we were both in the Adirondacks, but mostly it was the old men who liked me. You've heard the story about the young waitress who meets the rich man's handsome son and marries him. I never got the sons. I always met old men in their eighties who'd pull up a pant leg to show how firm their flesh was. You know I was very shy and straitlaced, and that kind of girl appeals to that kind of old man.

But for the most part my customers were my friends—even when they didn't know me. I enjoyed them. I loved what I did and, frankly, I made myself tops . . . I knew every bit of beautiful service and wine.

Every holiday—Thanksgiving and Christmas—I worked. You see, I didn't have a family or a home like some of the others, so I thought working was better than sitting home. And I saw my customers having fun, and I was a part of it: in a way I made it possible. Working compensated for a lot of things in my life.

Chapter Ten

THOSE WHO ENTERTAINED

I TALKED WITH JEANNE HUTTON in a church basement during a Wednesday all-day crafts session for senior citizens. The hall buzzed with conversation and activity. Tuna casserole and orange Jell-O squares were served at noon for thirty-five cents. In a far corner, one group worked on glazed ceramic roosters.

Jeanne had the kind of imposing good looks some call "handsome" in a woman. And though she'd recently broken her nose in an accident and wore a bandage, she walked in like she owned the place. She was popular with everybody. As we talked, several stopped to say hello and each in her way reached out to touch Jeanne.

"Isn't this fun?" she asked, staring at her half-finished painting, which I could see pleased her. "Oh, it is," she said, answering her own question. "You know, I never had time to do this when I was young. I was too busy with my music."

Jeanne was twenty-five years old in 1930. After three unfulfilling years teaching school, she "sat-in" one night for a sick piano player in Johnny Green's sixteen-piece dance band out of Kansas City. She stayed on for fifteen years.

JEANNE HUTTON'S STORY

It doesn't matter where you are or who you're with. You can still be a lady.

Yes, we were well known in the Midwest. Never played any city under 10,000. No small towns. 'Course, they couldn't afford a big band.

Our first date was Chicago, and I was appalled at the breadlines. My home had security, and I'd been educated in a boarding school. I never realized how the other half lived.

When I stepped off the band bus we traveled in, I saw women in minks and diamonds waiting in long lines just for a little cup of soup. Sure, some people still owned material things, but they couldn't sell them. Nobody had any money.

But the Depression wasn't bad for me. Actually, it was the greatest time in my life. I had a ball.

Got good money. It usually ran around $160 a week plus side benefits. Sometimes we got our room rent.

And I loved traveling. Before I was through I'd visited every state and all the major cities in the United States. Spent two and a half years in Honolulu, a year in Mexico City, and a year in Toronto.

But it was hard to meet young people my age, especially men. We had absolutely no association with anyone outside the music business. Oh, it was different for the men. They got out and ran around, but it was not the same for me. I had to take care of myself.

When we played one-night stands, I couldn't bear that bus because the men would throw their feet up, you know, and one thing and another. I was taught *that* wasn't ladylike so I bought a car. It was a beautiful, new Oldsmobile. I had to have some place to keep my clothes because I always liked to dress fine.

Well, when I bought that car the boys all wanted to ride with me. They didn't like that bus any more than I did. So I sold the mileage. Yes, ten cents a mile for each of them—and if I had flat tires— well, it was understood that they would fix them. I couldn't get dirty and then get back in the car because nobody drove my car but me. I really loved that car and wanted to keep it nice and clean. God, I was particular—always telling the boys to wipe their feet.

They'd gripe and fuss, but they were always there when it was time to go again.

When we were playing Chicago or other big cities we usually got the supper club crowd; but when we were on the road we got the people who'd saved all month to come. It was a tremendous social event in their lives.

I remember watching people coming into those big halls. At first they looked glum. But after a few drinks the party started to liven up. We kept the music gay, and we kept it moving.

We must have played "Star Dust" every five minutes in those early days. And we played all those popular numbers and the old World War I songs like "Hello Daddy." Of course, we jazzed them up.

And, hey, remember, "It Looks Like Rain in Cherry Blossom Lane"? I remember it well because it was Martha Raye's number.

One night in Chicago she came in after her late show, had a few drinks, and walked up to my piano. Gee, I felt flattered. I just adored her. She had this absolutely fabulous voice. I couldn't believe it. I always thought of her as being a big person, but she was really tiny. She'd just stretch her little legs out—she wasn't one to put on, you know—and sing, "It Looks Like Rain in Cherry Blossom Lane." It was so great, I'd cry until my blouse was wet. I told her, "You'll just have to quit singing because I can't quit crying."

I was supporting my mother at the time, and she had just come up from Key West. When I told Martha, she gave me tickets and told me to bring mother backstage after her show. Oh, it was the greatest thrill in mother's life.

But I met a lot of famous people in my business. I always sat sideways on the stage so I could look out, and I remember one night I saw B-O-G-A-R-T. Oh, yes, Humphrey Bogart. "Hey," I said to one of the sidemen, "don't freeze but that's Humphrey Bogart out there."

When we played, we played seven nights a week. But when we'd break for vacation, we'd take three months. Usually in the late summer and fall we'd take off so we could get rested up for the holiday season.

During this time I'd find myself alone, very restless, and unhappy. I couldn't seem to relax. It seemed like I needed the music to keep going. So I'd look around for other jobs, just for a different experience.

My goodness, one time I had just come from Chicago, and right back to Chicago I went, with an all girls' band. We called ourselves the "Tunnerees," named after Tunner, the woman who booked us.

I just loved it. We wore A-shaped leather skirts, vests with fringe, boots, and silk western shirts, all made to order. There were fourteen of us, and let me tell you, it was the first time I ever saw girls run around nude in front of each other. I could never do that. And I thought, "Wow, how'd I get in this jackpot?" But I weathered it. Always did.

I wouldn't room with any of them because they were careless about leaving their irons and dresses around the room. Well, they started calling me "Miss Uppity," but before we finished that tour we were all good friends.

Another year I played with a group booked into state fairs. That took me around carnival people, and I picked up their slang. Learned to talk "carnie" real good.

And that was the year I met a "Stage Door Johnny" to end 'em all. Oh, I'd gotten notes and stuff from guys. But this note was different.

We were playing a town in South Dakota when this Indian, Chief 'Fraid of the Eagle, saw me. He was the big chief there. Ha! He sure tried everything he could to get me in his tepee.

Well, he was close to ninety, mind you, and didn't talk English, but he and his interpreter followed me all over, proposing to me.

That old chief followed me all the way to White Cloud, Kansas, and I didn't get rid of him until after we had our picture taken together. Oh, that was a kick, let me tell you.

The chief and I corresponded a couple of times after that. I was playing Chicago when I heard he was killed on his way to the Chicago World's Fair. Had an automobile accident right down in the Loop. I felt real bad about it.

I remember another time we'd just finished twenty weeks in Chicago, and all the guys went on vacation. Not me. I entered a marathon contest in a furniture store window. Believe that? Well, it was good advertising for the store. Played seventy-two straight hours. They told me it was a world's record at the time.

I made the newspapers. Even the newsreel guys came out. Oh, everyone was applauding me, and there was a gang of people blocking the street. I'd look out and smile at them. Wow, it was a lot of fun. And I made $500 which wasn't hard to take. My land, I was so proud of that $500.

Let me tell you about the year I spent my vacation running a dance hall. Oh, that was an experience. Goldie Meet was our girl singer, and we got together and decided to go into the taxi dance business in Kansas City. So we rented this dance hall at 1319 Walnut, right downtown.

We were in the big time right from the start. Had about sixty girls working the taxi, and in three months we'd tripled our money and sold the thing. By that time, we wanted to get rid of the headaches all those girls caused. And we really had 'em.

But one thing I learned in Kansas City was *longevity*. It's all in the approach, you see—the fingers—the position of your hands. Since I was half-owner, the more dances I played the more money I made. And I wanted to make the money so I really played on that piano. I had a pick-up band of ten and would give the other musicians a number or two off. Everybody got a break since I didn't expect them to work as hard as I did, but I barreled on through.

Trouble with taking on local talent was getting into a little marihuana. I'd look around and say, "Well, I see Mary's here tonight. You'd better hold it down." This one fellow told me that it was almost impossible for him to really get hot on his clarinet unless he had a little stimulant of some kind.

It was all an experience. All these things sort of built my character.

I guess mother was the big reason I stayed single. I took care of her because my father had died in 1918, and she had raised three girls alone. But even with father gone, I had a pretty strait-laced upbringing. Never smoked or drank. And I didn't change on the road.

When I first went with the band, mother was very much against it, so I sat her down and gave her a few thousand words. "Mother, it doesn't matter where you are or who you're with," I said, "if you're properly raised, you can always be a lady."

Well, she didn't want me to go, but she finally agreed. I never forgot what she said when I left home. "You have one body and one soul," she said, "and you have to feed your soul like you do your body. You'll turn out to be just whatever you make yourself."

PEGGY GILBERT still blows a mean tenor sax, mostly in weekend jam sessions with "the girls," but sometimes for pay. "We just did a Coca-Cola commercial," she told me. "They flew five of us from the old group up to San Francisco and filmed us on the porch of one of those Victorian houses up there. We were playing pure Dixieland jazz. You don't see too much of us—they kept panning from one corner to another. All you can see is me and the tips of some of the horns.

"But they loved us and might even use the group in another commercial, because they think we're such a novelty."

She had trouble straining the irony from her voice at this last sentence. Peggy Gilbert led one of the big all-girl swing bands of the thirties, booking the same ballrooms as Goodman, Shaw, Dorsey, et al.

"When the big band era died after World War II," she explained, "all-girl bands disappeared, too. Oh, I organized small groups now and then—one called the Frivolous Five for Jack Benny when he went into television in the early fifties—but by that time I was a secretary for the union and couldn't go on the road myself, anymore. I figured it was all over for me."

Although semiretired, Peggy Gilbert remains active on the board of Local 47 of the Los Angeles musician's union. "I'm busy enough," she says. "But I dream about taking a big band out again —just like Bob Crosby and some of the others are doing. And I could. I could get them together—but you see, they'd all be *old*. It's OK for Bob Crosby to have white hair, but when it comes to women, well. . . . Audiences will accept old men playing good, but if it's old women then it's got to be comedy. That's the way it is. I fought that for many years, and finally gave up. Women have always stood for beauty and romance—that doesn't go with old, I guess."

PEGGY GILBERT'S STORY

We were swinging good. Real good. I think I had the only girl band on a big session with Goodman. It was a great time for music —the late thirties.

I was born in the Midwest—Sioux City, Iowa. You can't get any more Midwest than Sioux City. I grew up there, and since father was a violinist, I grew up with music. He wanted me to study piano, which I did, but later I became more and more interested in horns, much to my father's chagrin.

There were a lot of girl bands coming into our city on the Orpheum vaudeville circuit. Girl bands were big in the twenties. Once I heard a girl playing saxophone, and I immediately started going with it.

In 1927, I organized my own band—all girls—and played for the Eppley hotels all through the Midwest. Nice hotels in those days served you live music with your dinner.

There were five of us—piano, violin, drums, guitar, and myself on saxophone—and we called ourselves the Melody Girls. We all wore long white satin pants and sleeveless vests with glittering buttons down the front—that was something new in the twenties— pants. Nobody was wearing them in those days.

My family moved to Los Angeles in 1929, and I had to leave my group to go with them. So there I was in California, right in the beginning of the Depression: a girl with a saxophone, wondering what to do.

My first job was at MGM studios. Not to play, because they wouldn't have a woman horn player. Studios were all for men, except for a few women who played string instruments—violin, harp, or viola.

I got a job as a sideline musician. That means I was in a movie scene playing real music, but it wasn't being recorded. The actual music that was heard was recorded by a male studio orchestra and dubbed in. We women musicians were only acting.

Up to that time, the studios used extras who held the instruments and made believe they were playing. Well, that was bad because they'd pretend to play when they weren't supposed to, and vice versa. To a music lover or musician seeing the picture, this was terrible.

The union forced the use of real musicians. Petrillo, you know, made our union one of the strongest ones. He really put us on the map, regardless of what people thought of him.

The union forced studios to use union musicians, but never forced an employer to hire a woman musician. They didn't really try because the union wasn't too sympathetic to us women. It's only been within the last few years that they've had women on the boards. It's taken a long, long time.

We got eighteen dollars for an eight-hour day. It was good pay—studio work was the highest priced work you could get—but the orchestra that did the actual recording got paid more. We women felt the unfairness of it way back then—back in '29 and '30. For instance, in the *Great Waltz,* I had forty girl musicians in the beer garden scene. We really felt put down. We knew we could have played as well as the studio orchestra—and earned the higher recording fee.

Of course, it was discriminatory. And they gave us the most ridiculous reasons for it, like . . . , "Men don't want to have girl players sitting next to them," and "Men don't like to feel stymied by having to watch their language." 'Course, it was ridiculous. There wasn't one of us who couldn't have held down a chair and done as good a job.

I left the studios in 1930 and took an all-girl orchestra into the El Mirador Hotel in Los Angeles. We played in the lobby before dinner, then in the dining room during dinner, and in the ballroom on Friday and Saturday nights for dancing.

The El Mirador was a fabulous place in the thirties and we were the only band in the house. The people loved us.

After that, I went on to Fanchon and Marco—they had theaters all over the place way up to Vancouver. At first, I went out with Rudy Weidof as part of an all-girl saxophone sextette. He was a famous saxophonist—the only one making recordings in the early thirties.

After a few tours with Rudy, I went on the road for three years with an all-girl band, a big band—sixteen pieces. We played all the acts and then did our own thing on stage. We'd just finish one tour and come back to Los Angeles and immediately go into re-hearsal for the next tour. It was a grind, so when E. K. Fernandez—he was called the Barnum of the islands then—offered me and the band six weeks in Hawaii, we jumped at it.

I had no idea what we were going to play. We were a stage band, and thought that's what we were going to do, but we wound up playing for a three-ring circus. My brass players' lips were hanging down to their shoes. You know, circus music is grueling—one of the worst things in the world. But that was only for six weeks, and we survived it; I'll never know how. But from then on we played theaters at night and lived on the beach during the day, and ended up staying a year. And it was a great year.

When I got back from the islands, I put together a new band and we played theaters. We played Warner Brothers, we played Pantages, Orpheum . . . we played up and down the New England coast. But that was it—just the chain theaters.

I didn't start going into the ballrooms with all-girl bands until 1937. That was the start of swing—we were right there in the beginning with Goodman and Dorsey, and when Ada Leonard and Ina Rae Hutton came on the scene. Ada had been a strip artist in Chicago before she started her band. She had a fabulous figure and she could sing. Ina Rae was already a featured singer when her booking agent told her she should get a girl band to front.

All-girl bands were popular; always had been. Babe Egan and her Hollywood Redheads were the first girl band that I ever knew back in the twenties. She was so popular they booked her all over Europe. She played for Hitler when he first became a big man over there.

By 1937, I was doing the ballroom scene. I never had trouble finding girl horn players or percussionists or bass players. In those days there were many girl bands playing theaters and many with a vaudeville background. Yes, there were some wonderful women instrumentalists.

It was a great time—the late thirties. We'll never see a time like that one again. We were swinging good. Real good. I think I had the only girls' band that was on a big session with Goodman. I still have the program and it's just fantastic. I look at it now and I can't believe it myself.

Yeah, we were swinging. We did our own singing and our own performing, too. Remember Charlie McCarthy? Well, I had a girl dummy sitting on the bandstand dressed in a gown exactly like the band's. And I had her wired for sound. She had a little speaker in her chest and the line was run back to "Pee Wee" Preble, one of my trombone players who was her voice. I'd take the dummy up to the microphone with me and we'd sing duets together. This would absolutely floor everybody. It was a real cute act.

We barnstormed all over the country. We played the Trianon

in Chicago and the Palomar and Palladium in Los Angeles—all the big ones. I had the band booked into the Zenda ballroom in Los Angeles for two years, and we were doing other things on the side—like playing the Paramount theater and making pictures. We were ambitious and we loved to play; the whole band loved to play. We even took the staff band job at KETC radio—seven of us. We'd play all night and then play from seven to eight thirty every morning at the station—six mornings a week. You had to have a lot of stamina.

When we were on the road, we'd ride all night on the bus and then we'd get to the hotel and sit in the lobby until check-in time, so we didn't have to pay for two days. We'd bunk anyplace in the lobby just to save the money. Sure it was hard, but we were young and we were doing what we wanted to do.

It was all worth it. Especially when you stood up on the bandstand and felt your music moving people, watching them get up and dance, really getting going. It was beautiful, like painting a picture.

I won't say there weren't problems for women. A man was hired for his ability as a musician but a woman had to be attractive. She had to have a pretty face and figure. She had to be a showgirl as well as a musician. Yeah, we not only had to play as well or better than men, but we had to look beautiful while doing it.

How many great male musicians would have been eliminated if they were judged like us? Take Benny Goodman himself, standing there with his stone face, with no personality at all. He was expressionless, and rarely smiled at the audience. He just stood up there playing a great clarinet.

But when a girl stood up to play a horn . . . I can't tell you how many times I've had managers say, "Peg, the band sounds great, but get the girls to smile more. Tell 'em not to take their music so seriously." Now I'd ask, "Well, how can they smile with a horn in their face?" They didn't care, they'd say, "You've just got to find a way to make them come across better." Now isn't that ridiculous?

I had a fantastic first sax player. She could have held down first chair in any big band around—any of them. But she wasn't pretty. She was attractive enough and sang great, too, but every now and then I'd have a manager! One of them right here in Hollywood who had the Club New Yorker where all the stars came, would say, "Peg, can't you change her for a prettier saxophone player?"

Even the girls who were pretty had to keep looking their best all the time. If Gene Krupa had been a woman, how long do you think he'd have lasted? He had bags under his eyes—wow, all those fellas led wild lives, but if a girl came on she'd better look good.

You see, that is what girl musicians had to live with.

I'm not knocking it. I made a darned good living. It was a thrill, believe me. Every night I couldn't wait to go on. Really. Because I loved it every time we played one of those great, great arrangements and we did them all. We associated with all the musicians—fraternally, you know, on the outside. Even though we couldn't sit in with their bands and play with them, we'd often exchange arrangements. We'd be sitting up all night copying music together.

We were booked right along with the big men's bands—Ina Rae was, too. She didn't play as many ballrooms as I did, because she was a show leader and I was a musician leader. How I went for those dancing crowds. I loved to play dance music, to see the people out there really swinging.

But women musicians were considered inferior to men—some kind of virility factor entered into it—and they wouldn't let us in the recording studios. Not even Ina Rae could record. And so how could we build the kind of following the men's bands had? It was impossible. We had radio remotes everyplace, but that's here and gone if you can't follow up with records.

Sometimes we'd get a heckler because we were women. Young men would come up to the bandstand and challenge us to play something that Dorsey or Shaw or Goodman had out on a record. You know, some smart aleck who'd come up and say, "All right now, let's hear you play 'Sing, Sing, Sing.' " I had a girl on horn who did the trumpet bit—you know, *da-dadada-da-da*—just like Ziggy Elman. Those guys would look sorta sheepish. "I'll be darned," they'd say, "I didn't think you could do it."

Organ Music Under
Announcer: And now . . . Oxydol's own . . . Ma Perkins.
As we join Ma, we hear her saying to Shuffle . . .

THE VOICE OF MA PERKINS talking with Shuffle Shober is as much a part of my childhood as the memory of string beans snapping, screen doors slamming, and my mother warning me not to get dirty. Once I stayed home sick from school an extra day to see if Ma Perkins would discover a poison snake some no-good sent her in a package. She did.

Today, Virginia Payne, who played "Ma" in over 7,000 broadcasts, from December 1933 to December 1960, lives in New York City. She is not retired. And she is not the wizened, white-haired lady most fans think she must be, remembering the radio grandmother-figure of three decades. "When they're casting little old ladies, I get called," she says with a laugh. "I know the minute I arrive—and I'm surrounded by feeble, elderly actresses—that I'm not going to be right visually for the part. I can sound it but I have a full face and I'm active and hardy. I guess since I played an older woman for so long, they assume I'm quite old by now.

"Nobody realizes that I was only nineteen when I started the Ma Perkins role.

"Radio was a wonderful actors' medium, because anything you could sound, you could play—there wasn't the typecasting there is now. I appeared on many programs other than "Ma Perkins."

"After the show went off the air in 1960, I moved right into theater work. My main reason was to establish an entirely different image. I always ask television interviewers: 'Please don't reveal I'm Ma Perkins right away because the audience will spend the first ten minutes trying to catch the Ma Perkins voice.' Instead, I ask them to mention Ma Perkins at the end and put all my other credits at the beginning."

In spite of her desire not to be stereotyped, Virginia Payne was delighted when I told her that thirties women remember Ma with affection, as she herself obviously does.

"We tried," she said, "we really tried to reflect how those times were for women. I am surprised to hear critics today say we weren't relevant. The very first script had Ma coming down to the lumberyard. The yard had been closed since her husband died three months before and business was in a great slump. Ma was determined to re-open the business and run it herself. And the question at the end was: Can a woman run a man's business in a man's world and not neglect her family?

Now that was relevant in 1933, and it's just as relevant today."

VIRGINIA PAYNE'S STORY

Mother's Day was a big day for Ma. Cards and gifts poured in—
aprons, potholders, handkerchiefs. They never gave Ma anything
that wasn't useful. If Roosevelt was the thirties father figure, then
Ma Perkins was the mother figure.

I studied acting from the time I was five or six years old, even
though my family was all in medical professions. My father was a
doctor, my brother is a surgeon, and there are many nurses in my
family. But I had a bent for acting from the very first. I'd do
recitals at church, parent-teachers meetings—that kind of thing. I
went to drama school in Cincinnati; and then I studied at the Con-
servatory of Music, singing and playing the piano.

When I was growing up, we had a full musical and dramatic life
in Cincinnati and a very good stock company. I was still in high
school when I became an apprentice for the stock company. During
that time radio was emerging and WLW—an excellent station—
invited the company to come down and do some plays. We per-
formed late at night and I remember we were only paid cab fare.
But I loved radio right from the start . . . it never occurred to me
that it might be profitable. I just thought it was a big kick.

I took a heavy schedule of liberal arts courses at the University of
Cincinnati three days a week; went to drama school for two days;
and then in the summer, I added the stock company. I always
worked at acting.

More and more I was given opportunities to appear on WLW.
It was a great station, very large, with its own orchestra and dramatic
staff. A lot of people got their start there, including Eddie Albert
and Rod Serling. My point is that by the time I auditioned for "Ma
Perkins," I had a great deal of experience in the medium, even
though I was young for the part. I'd never have been able to play it
on television. I was only 19 years old, just a kid. Isn't that unbelievable? But true. And I really had to reach out to make it.

It was on a Monday—the 7th or 8th of August—in 1933, when I
auditioned for the part of Ma. I didn't know it at the time but about
500 other actresses in New York and Hollywood, as well as Cincinnati, were trying for the part. I had some tough competition.
Violet Dunn, an actress friend of mine, told me later that other

actresses were furious at the idea that such a young girl got the role.

But it was a thrill for me when they told me I had the part. I didn't realize what I'd landed. I think I would have been petrified if I had. I sort of took it all in stride. I remember calling my mother and saying, "Well, I got it," kid-like, you know, thinking I could do anything.

We went right into rehearsal for the first show. Procter and Gamble was already interested in it, and we did a 16-week tryout at WLW. That's when I found out that lots of others, even wives and girl friends of the station's executives, had tried for the part. So there was a good deal of hostility at first. The director said to me quite openly the first day, "Well, you got this away from a damn good actress, now let's see what you can do with it."

It was sticky for awhile. In the first place the role itself was difficult; I was really reaching out for something considerably over my head. Consequently, once in awhile the director would say, "You've lost it, you've lost it." And I'd think, well, I guess I have—and I'd go back and try it again.

We rehearsed five hours every day for a fifteen-minute broadcast, and at one time I thought I was going to lose my voice because he had me shouting and. . . .

But eventually the agency people told us we were going to the network and the show would move to Chicago. The agency was Blackett, Sample, & Hummert, and we were part of Mr. Sample's group. Some radio history books say the Hummerts had something to do with the show, but they didn't.

This same agency had just developed "Little Orphan Annie." Their idea of telling kids to ask mom to buy a product was new and a big advertising success.

During the show's tryout, I completed my bachelor's and master's degrees, interestingly enough in English literature. I teased one of my professors who taught the history of language. I told him that I felt—as Ma—that I'd probably put the language back a hundred years. She started, you know, with quite a dialect.

I moved to Chicago; and that was cute. My father and I got a map of the city and tried to find a hotel near the Merchandise Mart where we broadcast. My father didn't know the city any better than I did. It turned out that the hotel, although nice, was in a rather Bohemian section on the Near North Side. Soon after, I moved to an apartment a little farther away and my family was a little concerned about that; they were always protective.

The move to Chicago was a difficult one. We got a new director and, except for Charlie Eggleston, the man who played Shuffle, and Marjorie Hannon, who played Faye, all the rest of the cast was new—announcer and all. I was meeting these people for the first time, and it was quite a change.

Charles was older and a wonderful man. During the run of the show he celebrated fifty years in show business. I would say that when we started "Ma Perkins," he was in his forties or possibly fifties. Charles was wonderful about our difference in age . . . he was helpful and we played together beautifully. There was considerable interplay between Shuffle and Ma. Everybody always looked forward to those scenes between them.

The show was broadcast from the Merchandise Mart for thirteen years. The place was enormous; at first I used to arrive early so I'd have time to get lost.

Not too many people remember that we were on both the NBC Red and Blue networks before they were separated—the NBC Blue network became ABC. That was very unusual, even then. We also recorded the show for 228 stations. These recordings were shipped to Hawaii, Canada, and other remote places. Right from the start, we had a wide following. We were on live fifty-two weeks a year, until the very end when we taped the day before. It was a tremendous load. We were in the studios all the time. We did three broadcasts every day. In the morning we went to World studios to record—six weeks in advance for the far-flung places; next we did ABC; and then over to NBC to do it again with a new organist, announcer, and so on. We were busy from nine in the morning until three thirty in the afternoon. For radio, this was a long day.

At the same time, I was doing "First Nighter," "Grand Hotel," "U.S. Steel Hour," "Cavalcade of America," and "Eternal Light": I loved that last program. You see, my voice wasn't recognizable; I could change it for the character I was playing. I also did "Today's Children" for Erna Phillips, and I did "Jack Armstrong" for a while. I was a very good sight reader. We all were; we had to be.

Of course, "Ma Perkins" took most of my time since the show took hold almost immediately. Years later I saw a mail map of those early days and it was amazing. I remember we had a couple of offers, like a clothespin apron and my picture for a boxtop and a quarter or something like that. Well, it brought a great mail response. The picture of me was in full makeup, of course. We went down to a lumberyard to take it. You see, I was always in makeup whenever pictures were taken for fan magazines or during personal appearances.

When the network sent out my real picture they'd identify it on the back as Virginia Payne of the cast of "Ma Perkins." They'd never identify me as Ma—it took me a long time to get any kind of billing on the program. It was in the fifties before I finally got billing as Ma.

I admit that it was hard not to be myself, but then I was able to do other parts on radio so I didn't feel quite so bad. Those parts were imperative because they kept my identity alive as a young actress. It wasn't that I got so much billing, but it helped my own feeling about it.

After playing a role for so long, older men, much older than me, were saying, "Hello, Ma." I kind of resented that, but at the same time the whole thing was really thrilling and the recognition was good.

The cast was very close, like a family; players stayed with the show for such a long time that we went through a great many real life things together—births and deaths, divorces and marriages, successes and failures.

For a long time Charlie was ill—having heart palpitations—and I kept working to get him back on the program. We did personal appearances so he could see he could work without the palpitations. Eventually he did get back on the show.

Murray Forbes played Willie for twenty-five years. One funny thing—in the script Willie Fitz was always dreaming dreams and making big plans, most of which never worked out. So when the program went off Murray took one of Willie's dreams: he went into real estate and today is very successful at it. It was so funny; I guess he talked about it so much he convinced himself.

We were all proud of the show and ambitious for it. We wanted it to be good. We had one writer, Orin Loveroh who was with us for twenty years, and he had lofty ideals. As a consequence, we were in first place among the daytime serials most of the time, and I don't think we ever fell out of the top ten. We were usually in the first three. And believe me, points in the ratings were fought for, just like they are now.

Ma was a very believable character, and her problems were very real to women of the thirties. We tried to keep the plots moving, even though they usually centered on Ma. The point of interest did change, and we had other people come in. Plot lines were usually conceived for a thirteen-week period. We tried not to have terribly drawn-out plots, even though they teased us that we did. For example, when Faye had her baby, she said to her husband at the fade out, "Hold my hand," and the next day the baby was there. As I said, we tried not to do these long drawn-out things, like murder trials; and we didn't have amnesia. We really tried hard to get away from those aspects of daytime series shows, so it's funny that we should be tarred by the same brush.

The critics of "Ma Perkins" should remember that during the thirties there was a much more extroverted society. Ma was a friend to everyone in town. Most of the things that interested her didn't have to be about her. Sometimes she was concerned about her children. Evie was a particularly difficult daughter; they would be estranged from time to time, but you had the feeling those misunderstandings wouldn't last long, and that they would be resolved, like most family problems. Things that happened to her business partners, her family, or to the people in the town concerned her. She had a sense of community, as did a lot of people in those days.

Rushville Center, of course, reflected the prejudices of the thirties. We had the banker's wife who was snobbish, and her daughter who had everything, versus Faye who had very little. That kind of thing was standard then. In those days, bankers were not held in such high esteem, and it was interesting to see how that character changed over the years. My father told me that he thought the banker was the villain of the program because he was always foreclosing mortgages; but that changed as the Depression eased. We had one plot where he was interested in a lady piano player and we began to see a deeper side of the man, a more human side. So there again, our program changed over the years.

We tried to get away from ethnic and racial stereotypes too. In the early days, we had a boy who helped at the lumberyard. He was a black named Rufus. That part was originally played by a white man from North Carolina who had an excellent dialect, but we departed from that after a time. I remember early in the show, we had a character named Ole Swenson who did a Scandinavian dialect which was the standard for comedy then. But we really did reflect the changes in people's social thinking, like a folk art should. When we began the show, we all had names like Perkins, Pendleton, Phipps, Farnum—they were all simon-pure American names. And then gradually we began to try to get an ethnic mixture into the town. We had names like Zambrini, Ivanov, and so on. In the early times those characters were all done in dialect, but as time went on that changed: a factory moved into the town, and we began to have Slavic names, and the dialects were eliminated.

We did try to point the way when we could. In a humorous way we tried to point the finger at gossip, which was a particularly destructive problem in small towns. And I think the show was moralistic. Ma, particularly, was a tolerant, understanding woman; she was slow to judge. This was very admirable to fans. She was always counseling, "Wait till the facts are in." When you talk to daytime serial critics, they act as if that was very unreal. But I don't think it is with wise people. I think people who have been around awhile keep their counsel until they really know. Ma was a very mature person, after all . . . a mother, grandmother, and experienced businesswoman.

I loved to read our mail. And I answered a lot of it in longhand, particularly when fans sent gifts, like when a woman went to the trouble of tatting the edges of handkerchiefs or making potholders. Around Mother's Day, the mail poured in; Mother's Day was a big day for Ma. If Roosevelt was the father figure of the thirties, then Ma Perkins was the mother figure. The cards and gifts overwhelmed me. One of the most unusual gifts was from a woman who sheared her own lambs and made a pillow for me. And there were countless handkerchiefs with embroidery and sketches of flowers and, of course, there were aprons. The gifts were pretty down-to-earth things. They never gave Ma anything that wasn't useful because that's the kind of person she was. As for the Mother's Day cards, they were fabulous. I really got the feeling that kids, especially, had spent their entire allowance getting the fifty cent cards—you know, very elaborate ones. But they came from all kinds of people—men and women and children.

Men would become attached to the program because of their mothers. Or, for example, salesmen wrote me that they couldn't make a housecall when we were on the air, especially if there was some kind of climax. They'd tell me every house would be tuned to my program . . . women of the house were listening and didn't want to be disturbed. So these salesmen would listen in on their car radios so they'd know when they could safely make their calls, and a lot of them got interested in the program that way.

When so many people identify with a character you're portraying, there's no doubt you develop a sense of responsibility toward your audience. For about the first seven years, I didn't have any vacation unless I just happened to be out of the script that day. And that was fun, because in the fan mail the next week would be letters from people who'd report almost verbatim, "while you weren't there, he said, and she said, and then he said," they were on my side and wanted me to know what went on while I was away. Some would add, "but I won't sign my name because she's a dangerous person."

The fan mail had great variety—the naive letters and the very intelligent ones. One woman started writing me when her boy was little; when he was in the service she asked if he could meet me when he passed through, and we did. She sent me an invitation to his wedding. This woman and I continued to correspond for about twenty years.

I had a secretary but I tried hard to answer personally. I don't think we were as remote—in radio—as today's television stars.

Most of my mail wasn't composed of pleas for problem solving. Most was simply identification, like, "I had trouble like that with my daughter, too." I never wrote anything specific; I'd just write that I hoped things were working out. I found there were many, many lonely people all over the country who turned to a fictional character to fill their needs. Perhaps they had lost their parents. And I'm sure there were people, too, who just preferred Ma to real people. And there was the nostalgic turn to it, too. They'd say, "You remind me so much of my grandmother or my favorite aunt,"— Rushville Center was that little town that everyone was from or wanted to be from. Nostalgia is nothing new.

When the critics try to analyze radio's daytime serials, they keep turning to the plots. And I don't think the plots had a great deal to do with it. I think it was the characters. You're really not interested in your friends for what happens to them but for who they are. Anyone analyzing the show always talks about the plots' repetition and unreality. I don't think plot was "Ma Perkins'" appeal at all; it was the characters. People would tell me where they were when they'd experienced a similar problem or life change. I'm sure that the continuity of the program helped people during the Depression. We were their link and we were something to cling to.

Our sponsors had a lot to do with it, too, because we never changed our time. They were wise not to dabble around. We were on at 12:15 Central time and 1:15 Eastern time for all those years. And it wasn't just the continuity, but the time itself—lunchtime. Many people heard me when they came home for lunch, especially children, so we were associated with food and home and love.

My life has been mostly work-oriented—we did have a heavy schedule. Most of my friends were in the business so a lot of my associations were within the business. I remember when we moved the show to New York in 1947, Mr. Wolfe, our director, told me that I depended too much upon my work.

Naturally, the tough schedule eased; it had to. After the first few years, I'd be written out for two weeks and I'd travel, which I dearly loved. And, I did make a few personal appearances—Charlie and I did a big appearance in Des Moines, Iowa—buses came in from all over the state. I had a whole outfit, you know; an older woman's clothes, a wig, and stage makeup . . . I really dressed for it. People didn't know my age. I did it as a stage appearance in a large auditorium so people wouldn't know I wasn't an elderly woman.

Women in the thirties: when I think of them, I think they were courageous and achieving. And when they couldn't achieve themselves, they were anxious for their children to achieve. So many of today's accomplishments started from the ambition of those mothers for their children. They made tremendous sacrifices. I'm not sure we'd be willing to do that today with the philosophy of doing your own thing first.

But those women were very giving. And I don't think Ma was that different from the average thirties woman. I never saw her as unrealistic; if she had been she wouldn't have had the following she had for as long as she did. She represented what a great many women were doing, and she lived their experiences. She also believed in prayer. You see, it wasn't a cynical age. They had to hope, they had to believe. Ma was one of them. She wanted things for Faye and Evie and John—at the same time that she was coping with her own life. Ma handled so many day-to-day, basic problems of survival like most women that she didn't have time to consider her own feelings.

PART FOUR
WOMEN INFLUENCING THE WORLD ABOUT THEM

IF THE FORCES OF ECONOMIC EVIL were prepared to defeat Depression America, then the righteous legions of the Lord also were ready to do battle. In addition to their traditional care of the old and sick, church women in many communities organized relief for families of the unemployed.

But the armies of displaced and jobless soon overwhelmed the meager resources of most churches, forcing women's groups to adopt a desperate new fund-raising approach—selling overpriced merchandise for a percentage cut. *The Christian Century* chided these "artless . . . naive" women for bringing the silk-stocking merchants into the temple. Yet even these frankly commercial innovations failed to feed the multitudes.

Alas, if the church could not fill all the hungry bellies, it could nourish many hungry souls. To some, the Depression appeared to be the wrath of God visited upon a modern Sodom and Gomorrah society. Regular church attendance rose in the early thirties. But it was the prophets promising salvation from disaster who drew crowds of penitents. The hot wind of religious revival blew across the country, carrying countless tent meetings and evangelists from town to town. "Can a Bobhaired Woman Go To Heaven?" was the provocative question asked by one preacher. His answer, unfortunately, is not recorded.

Nothing could squelch the believer's desire to believe. Father

Divine had chronic headline troubles with the female "angels" of his kingdom. Sister Aimee Semple McPherson—twice sued for slander—was bailed out by her Angelus Temple faithful who filled collection buckets with cash, watches, jewelry, and even their gold teeth.

Less flamboyantly, many thirties women found church offered more than solace for their soul. Bible and women's groups provided intellectual and social companionship, and the church "Cradle Roll" department baby-sat while mom attended services.

Young women and girls were included in the wide range of church activities. The Methodists had their Epworth League, the Baptists their Young People's Union, and the Catholics their Catholic Youth Organization. The Catholics were the liveliest with Saturday night dances and bingo. Young Baptists were more likely to face long evenings of such topics as, "What was the significance of Paul's letters to the Ephesians?" punctuated midway with lemonade and cookies.

It may stretch a paraphrase to say, "There are no atheists in a depression." But many women during those hard times found the "old time religion" the best way they could make do in a hostile world.

Outside the church, women have often banded together to work for social progress. Better care for the insane and indigent, the abolition of slavery and child labor, temperance, universal education —all these causes were promoted by organized women.

During the early decades of this century, as woman's leisure time increased, so did her public spiritedness. By the 1930s, her interests had evolved into an endless number of organizations, both serious and pleasurable.

Cleaning up the movies was one such successful thirties venture. As guardians of the nation's morals, women were alarmed about blatant sex being projected at the neighborhood movie palace. Although motion pictures always portrayed the back-street mistress suffering and the unwed mother secretly giving up her child (later to painfully watch it grow up from afar), the suggestion of cinematic sin was all too frequent for the National Legion of Decency. Nonsectarian and largely female, the legion and many women's organizations protested advertisements like:

AN ARISTOCRATIC LADY
WITH DEMOCRATIC LIPS
SHE TURNED A COLD SHOULDER TO A WARM-HEARTED
NOBLEMAN, BUT BLISTERED THE LIPS OF A NOBODY
WHOSE CALLING CARD WAS A RED HOT RIVET.

And they won. The legion's vocal censorship caused the movie industry to set up its own production code for self-regulation.

Nobel Prize recipient Jane Addams, famous for her pioneering social work at Hull House in Chicago, should be remembered equally for her pacifism. Long the president of the Women's International League for Peace and Freedom, she influenced a generation of women and youth.

The climate of pacifism Addams and others helped to create brought startling results: thirty years before Vietnam war protestors took to the streets in the 1960s, young people swore the Oxford oath . . . "We will refuse to support the government of the United States in any war it may undertake."

The early thirties found the country awash in bathtub gin, bootleg hootch, and gangsterism, but Prohibition's repeal in 1933 was a mixed joy for some. It drowned the hopes for a dry America for which the Women's Christian Temperance Union had worked so long and earnestly.

In 1974, while Mrs. J. Fred Tooze was president, the WCTU, still 250,000 strong, celebrated its hundredth anniversary. Mrs. Tooze recalls the time of repeal: "Naturally, we were disappointed, but we weren't discouraged . . . we went right back to work."

But the WCTU of 1934 did not pick up the saloon-busting axes of old; instead they picked up the mightier pen, printing reams of educational literature, some of which is still turning up in high schools.

Women's clubs gained popularity in the 1930s to the extent that one psychologist expressed fears that too much outside-the-home activity could cause nervous breakdowns among the middle class.

On the other hand, *Woman's Home Companion* considered women's organizations so important that the magazine gave the subject an editor and a regular feature section. In a guest column, one young club matron marveled at the scope of women's groups:

"It's amazing," she wrote in 1937, "to see all the societies that are helping women in their self-imposed task of enriching American life. I had no idea so many women were interested in civics, government, and the nation's political problems, to say nothing of international affairs."

One issue of the *Companion* advised a woman in Texas on how to organize a club for young mothers; gave a North Dakota woman information on modern art; answered a Mississippi housewife's question about the Spanish Civil War; and helped a New England woman with luncheon ideas.

A club woman writing at that time explained how organizations throughout the nation helped fulfill a need in women to run things: "Executive ability is rated high in this country," she explained. "Where else can a confident woman exercise so much of it?"

The uncertain times of the Depression decade drew women together in a companionship that suburban isolation and our national addiction to television have largely erased. Though few women of the 1970s would want to return to ten-dollar-a-week jobs and outdoor toilets, it is easy to envy our foremothers their togetherness.

During the thirties, women began to influence their world in an entirely new way. When Franklin D. Roosevelt was elected president of the United States in 1932, it was not only a new deal for the country, but also a whole new deck of political cards for women.

One of his first cabinet appointments was a tough, shrewd, and rational secretary of labor—Frances Perkins, the highest woman political appointee up to that time. During her twelve years in office, she fought for better minimum hour and wage laws, and was instrumental in the passage of the Social Security Act.

But she was only the first of several women elevated by the Roosevelt administration. Florence E. Allen was appointed to the bench of the U.S. Circuit Court of Appeals—a judgeship just one rung below the Supreme Court; Ruth Bryan Owen became the first woman minister to a foreign country (Denmark); and former Wyoming Governor Nellie Tayloe Ross stepped up to be director of the mint.

Did women have political power? According to a survey by the

League of Women Voters taken in the mid-1930s, between 20 and 25 million women were registered to vote. Of that number, the upper class, "clubby and well-lettered," were most likely to vote with their husbands; the lower class, "mill workers and domestics," were not likely to vote at all. But the middle-class women—the majority of women voters—were "independent." Political observer Bob Considine thought these women held the balance of political power but didn't know it: "In 1932, they turned out Hoover," he said. "All they have to do is make up their minds."

When women do, Considine predicted, ". . . we shall have a woman president and perhaps a balance of sexes in Congress and the Cabinet, and the country will be a little better for it."

But before this bright future could be realized, constitutional freedoms would have to be extended. In the South, the poll tax and property laws, meant to deny Fourteenth Amendment benefits to blacks, had successfully disenfranchised women as well. Poor laws prohibited balloting by "paupers," about 25 percent of the nation's voters, both male and female.

Perhaps spurred by Frances Perkins's ringing denunciation of the law as medieval viciousness, Massachusetts was first to decree that those on relief could vote.

What did women want in the thirties? According to another League of Women Voters' survey, they wanted:

- Qualified people in government
- Public funds for education
- Child labor legislation
- Protection of consumers including the regulation of advertising on foods, drugs, and cosmetics.

If these were women's political concerns, they had a champion in the form of a president's wife.

Eleanor Roosevelt was not an imposing woman. Her teeth protruded; she wore plain dresses and low-heeled shoes, combed her hair in a nondescript fashion, and spoke in a shrill voice.

By all appearances, she was a likely candidate for mediocrity. Instead, she dominated the decade and provided inspiration for women all over the world. Helen Gahagan Douglas sums up: "She set a pattern for us."

To the point of being a target for ridicule, Eleanor Roosevelt befriended the flotsam of society—the Okie, the black, the unemployed.

Her faith in the young led to her patronage of the controversial, left-leaning American Youth Congress, and her personal efforts helped establish the CCC and National Youth Administration programs.

It bothered her that the CCC would not provide help for young women, so she became active in the establishment of camps, such as Camp Jane Addams in New York, for girls. But this effort was unsuccessful, because no work could be found for women equal to that given to the CCC men.

At a time when blacks were publicly epitomized by Step 'n Fetchit and cinema mammies, and *Time* magazine could write about "fuzzy-headed Negroes" without fear of protest from the NAACP, Eleanor Roosevelt was color blind. When Marian Anderson, the outstanding singer, was refused permission to use the DAR concert hall in Washington, Mrs. Roosevelt invited her to use a more fitting stage—the Lincoln Memorial. In 1936, her dining with black guests in the White House set off reams of racist unpleasantness in the press, North and South.

Her feelings about a woman's place were not as clear cut. According to newswoman Lorena Hickok, she envied women in business or the professions who could make their own living. "If I had to go out to earn my own living, I doubt I'd even make a very good cleaning woman," she once said, somewhat bitterly. "I have no talents, no experience, no training for anything."

However, this was not feminism, even thirties style. "Men and women are different," she stated firmly. "They are equals in many ways, but they cannot refuse to acknowledge their differences." However, her traditionalism was ambivalent, because she added in the same quote: ". . . certain questions are waiting to be solved until women can bring their view to bear. . . ."

Despite her strict, Victorian upbringing she was hardly a typical woman of that time. She could scarcely cook, being confined to an occasional omelette; her child-rearing views were decidedly permissive; and she was often away from home.

Her trips when she acted as her husband's eyes and ears, became a national joke. One of them was funny:

MRS. ROOSEVELT: I am very happy to buy this ticket from you,
Mr. Benny. How much do I owe you?

JACK BENNY: Well, that's twenty-five cents for one ticket.

MRS. ROOSEVELT: Can you give me change for a dollar?

JACK BENNY: Well, I haven't the change with me just now, but
I'll send it to you . . . if you'll just stay in one place.

In political matters she interfered on behalf of women. Although
she denied it, it is believed that she lobbied for Frances Perkins's
appointment. In a 1933 note to Secretary of the Interior Harold
Ickes, she was quite direct in stating her preference for a woman
as assistant commissioner of education, and adding that half the
positions for unemployed teachers should go to women.

She was openly active in the women's division of the Democratic
party run by the savvy Molly Dewson, allowing Molly to introduce
her Reporter Plan at one of her "First Lady" press conferences
where politics were usually "out."

The plan, reported Emma Bugbee of the New York *Herald
Tribune,* aimed at organizing Democratic women and proselytiz-
ing Republican women as well. The *Tribune* quoted Miss Dewson:
"If the administration policies are really understood by Republican
women, they will discover that at heart they have been Democrats
all along."

Through it all, according to reporter Bugbee, Mrs. Roosevelt
smiled quietly, allowing the party's women's division to walk off
with all the publicity.

By the end of the Depression decade, Eleanor Roosevelt was
being seriously proposed for national office—an unexpected political turn that greatly embarrassed her. But it's no wonder. A Gallup
Poll of the time gave her 68 percent popularity, topping the president's rating by 4 percent.

And she continued to grow in the esteem of her compatriots.
Before her death in 1962, she was to become an international states-
woman—universally revered. Adlai Stevenson eulogized her memory, saying, "She would rather light candles than curse the dark-
ness."

Some of the candles she lit in the thirties are still shedding light
on women today.

There were many other strong women who left their mark on the 1930s. The comic book character "Wonder Woman" appearing at the end of the Depression was a logical outgrowth of the strong-woman image no one considered unusual during the thirties.

Hollywood's reigning royalty included top dramatic stars Bette Davis, Katharine Hepburn, Joan Crawford—all playing assertive women with wills of their own. Even comedic talents like wise-cracking Joan Blondell and super-sophisticate Myrna Loy arranged their own screen lives and often those of their movie men.

Two major heroines emerged from the decade, both for very different reasons—Anne Morrow Lindbergh, martyred mother whose tragedy every woman could feel, and Wallis Warfield Simpson, captivating commoner who usurped the heart of a king.

For Depression-weary Americans the love story of Mrs. Simpson and Edward VIII was a "foreign entanglement" in which they very much *wanted* to become involved. That headline was a welcome change from those concerning war in Ethiopia and China. On Nov. 9, 1936, a month before abdication, the International News Service even abandoned standard journalistic prose with this breathless Byronic picture caption: "The photo of Mrs. Wallis Simpson shows the Baltimore beauty in her most charming mood. Observe the soft, sympathetic eyes; the humor of the lips; the breadth of the forehead. . . ." A few weeks later, after Edward gave up the throne for his "woman I love," *Time* magazine named her their first "Woman of the Year."

Other, literally strong, women emerged into the world of sports early in the decade. Swimmer Helene Madison McIver held fifteen of a possible sixteen women's free-style records. Not far behind, the beautiful Eleanor Holm won a gold medal for the 100-meter back-stroke in the 1932 Olympics and later swam to professional fame in Billy Rose's Aquacade.

On the tennis court, two Helens, Helen Wills Moody and Helen Hull Jacobs, between them won nearly every title in tennis-dom. A famous feud fueled by newspaper sportswriters developed between the two when Moody, complaining of a bad back, defaulted at the women's Singles Championship in 1934.

But the darling of the sports world was undoubtedly Mildred "Babe" Didrikson—the "one-woman track team." At the '32

Olympic Games in Los Angeles, she won both the javelin and low hurdles, plus tying for first place in the high jump.

A typical Didrikson news story of the early thirties usually had her exhibiting her prowess in a "male" sport—baseball, football, or even putting on the gloves with Bill Stribling, the light heavyweight champion whose lip she split. Although obviously the superwoman athlete of the century, these stories never failed to mention that she was also a gourmet cook and a sensational ballroom dancer.

Golf became her game after 1935 when she was the first woman to win the British Amateur. By her death in 1953, she had won eighty-two tournaments.

In the 1930s, women's brawn was more than matched by their brains. Six out of ten Pulitzer Prizes for fiction went to women and two Nobels—one to Jane Addams for peace in 1932, and one to Pearl Buck for literature in 1938.

The rise of gangsterism during the early days of the Depression produced another kind of strong-woman—the moll—as depicted in hundreds of pre-Hays office flicks. Clyde Barrow had his Bonnie and Alvin Karpis his Ruth, but the mother hen of them all had to be cigar-smoking, tommy-gun-toting Ma Barker, who died in a flaming shoot-out in Florida.

Another strong woman emerged in the thirties who was some-times the target of company goon squads, Pinkerton agents, and police. Union members, representing needle trade and factory workers, marched, picketed, and organized—an important part of labor's victories.

Still, the big news during those desperate years was aviation . . . and if the twenties belonged to the Jenny-flying barnstormers and ocean-hopping Charles Lindbergh, the thirties belonged to the women fliers. Amelia Earhart, a Lindy look-alike, flew the Atlantic solo in '32, then from Honolulu to the mainland, followed by flights crisscrossing North America. Her disappearance during a 1937 round-the-world flight created something of an Earhart cult, many people refusing to believe she was lost.

Also during the thirties, aviatrix Ruth Nichols set an altitude record of 21,350 feet; Louise Thaden and Frances Marsalia stayed aloft for an eight-day endurance record and Mae Heaslip flew at a sizzling record speed of 252 mph.

But in the field of air-racing, Jacqueline Cochran holds the decade's top honor, winning the Bendix Trophy and $12,500 in 1938 against an all-male field.

Many women during the decade, worrying about their next meal or their next job, still found time to copy their favorite heroine— maybe the independence of Bette Davis, the backhand of Helen Moody, or the golf swing of "Babe" Didrikson. And hundreds of women, following the lead of Earhart and Cochran, qualified as private pilots.

These wonder women of the 1930s mortally wounded the do-nothing ideal of Victorian womanhood, changing women's role for good—and for its own good.

Chapter Eleven

GIMME THAT HARD TIME RELIGION

"I FIRST JOINED the Evangelical church in 1908," she said with pride. "I guess about seven or eight years ago they had a little celebration on my fiftieth anniversary. Gave me a corsage and a little speech . . . took my picture."

Oleta Hagens is a woman of rockbound ideas. She believes in God and Christian charity; that sparing the rod will produce sassy children; and that automobiles and airplanes cause people to go so fast they can't enjoy their lives.

"I've lived in the most wonderful years that ever existed," she added. "We had to walk twenty blocks with my husband carrying Howard and me carrying Florence, just to catch the streetcar for church. Never missed a meeting. Think anybody would do that nowadays?"

OLETA HAGENS'S STORY

When I did anything for others, I always got paid back almost double. I think God did that for me.

All my life, I've always tried to give where I could, especially during the thirties. Seems to me when there's making do to be done, women are usually the ones who do it—scrimping and raising our families with whatever is available. If there's a lot, fine, but if there's a little, we do it then too.

I remember women in the 1930s were just pluggin' along as we always did. I had a house that I was renting and there was a family with three children in there. Well, the man lost his job and there were five months when I didn't get paid, and I was hauling food over there every week besides. Then I finally just couldn't keep it up because I had my own family to feed, so I got tickets for them. There was a soup line over in town, and if you had tickets you could get meals every day. She was sweet and did what she had to, but it was kinda pathetic because I could tell everytime I came she hated to face me without having the rent. And finally her husband, he just up and left her. He couldn't take it, but she had to stay with those three little children.

Oh, I'll never forget her baby. I thought about him for the longest time. He was just crawling around on the floor one day, picked up an ironing cord and put it in his mouth. It was still connected to the wall—and it burnt off half his tongue. Of course, she couldn't get no help, had no car or money.

Anyway, her husband had been gone about three months, when he called her and wanted to know if she would forgive him for leaving—told her he just couldn't stand the pressure. Well, you know she *was* willing, and she packed up—bag and baggage to go to Oregon where he had a job. She left all her furniture in the house so as to pay me for the back rent she owed, and that meant I could rent it for fifteen dollars more a month, it being furnished and all now.

Even with all I did for that family, I got paid back almost double. I think God did that for me.

People shared in those days. Even though none of us had a lot, we helped some mighty poor families in the church. My mother-in-law couldn't afford much—her husband was just a laborer for the Southern Pacific—but when I'd tell her about a hungry family, she would go to her pantry and hand me something. Yes, church people always pitched in.

It never occurred to me to turn anybody away from my door hungry. One day this bum came to my kitchen door. It was in '36 because that was the year my husband, Will, took sick with TB. Well, this bum said he wanted old clothes or money or something to eat. I told him I didn't have any money, but I'd fix him some fried eggs and bacon. You know, he was a ragged bum, but he made it plain he wouldn't eat unless he could do something for me. So after I fed him, he and I went out and found a shovel and he dug and worked all morning. About three weeks later he came back and asked me if I could feed him. Now, I recognized him right away and I says, "Oh, you back again?" He kinda hid his head, you know, he didn't want me to recognize him. So this time he went right to the shovel and started working again while I fixed his meal.

That got to be a regular habit and he was a godsend because my husband was sick for three years. Well, Jack, that was his name, kept coming for all that time and mowed the lawn and cut the bushes. He was a wino, you know, and he couldn't hold onto money.

Don't get me wrong, he was as polite as anybody and a good soul. Why, after he'd finish working in the yard, he'd come in and play cards with Will to keep him company and help him pass the time.

One day he came and I told him Will had just passed away. He stood there in the door and cried like a baby—'course winos do that, you know. He said he'd like to go to the funeral, but he had no clothes. I'd give him clothes many a time, but he couldn't keep them 'cause he liked his wine too well—but since this was a kind of sad affair I took him into the house. I gave him one of my husband's best suits and a shirt, a tie, and even a pair of socks and shoes—the whole outfit. He came to the undertaker's parlor and viewed the casket and well—it just broke me up. He stood there and cried as much as—more than I did. I'm not much of a crier anyhow and I guess I'd already done my share while Will was sick, crying and praying that the Lord would make him well.

Three weeks after my husband died, I just had to get out of that house—I couldn't stand it. So my daughter Florence and I got an apartment over a drugstore in town. We hadn't been there long 'til the doorbell rang and there was Jack, and so I had him come in and give him something to eat. But the landlord said he didn't want any bums in his building. I had to tell Jack, "You can't come here anymore. Will's gone and I have nothing for you to do." You know, he was really so proud he didn't want to take anything without working for it—so I never seen him after that. Funny, but I remember his birthday every year and I always have wondered what happened to him.

I told you I always get paid back double for all my charity work. That's mostly true, but I've had some hurts.

There was these kids, they had holes in their pants' knees and they were pitiful, really terribly underfed. Since they came to Sunday School, I visited their home one day because they looked so poorly. I thought sure I could help them in some way. The mother gave me this long tale of woe, that she didn't have no husband and the kids didn't have enough to eat. And they hardly had furniture in that place. Those youngsters were sleeping on an old mattress laid on top of some orange crates. Well, I carried many a box of food over there and when a friend of mine bought a new bedroom set, I asked him: "Chester, what are you going to do with your old set? I know a poor family who needs it bad." He gave it to me on the spot. I thought Chester did a wonderful deed, because it was real hardwood—good stuff. Now, I borrowed a truck and lugged that set with springs and a nice mattress over there.

The next time I'm back, I was shocked to see the kids back sleeping on the old mattress spread out on the orange crates. So I asked them where their new bedroom set was and they said, "Mama sold it and put the money in the bank. She's got over $2,000 in the bank!" At that time I didn't have $300 in the bank myself, and I spent my time out beggin' from everybody for people like her.

So with all your charity work, you still have some hurts—and don't think you don't.

A CATHOLIC WOMAN

At that time the Catholic Ladies' Relief Society was an agency of the Community Chest. Like everybody else we were trying to help where we could, but there was never enough money or anything else to go around.

We had a shoe fund—a Jewish man named Cohen gave us $500 for children's shoes. I don't know why, except he was a good man and was interested in helping poor children.

I'd hear about a child who couldn't go to school because he had no shoes. In those days kids had to walk to school . . . they couldn't go barefooted. So I'd take this child to the store and buy him good sturdy shoes, not cheap ones.

And sometimes we'd take food—not very fancy stuff, but good and wholesome. Those poor people were proud then. You know, they always used to invite me to eat with them—and they'd be insulted if I didn't. They'd bring down their china—it would be all cracked and chipped, but there was a sort of dignity about it.

Once I took a pound of butter to a woman who couldn't get over having so much. She'd been buying it by the ounce and melting it so it would go farther. That house, I remember, had cracks in it so wide I could feel the air coming through.

Some of the stores would give us leftover yardage—remnants —and we'de make up little shirts and dresses and pajamas for the orphanage. Every Ladies' Society in the diocese was alloted so many garments in different sizes to make. I got so I made the best button-holes out of real fine crochet thread. "Those buttonholes last even after the shirt is worn out," one of the sisters told me.

HELEN BARTON AND HER HUSBAND, Randall, live in a pink house in a Portland, Oregon, middle-income suburb. Little of Helen's Tennessee accent remains, but she still has all of her traditional mountain hospitality. "Come right on over," she said when I tele-phoned and mentioned the name of a close mutual friend.

"Do you mind having weiners for lunch?" she coaxed, popping them in the broiler. No, and I didn't mind fixing a salad and brewing a pot of coffee while Helen answered one telephone call after another.

"There," she said, "I've taken that thing off the hook so we can talk. You know, I'm the neighborhood problem solver."

I could see how that job might have fallen to Helen. She looked like Ma Perkins should have looked, and probably didn't—large, bosomy, and confident—the kind of woman who elbows others out of the way, saying, "Let me do that for you, dear."

"You have to understand the Depression," she explained during lunch. "Almost all the families in my town were on WPA or some kind of relief. Religion was the only thing that gave them any answers."

Helen had put more than distance between her present and past —her self-perspective proved to be brutally honest and amusingly tongue-in-cheek. "But don't get me wrong," she assured me, "dad was right all the time. And I've made the church an important part of my life since that night in '37 when I came back home a sinner."

HELEN BARTON'S STORY

My dad always told me, "A woman who'd smoke a cigarette would do anything."

Dad just couldn't forgive me for running away and getting married—and to a drinker at that. But I was seventeen and so tired of the strict way he made me live. I couldn't date, keep my own money, go dancing, or anything. The only social life I had was wrapped up in the Southern Baptist church in our small town.

So I married the first man who asked me. My life really changed after that, because I didn't have dad to keep me on the straight and narrow. So, let me tell you, I became a lot less straight and not so narrow. Pretty soon, I even took up smoking.

Of course, dad heard about this, and the next time I visited home, he wouldn't talk to me. "A woman who'd smoke a cigarette would do anything," dad said.

After that, I set out to prove he was right. I started sinning, yes, sinning—smoking, drinking, dancing—all that.

My first husband and I lived together thirteen months. We argued every day. Every weekend was a brawl because it was one big drinking party—the money we'd worked so hard for all week went for booze. Oh, we made news—everybody in town knew about us.

The fighting kept getting worse and *my* drinking was catching up with my husband's, so one day while he was at the corner bar, I left his hot lunch sitting on the table and took off. I never went back there again.

At midnight I was on the road thumbing with a girl named Dolly. She turned out to be some dolly, all right, entertaining a different guy every night. I still had better principles than that.

But anyway, we left together and were hitchhiking toward Chattanooga when a car came along . . . going in the opposite direction. A guy stopped to ask where we were heading. Then I blithely asked, "Where are *you* going?" Well, he was on his way to Richmond. I asked Dolly if it mattered which way we went. She said no, so we ended up in Richmond.

I got rid of Dolly soon. I guess I was still pretty prudish, even though I felt like a sinner all the time, because I was doing things I'd been taught all my life not to do.

The best job I could find was as a combination waitress-bar-maid. I made enough to pay for a room and I got free meals in the restaurant. But worse, I began getting a lot of free drinks in the bar.

I thought I had it made. I was showing dad I didn't need him or his religion. I could get high anytime I wanted. And I seemed to want to—more and more often. It wasn't long before I began getting sick. I couldn't eat. I'd been living on cigarettes and liquor for six months. I was just bones—only 118 pounds—and I'm tall. Several times I passed out. Then I blacked out completely from drinking. But I didn't call it blacking out; I called it fainting so I wouldn't have to face what I was doing to myself.

One night I came to the end of my road. I collapsed on the bar-room floor. Next thing I knew I was in the back seat of my girl friend's old Chevy . . . she was taking me home to my parents in Tennessee.

My mother, bless her, nursed me for a month, until I built up my strength. My father was very stern, but sometimes I'd see him peek into my room when he didn't think I saw.

Oh, I had black sheep status, all right. I was a Baptist sinner, in a Baptist home, in a Baptist community. Everybody in town was a Baptist those days, very fundamental.

I remember the first night I felt well enough to go somewhere, Randall came over to invite me to church. I went defiantly, with my cigarettes in my purse.

After the service the preacher invited me to the altar. Faces lined the aisle . . . faces of people I'd known all my life. They surrounded me and began yelling and screaming for God to cure me of my wickedness. You see, I was their big-time sinner, and they made the most of it.

Oh, I can see the humor of it all now, but the people patted me on the back, and they loved me. They were really warm, wonderful folks.

They changed my life. That night, kneeling at the altar, they prayed that God would take the terrible habits away from me. "Oh Lord," they hollered, "take the sin away from her. Take away the desire for cigarettes and liquor."

Later that night I lit up a cigarette out of habit. It tasted so bitter I had to put it out. I haven't smoked since.

GRETA JOHANSON TOLD ME she came from a line of women who did things: "My Swedish grandma, her husband was not healthy, had to take a hold of the family and make money tradin' cattle; and my ma, her husband drank, had to get out and be the bread-winner. I sure never expected my life was goin' to be any bargain."

At seventeen, Greta left home with one dollar in her pocketbook and train fare to MacIntosh, South Dakota, to marry a homesteader she'd met only once the summer before. It was 1917.

"We were married ten minutes after I got there," she said, "and drove in a wagon out to the little shack he was putting up. It was only ten feet by twelve feet and you had to figure out which corner you would put everything in, or whether you were going to put 'em under the bed or hang 'em on the walls."

By 1930, she had two boys and "a little bigger shack" with a lean-to kitchen and a storm cellar. She also had the religious faith she'd need to survive −52° winters, 115° summers, hordes of garden-devouring pests, and the sure knowledge that she was gradually losing her home.

GRETA JOHANSON'S STORY

"He don't take our troubles away from us, but He helps us through them . . . sometimes He even makes us miracles."

That winter of 1930–31, I spent wrapped up in a sheepskin coat, plugging the cracks in my walls. It was cold as blazes. Everything froze in the cellar, and we had a hard time to rustle up enough food. Had no money. Couldn't even pay our mortgage that year, and all we heard was Hoover sayin' prosperity was around the corner.

The boys slept on a fold-up couch at one end of the kitchen because it was warmest in there. We burned lignite coal. It's mighty hard to start, but those ashes hold fire all day and all night.

The big room we used as our bedroom and front room. We got along pretty good. Had to. 'Course, I couldn't have a lot of keep-sakes or anything like that; any extra things around would just take up room. Mostly they got broken up and burnt in the stove.

That was the year I almost died from fibroid tumors. I hemor-rhaged for twelve days until my blood was just the tint of milk. I didn't expect to live. I hurt so bad, I was just done with this life. I kept a-praying, "Lord, take me home to live with you."

But it was the Lord's will that I live, although the doctor said I'd never do a day's work in my life. He kinda fooled himself. The next summer I was working in the fields, disking, mowing, raking, driving the header box. I learned in this life to trust the Lord. That don't mean He'll take our troubles away, but He will help us to get through them, and sometimes He'll make us miracles.

Saving my life was a miracle He did. Another was my friend Ella. She had six children and was expecting another one. I think she had two weeks to go. Well, it was close to a mile or maybe even more that she lived from our place and this one day she led her horse and walked over.

Now, she wasn't a woman for visiting. But she came in the morning, stayed for dinner, and stayed for supper. After we washed the dishes, I asked her what was troubling her. And she started telling me. She didn't have a stitch for that little child to come, no doctor, and no money. Well, I had some leftovers from my two boys. I gave her ten yards of flaxen for little gowns and some flannel for blankets. I dug out a fifty-pound flour sack and put it all in there, and it was full to the top. It was 'bout close to midnight before she ever decided to go home, and she was still in such a state that I walked with her and the horse.

We came to a tree there in the big pasture, and she says, "See that tree, Greta? See that rope on the saddle? If I wouldn't have got any help from you, I had planned on hanging myself to that tree on the way home. I didn't see no use in livin' anymore with all those children and nothin' to give them."

When we came in the house, her husband Alfred was asleep, so I called him, and I said, "Alfred, you take good care of Ella and you watch her." Didn't tell him anymore. Just that.

The next day her oldest girl rode over after school. She says, "Mama doesn't have any thread. Could she borrow 'til she gets some." Now I used to get my thread by the box because I didn't go to town but twice a year, and there was always a lot of mending to do. So I sent over white thread, and after a couple of days I came along to see how she was doing. Miracle of miracles what that woman had done with the old material. She'd cut out little gowns and shirts and faced them with tape; made flannel blankets crocheted around the edges—all pretty as a magazine picture.

Come to find out there were three more women in that part of the township that were in the same condition. I tried to help them as best I could, because I knew the Lord had let me live to witness for Him.

The summer of '33 was the worst year, and the last we were able to hold on to our homestead.

That was the year the blister beetles came. They were—oh, about one-third of an inch long and they had big broad backs. When they came, they just came in droves. They cleaned out our garden in a day. One thing that got to me was when they ate the onions right out of the ground. Onions is so strong and how they ever. . . .

But we'd joke about it. We still had our potatoes and my husband would say, "Some is the size of a pea and some is little, bitsy things."

And we had our milk and eggs and our rice. I traded churned butter for sugar and coffee. Some of them women roasted wheat for their coffee, but I'm a Scandinavian and I had to have the real thing.

As I was sayin', that last year of '33 did us in. The hot winds came in for twelve days and turned our beautiful green fields of rye red. There was no grass and the cattle was eatin' dirt. We hadn't had a drop of rain when the Wesleyan Methodist revival came for a tent meeting. For two weeks us women would gather during the day to pray for rain. At night the menfolks would join us and we'd all pray. My husband didn't come with me. In those days, he wasn't saved. I had to pray twenty-nine years for that man until he became a wonderful Christian.

Now the Bible says to come to the Lord as a little child. That's what we did. We prayed just like you'd come to your own father. Anyway, after two weeks of that, the evangelist was very burdened. He saw the need of the farmers, and he couldn't expect to win souls for Christ where conditions were so withered. It was even hotter in that tent than it was outside.

Well, on the last night of the revival, I wish you could have seen that minister. He was so burdened down, I thought he was going to bend over and fall in pieces.

He called on us to sing, "Showers of Blessings."* "Sing all four verses," he said. Now, that was unusual—singing all four verses.

I looked out at the sky as we began to sing, and I want you to know there wasn't a cloud in it.

* "There Shall Be Showers of Blessings," McGranahan, Whittle, © Lillenas Publishing

But when we finished the hymn, he said, "Sing it again." That was the first time I ever heard any preacher ask us to sing a song all the way through twice. But we sang, louder this time:

There shall be showers of blessing,
Precious, reviving again.
Over the hills and the valleys
Sound of abundance of rain.

Once more he called, "Sing it again!" and this time—as we began to sing—drops of rain were falling on the tent, and people who'd gathered on the outside to poke fun at us crowded inside.

Then for the fourth time, he shouted, "Sing it again!" and as we sang the chorus . . .

Showers of blessing,
showers of blessing we need,
Mercy drops round us are falling,
but for the showers we plead

. . . the rain was a-comin' down harder and harder.

Why that tent was filled up with people singin' and praisin' the Lord. No Pentecostals ever had a better meeting than we did that night.

AN OHIO WOMAN

I tried always to live a Christian life and give my children something to depend on. I taught them the beliefs of the United Brethren and the New Testament. And I took them myself to church and Sunday School and on Wednesday night to prayer meeting. I didn't believe in sending my children while I stayed at home like some mothers. A woman doesn't have a lot of time to raise her children, and when they're gone it's a real comfort to know you did your best while you could.

SHE LIVES AT THE HEAD OF THE STAIRS on the second level of a nondescript apartment house with one of those arboreal names like

Garden Terrace or Pinewood Glen. Every other door is painted yellow.

The day I was taping her memories, Arlie Coons was all dressed up in a beige knit suit with a bouquet of artificial flowers pinned to her lapel—her white braids folded back and forth across her head, one on top of the other, until they stood as tall as a fine Spanish comb.

"I married the first time when I was twenty-three; that was in 1913," she said, "but my husband lived only six months. I had been a widow nearly fourteen years when I married Mr. Coons.

"Now don't ask me why, but it just didn't dawn on me that I'd ever get pregnant. Even though my menstrual cycle was regular, I thought I was too old. Somewhere I'd got the idea I couldn't have a baby because I was too near forty. But I did—two of them—and right at the beginning of the Depression."

ARLIE COONS'S STORY

Sometimes we'd be stuck in a town for two or three weeks after the meeting was closed because we wouldn't get enough in the collection plate for gas to get out of town.

We were living in Chicago when Mr. Coons had his "saving experience." In the Pentecostal faith that's what we call conversion. He then went into "speaking in tongues" and healing. He put himself more and more into the Lord's work and did a lot of rescue mission work, but even that was not enough. He wanted to preach so he built a regular house on the back of this big truck. He bought an old, White truck with a bed, built a house on it, and behind that we pulled a small trailer. He built that, too.

His brother was a sign painter so they got together and painted scripture verses on every bare surface of the truck and trailer. *Jesus Saves. Ye Must be Born Again.* They were both very good sign people and added big hearts and crosses and flowers and a lot of artistic work with beautiful lettering.

Then we drove south to Texas where lots of Pentecostal people lived. I remember there was a good deal of taunting from alongside the road as we drove south. But I can't remember that this especially bothered us. The Bible says, "They that will love God and Christ Jesus shall suffer persecution."

By 1931, I had two babies in diapers, and we were doing gospel work, going from town to town, holding meetings in little towns not too far from Houston. There was Pelly, Kilgore, Goose Creek, Huntsville, and lots of little towns—I don't remember their names anymore.

We didn't have a tent, so whenever we got to a new town, Mr. Coons would just preach in whatever place there was, sometimes a house 'cause Pentecostal people then, they didn't all have churches. Sometimes a tabernacle, or maybe somebody else would have a tent to put up, and he'd preach in that.

Usually we stayed about two weeks, but sometimes we would get stuck and stay two or three weeks after the meeting was closed because we wouldn't have money for gas to get out of town.

Nobody had hard money in those days, and sometimes there wouldn't be enough in the collection plate—five cents and ten cents and twenty-five cents maybe, but hardly ever a dollar. A dollar was just the biggest thing. You could buy an awful lot with it. Once I bought a pound of first-grade steak for fifteen cents and a dozen eggs for ten cents and still had money for gas to get down the road.

But mostly we ate dried peas and beans, especially in the winter. Do you know there was nineteen different kinds of peas through that country? And most of those poor farmers couldn't bring us money, so they brought us peas—chick peas, brown crowder, speckled crowder, whippoorwill, yard peas, and purple hose, and I don't know what else; but they was all good-tastin' peas.

They did get monotonous, but when you are hungry 'most anything tastes good. And then sometimes we'd be supplied with sweet potatoes and, if I could afford the eggs, I'd make sweet potato pie.

In the beginning, my husband would lay hands on people and they were healed, but primarily he would just preach the evangelistic messages. Of course, if anybody wanted to be prayed for in a healing way, why we did that, too.

Usually I played piano—I played hymns and I testified, but with two babies in diapers there wasn't much else I could do.

Bonnie Jean wasn't two yet when Virginia came. That oldest girl was nervous from the day she was born. She wouldn't sleep. Never would take a nap. I'd rock her and walk her, but the minute I tried to put her down in the trailer bed, her eyes would pop open and she'd start crying. Finally, my husband brought home a bed—such a bed—I never seen the like of it before or since. It was mechanical and he could wind it up and it would rock her for hours without stopping. I just knew the Lord sent that bed to me.

Now, when my youngest was five months old, I thought I was pregnant again and I just nearly cried my eyes out. There I was climbing in and out of that truck and trailer house. We had steps but it was still a strenuous climb carrying the babies, and I always felt a kinda catch in my hip. A friend of mine said she had the same thing and the doctor told her that it was just some suffering she wouldn't have to do when her next baby came. He meant her hip was expanding.

Well, when I thought I was pregnant, with two babies in diapers already, what could I do with another baby and living in that rig and traveling and all . . . I just . . . for three days I. . . . One day I didn't stop crying all day long. I felt despondent and discouraged, nervous and irritable—and every kind of a feeling but a good one.

My husband couldn't help me. What could he do? I thought I would lose my mind. I felt like maybe it was going already. I tried to keep it hid, but I felt like anybody could tell by looking at me. Finally, I met this wonderful Christian woman at a place where we stopped and I talked with her and she began telling me a story about her very own mother. This woman was young and had a child, but she said her mother had had ten children and had thought she was pregnant again. Now this young woman—her name was Viola —was serving the Lord and had a lot of faith, but her mother hadn't accepted the Lord. Well, her mother had told Viola if she was pregnant she was going to kill herself. She'd already had ten children and she didn't intend to have eleven. Viola knew her mother well enough to know she meant exactly what she said and it just worried her sick. Viola spent one whole day with her, pleading with her to go to church. And she wouldn't leave until her mother had promised to go to this cottage prayer meeting they were having that night. Viola felt like if her mother would go to the meeting and get saved and learn to trust the Lord, the Lord would see her through this thing. Well, her mother promised she would go that night—

and she did—and she got saved. That woman dismissed suicide right from her mind and trusted the Lord. And sure enough, you know, she *was* pregnant, but she lost it. Yes, the Lord aborted her. She had an abortion just from trusting the Lord.

Now the Lord had done miracles for me before, but somehow my faith had just weakened. But when Viola told me that story about her mother, I thought—well, if I am pregnant, I'll just trust the Lord and let Him do it for me. And so I think I only went two weeks overtime and then I came around. It was menopause that started on me—that's what it was.

Mr. Coons stopped preaching about that time. Just like thousands of others in the Pentecostal movement, he lost the call. He had great ups and downs in his spiritual life—he went from great highs to great lows. Oh, he never lost his faith in God and all, but he lost the power that he had. There's power in the spirit of God if anybody can get in that attitude to receive it. And he had that power. But he lost it.

A GALLERY OF PICTURES showing her late husband "T. J." behind a dozen or more Baptist pulpits, line the hallway just off the living room. A widow for only fourteen months, Maxine DuBose still spoke of him in the present tense, and when she did her loving memory of the man was as prominent on her face as the deep burn scar which sweeps from under her blouse up to her cheeks.

"It happened on Halloween, the year I was four," she said, getting the unspoken question out of the way. "My brother and I were jumping back and forth over jack-o'-lanterns and my petticoats caught fire, under my woolen coat. It blazed up underneath—the coat acting like a funnel for the flames—and my arms and neck were burned very, very deep.

"My daddy had a specialist come from St. Louis and paid for him to stay in the hotel for two weeks 'til I got over the worst of it. But it left me like this."

Years later, after her marriage, a famous plastic surgeon came to visit her home town, Wichita Falls, Texas. "Daddy wanted me to have surgery then," she remembered, "but T. J. didn't want me to. He said, 'I love you just like you are.' So I never had it done."

MAXINE DUBOSE'S STORY

We were married five years before I became a Baptist. I realized all along that I didn't have what T.J. had; I didn't have this *love* for the Lord.

We were married when I was sixteen and he was eighteen. Ours was a teenage marriage that worked. A lot of them didn't in those days, either, but ours did.

He came from a deeply religious Baptist family. I was a Methodist but I never had been saved. I thought I was a Christian because I was a church member.

When the Depression hit we had a baby. We were really just babies ourselves when Patsy Ruth came along a year after we married. We used to laugh and say we all grew up together.

My husband worked in a Rexall pharmacy. He never had a problem getting a job—never. We really had no money problems. I don't know what those are. You see, my daddy always had money. He'd gone into the oil business back during the boom in '18—gotten right in on the ground floor. We had a big car and "nigra" maids and gardeners. Even during the Depression, things didn't change much.

After I got married, I didn't mend my spending ways. I still had my charge accounts in just about every store in town. One day I went out and charged three bathing suits to my daddy. When T. J. found out, it really caused a problem between us. "Now don't do that again," he told me, "because it'll give us trouble all our lives if you do." Well, of course, I never did that again.

We were married five years before I became a Baptist. I realized all along that I did not have the same thing that my husband did. I didn't have this *love* for the Lord\and *love* for my fellow man and a *love* to do the work.

During all that time, we were going to Sunday School, every church service there was, Wednesday night prayer meetings, and anything in between times. We didn't miss anything. It became our life.

It didn't seem like such a radical change for me then, but now when I look back on it, it was. My husband had never been with a group that drank and smoked and I had sorta run around with that group. I never did drink or smoke myself, but I had friends who did. I don't think I especially condoned those things, but I didn't have a double standard like my parents did. They believed a woman who smoked and drank was going straight to hell, but a man could do these things and get away with it.

I believed that in the sight of the Lord it was just as wrong for a man as it was for a woman. He doesn't look on the sex of a person to see if it's right or wrong. The Lord just looks in the heart of a person. What's wrong for one is wrong for the other. Come to think of it, that's not really my idea. T. J. taught me that.

In 1932 my husband surrendered to preach. One night he made a public decision. That's how we do it in the Baptist church. T. J. just calmly walked the aisle saying he felt that the Lord had called him to preach. I can't remember even being surprised. But I still hadn't surrendered myself. So for a whole year, we read our Bible and we studied and we prayed before I was saved. I was seeking so hard it drew T. J. closer to the Lord helping me to find Him. I don't know why it took me so long. I just wanted to be sure. I didn't want to be a Baptist just because T. J. was.

Now, my brother did everything he could to talk him out of becoming a minister 'cause he thought that preachers' wives had such a hard life. He offered to send him to med school—pay all of his expenses and give us a family allowance so he wouldn't have to get a job after classes. Then when that didn't work, he offered to send him to pharmacy school.

But neither appealed to us. Oh, we talked about it and prayed about it, but by this time we were both wholly committed to T. J.'s ministry.

We moved our furniture to Ft. Worth, and all three of us went to school. Patty started first grade and T. J. and I went to Southwestern Seminary. I got my religious education degree there and then a BA at Hardin-Simmons University in Abilene. I have a teaching certificate, too, but I never used it.

We'd go to classes from eight o'clock in the morning until about two o'clock in the afternoon, then I'd come home to be there when Pat got out of school. T. J. went to work at a drugstore until midnight. I studied at night, but he rarely got to study except on the weekend. We worked like that for years, with hardly a sick day.

Now, that just shows you that the Lord blesses kids that don't have any more sense than we did.

It didn't seem like a big thing at the time. We didn't make a lot of to-do about it. But, my goodness, if I had to do it like that now . . .

T. J. was lucky he didn't have to wait 'til he got out of school to start preaching. Even though he was working full time at the drugstore, he took on two half-time churches—one in Dundee and one in Mankins. They were just small towns with sixty or seventy in their congregations. Of course, if we had a special service more of the town would turn out. They were the sweetest people. They had been hard hit by poor crop prices and wouldn't always have money to pay us, but they'd give us turkeys, chickens, eggs, and fresh vegetables. Sometimes they might give us ten dollars though.

We usually met in the schoolhouses and every Sunday night when we would get through the service, we'd have to take up our songbooks and lectern and put them all in the back so the room would be ready for school the next morning.

Generally, one of the families gave us a room in their home. But with Pat that made three, so we always kept a little folding cot in the car for her just in case they only had one bed. But it was such a wonderful experience and such wonderful fellowship. We got to know and to love those people.

Now I was a city girl and I'd never visited a farm in my life. I could hardly believe the breakfasts—fried chicken and hot biscuits with cream gravy. On the other hand, I *never* got used to going without electricity or an indoor bathroom. I didn't like that part of it.

Later we took a post in Eula and they had a little frame church. Oh, it was beautiful and we loved it. It hadn't been painted for twenty-five years and it badly needed remodeling. They didn't have any money but we went ahead just the same—did the work all ourselves. We'd go out there on Saturdays, take our lunch, and Pat would play with the town kids while we worked like dogs— painting and cleaning out classrooms that hadn't been touched since the year one. But we just had the *best* time, you know, working hard but still having a good time.

Sure, there was always the problem of the shortsightedness of people. They could not see into the future. They could not see what the Lord had in store for their church if they would only depend on Him. T. J. would tell them, "Just step out on faith and the Lord will provide." And he believed it so fully and his enthusiasm for it would get to them, even though some would always drag their feet.

I guess I didn't always believe I was an asset to him, but T. J. did —he really thought I was. I took a number of courses just so that I could help him with his work, not realizing how much it would help me too. I have the same education as most pastors. Sometimes, when I'd speak at different meetings or teach a book—I loved to do things like that—people would come up and say to me, "You ought to be a preacher," or "You missed your calling."

But I'd always answer, "One preacher in the family is enough," and T. J. would say one of the reasons I didn't want to was that I did all my preaching at home—to him.

I guess I just never could do it. I thought I could be just as effective for the Lord in other places of service as in the pulpit. I don't think I would even want to belong to a church where a woman was a preacher. I'm narrow, maybe . . . call it what you want.

But when I remember the thirties, I remember it was all just so much fun. I was doing the things I wanted to do; the things I felt the Lord wanted me to do. So my life was a joy to me. T. J. and I have had an exciting life from the very beginning—it really has been—right from the very beginning.

AN ARKANSAS WOMAN

Quite so—the church was a comfort to me. In fact it was to ever'body I knowed. We could only afford to have a preacher one Sunday a month . . . usually a student still in training. All the members of the church would take turns havin' the preacher to Sunday dinner. Sometimes we'd have him for Saturday night, too.

There was about thirty-five or forty members and we all gave one dollar a month—even that was hard to come by some months.

But there were lots of Sundays we had no preacher and we still had Sunday School every Sunday. My parents went to that church and my mother taught the Bible class while I taught the younger kids. It was just one great big room—plain pews, one piano—with two big, old wood stoves in there. We'd have wood-cutting days to keep firewood put by. And spring cleaning days . . . us women would all go over there and wash windows, scrub floors, clean it out good. We *worked* in the church in those days.

And we didn't leave our youngsters home. Shucks, I used to lay my babies on the seat right there next to me and give them a bottle or a toy. Then when they got a little older I'd take along pencils and paper. Oh, they were a-listenin' and a-learnin' all right, because when they got to be about eight or nine they knew all four verses to every song.

But, in them days, we kept our socializin' out of the church. I don't think God finds any fault with square dancin' or card games where they ain't no gamblin', but when they bring it in the church —He goes out.

Chapter Twelve

THE ORGANIZATION WOMEN

WHAT HAPPENED, I wondered, to the WCTU after Prohibition's repeal? The national office in Evanston, Illinois, answered my question by sending me to one of its oldest active members.

In 1974, Agnes Hayes attended the 100th anniversary convention of the WCTU—an organization she had joined as a child of ten, seventy years earlier.

"It was a landmark convention, no doubt about it," Mrs. Hayes told me in her home in Hutchinson, Kansas. "But we don't get much publicity these days. There was a time when we had better public relations. When I was national president in the 1950s, I appeared with Dave Garroway on the 'Today' show."

Her mother was an early member of WCTU in western Kansas. "My mother's chief interest outside her home was the WCTU," she remembers. "So the natural thing for us children was to join the Loyal Temperance Legion, and then later as teen-agers, the Youth Council."

After five years as national president, Agnes Hayes became a legislative representative in Washington during the Kennedy administration, trying unsuccessfully to ban the service of alcohol during commercial air flights.

"I'm confident that people will wake up to what alcohol is doing to this country—someday," she predicted. "But in this permissive age, just hanging on is progress."

AGNES HAYES'S STORY

I won't deny repeal in '34 was a blow. It was devastating to me personally . . . but our president, Mrs. Ida Wise-Smith, said, "Start again."

We were living in Utica, Kansas, when the crunch came in '32. I was teaching and my husband was a principal. We decided that since teaching jobs were so scarce, I should quit so that a married teacher with a family could have my job.

Not working—and not having had children—left me free to work with the WCTU. During the thirties, I served as county president of Ness County, and finally in 1938 as Kansas state president.

Now most people who grow up outside the WCTU think we're a group of desperate drunkards' wives—and there were some of that type I'm sure, but largely we were women who had religious and total abstinent backgrounds.

Through the twenties we had lost membership, so we were at a low ebb when repeal came. My own aunt felt that when the Prohibition amendment was adopted, we had accomplished our purpose. People naturally felt it would be the end of the legal liquor business. Most of us always felt the problem was because of the open sale— an open saloon had been the symbol of the havoc wreaked by liquor. So many thought that when the saloons were closed, the problem was solved . . . but of course it wasn't.

As for myself, I had never seen a saloon. We had none in Kansas —no children carrying buckets of beer home or fathers lying in the gutter . . . in Kansas we didn't have things like that. . . .

I won't deny repeal in '34 was a blow. It was devastating for the organization and for me personally—there's no doubt about that.

After repeal, Mrs. Ida B. Wise-Smith of Iowa became the national president. I thought she handled it well. She said that we must enhance our educational program and expand it greatly. "Start again," she counseled. I did, but I suspect some just gave up —those who were not dedicated.

I know the arguments about Prohibition, and I don't believe them. They say it encouraged people to defy the law, but does a red light *encourage* you to break the law? Of course not, it encourages you to obey it. It's the same thing—exactly the same.

I never could understand why people apply the concept of lack of respect for the law only to Prohibition.

Now this might interest you. In the early thirties there was a lot of agitation for repeal . . . and unemployment—because of the Depression—was the main point in favor. The liquor industry assured the people that if they would relegalize liquor men would go back to work and there would never be a need for income tax. In those times they were convincing arguments.

Proliquor people said the law was unenforceable. It wasn't true at all. The problem was that the law was not evenly enforced—and the law itself was poorly written. The thing was that it was illegal for a man to sell alcoholic liquor, but not for a man to *buy* it.

Not many people know what the liquor industry did after repeal . . . you see, a whole generation of youngsters had been reared on the theory that the use of alcohol was illegal and not a good thing. So the brewers had to change that image, and they set about to do just that. They started what was known as the "Home Life in America" series of advertising in family magazines. They had beautiful color pictures showing beer in the home. . . . For example, here would come a grandmother carrying in the turkey *and* a tray of beer to the Thanksgiving table—and another one showed families singing around the organ, drinking beer. And they did a good job of it. Most people began to think of beer just like they did of Coca-Cola.

We knew WCTU had to do something to combat that. So a woman was hired . . . Rachael Palmer, who was the state superintendent of schools in Montana, and she went back East to a scientific temperance research library . . . in Boston, I think. She studied there for about a year. After that she wrote, and the WCTU produced, motion pictures for schools and an enormous number of pamphlets. So I would say, through the years, the name of the organization has expanded enormously.

We faced slick, professional advertising, and we made every attempt to use the same methods. Although we were mightily discouraged, believe me, we didn't stop work for a minute. One of the first things we got into was what constituted intoxication for drunken driving. We insisted on .05; others asked for .15. I think we were responsible for getting it lowered to .10. So we were a voice for temperance. Not even repeal changed that.

WHEN FERN YOWELL'S SON DIED in 1970 a few months after her husband had a fatal heart attack, she said she didn't know what to do. "Finally, I decided I could either go around to my children's homes being miserable, or I could find a new way for myself right here which is what I've done."

She guided me around her home while we talked. Almost every picture and every piece of furniture had a story behind it. Wherever a beam of sunlight filtered in, a potted plant was there to meet it. She saved the best 'til last, her most precious possession—the doll she got for Christmas in 1902.

FERN YOWELL'S STORY

When you had club in your house it was just the biggest thing that happened to you all year.

We had a quarter-section six miles outside of Anthony, Kansas, during the thirties. We knew everybody for miles around— they were good people, intelligent, fine people. And us women enjoyed each other's company so much that we started a club; and we called it the Community Helpers.

Women were encouraged to form clubs in those days by the state agricultural college. They'd have us send one of our members up every month to learn some kind of thing; and then she'd come back and teach the rest of us. It wasn't like a school, you understand; it was more like inspiration to get us to see that we could make do with very little.

There wasn't any money so most of what we did had to be done with next to nothing. One of our biggest projects was learning to reupholster with gunnysacks. Now, we had lots of big sacks that wool was packed in; we'd take them and bleach them until they were soft and just the most beautiful beige color. Sometimes we'd cross-stitch them. Anyway, we got so good at it this one year—'35 I think—that the Community Helpers won first prize at the Kansas State Fair. We had a complete room: furniture, wall hangings, pillows, and everything, all made out of gunnysacks.

We met every two weeks, and we'd always bring a covered dish. Now *that* was food, the best food in the world. Well, it was just the biggest thing that happened to you all year, when you had club, you know. You cleaned your house from top to bottom, and the men would always arrange to stay away in the fields on club day. The husbands were all for us—there just weren't any "stinkers" in the whole bunch.

The summer of '36, I think it was, we worked the whole time on a quilt. It was a Dutch doll pattern and we planned to use it as a prize at our Christmas party for the one who brought the best gift. Every year we drew names at Christmas and the only requirement was that it couldn't cost a penny and it had to be homemade. Well, every one of us got busy making footstools, pillows, all kinds of pictures, hangers—every kind of thing—because all of us wanted that quilt real bad.

Now, what I did, was to take an old jug and turn it into a kerosene lamp. My husband drilled a hole and put a cork in it so we could put in the kerosene. Then I got sealing wax off of old batteries and dripped it on—all over the base. Then I made a wire frame and fixed up a shade of real thin gauze cloth with little beads all over it.

Finally, I varnished the base and shook more beads on it and put on a little design. Well, you should have heard the raves—everybody thought the lamp was beautiful! And, yes, I won the Dutch doll quilt.

Christmas was a wonderful time in those days—we had so little and yet we had so much. The club even made Christmas trees and gave them away. Well, there weren't any pine trees in the middle of the Kansas plains, so we took old broomsticks, drilled holes in them so we could stick tree limbs in there, and made our trees that way.

"BACK DURING WORLD WAR I, I was one of the charter members of the Jane Addams International Peace Movement," she said. "In 1922, I spent three months barnstorming Ohio, West Virginia, and Pennsylvania. On any street corner where I could put up my soap box, I'd talk against war."

Like Jane Addams, Lillian Cantor Dawson* was schooled by Quakers. "I was Miss Addams's personal friend," she recalled with pride, "and organized her speaking engagement when she came to my hometown, Pittsburgh.

* Lillian Cantor Dawson: The story of her social work with the Workman's Circle is told in Chapter Eight.

"Pacifism was a dirty word, even after the Great War. I had arranged for her to speak in one of our school auditoriums and had sold over 1,200 tickets. The day before her lecture, I got a call from the superintendent of schools, saying he couldn't allow the school to be used by a pacifist. 'Someday,' I told him, 'you will rue the day you missed the privilege of meeting Jane Addams.' "

I asked Lillian: "We've had three major wars since you, Jane Addams, and other pacifist women worked for peace in the 1930s. Why?"

Her reply: "Because every time there has been a slaughter of innocents the world has stood by and let it happen—and the next time it was always worse.

"My biggest fear is that the world is getting ready to stand by again—with Israel."

LILLIAN CANTOR DAWSON'S STORY

Of course, our goal was disarmament—always disarmament. But we were never to see that . . . the most positive outcome of the conference was that women realized they were a power.

In 1934 there was a convention of the Women's International League for Peace and Freedom at The Hague—I was so happy to get to go. I had already met my future husband, but I left him and went off, and I was gone for almost eight months.

There were women representing some thirty nations, some of the finest women you ever would want to meet. Austria, England, and Germany were represented. Of course, Madame Doty from France was there . . . to this day I can see that flaming young woman—a wow of a woman.

Of course, our goal was disarmament—always disarmament. But we were never to see that. The most positive outcome of the conference was that women realized they were a power. Women, at that time, were finding that their natural female role of helping the culture survive might lead to peace. We were finding that we weren't prisoners—as Freud was saying then—of our biological selves.

After the conference, I went on to Palestine. I went for six weeks and stayed seven months. And there I met that superb pacifist,

Henrietta Szold, and I told her of my friendship with Jane Addams and the others; this was what she wanted to hear about.

Let me tell you about Miss Addams, while I'm on the subject. She was a little, nondescript, almost mousy woman. Not the fiery type at all—very subdued. You listened because of her sincerity.

It was obvious to everyone that she was genuinely devoted to the idea of peace. It was such a strong thing that you felt its power, even when she spoke so softly that you had to strain forward in your seat to catch all her words. Even when she spoke to a large group she didn't raise her voice. She was a Quaker, and Quakers believe the message speaks for itself.

When I came back from Palestine in 1935, Miss Addams took me to tea at the White House. She introduced me to Eleanor Roosevelt: "This is our baby pacifist and, just like all babies, she creates quite a stir."

I thought Mrs. Roosevelt was one of the great women of the day. In her heart she was a pacifist but, of course, she couldn't openly take a position. Here was a woman whose personal troubles never defeated her but helped her develop into a magnificent human being.

She had a despotic mother-in-law, and she had many more children than was usual in those days for a woman in her position. And then with her husband's polio—well, out of painful experience the great strength of the woman appeared.

I met her again two years later and she said, "Oh, here's the baby pacifist." She was a remarkable woman.

About that time—at the WILPF's 1935 convention—some of us in the peace movement began to be very concerned about the Nazis who were gaining at such a rate in Europe. We were hearing of the persecution of Jews and Christians, too. So we tried to introduce a resolution from the floor condemning the senseless, immoral things that man Hitler was doing. But Jane Addams, who was chairing the convention that day would not entertain the motion, and so about a hundred of us walked out—both Jews and non-Jews.

There was no effort to bring us back, and so that was the end of my contribution—although that was not the end of my pacifism.

I just could not believe that the world should stand by and let Hitler happen. But at the same time I thought war was the greatest scourge of mankind. It was, of course, a difficult personal decision for me.

The peace movement was one of the great experiences of my life; it also caused some of the greatest emotional disappointments.

"IT MUST BE this new hearing aid," she said, tapping her ear. With her husband John dead, Anna Hansen Hayes has moved from their spacious family home into a small apartment in Twin Falls, Idaho. At eighty-nine, she finds new things don't work as well as the old.

"I'll have to have the man adjust it tomorrow," she told me apologetically. "That's all right," I said, not minding at all. "I can speak louder."

Anna Hayes graduated from college in 1904 fascinated with the then avant-garde work of Maria Montessori, an Italian educator who believed children between ages three and six should develop through individual activity. "I loved teaching," she said, "and I'd started my second year when John Hayes suggested I might like being married to him even better."

She had three childen but her sublimated desire to teach found another expression. "When my children were in school in Denver," she told me, "I became very interested in the parent-teacher's organization. I joined the PTA in 1919 and held a post on either local, state, or national level until 1973, serving as national president between 1949 and 1952."

ANNA HANSEN HAYES'S STORY

The PTA, like most organizations during the 1930s, had no money so I rode with the educators, the health division, or whoever else was going in my direction.

During the thirties, I think the greatest satisfaction for me was talking about the profession of parenthood. I had been elected Idaho state PTA president, and I traveled around the state talking with dozens of local groups.

Professional parenthood was one of the themes I used, and I found in a good many instances that young mothers agreed with me.

They were interested in the idea that parenthood was a profession. You see, I have always felt one of the most important functions of PTA is to raise the standard of home life . . . and that is one of the things I worked for consistently right through the years.

I liked my role as a teacher of parents because I wanted them to understand their child's mind and behavior, that there was tremendous influence in the elements of the home itself. I taught that every child was deserving of understanding and should have the privilege of being part of the family instead of being completely ruled. I dare say, I believed in less authoritarianism than was normal then. I felt that a successful family gave importance, in the family structure, to every member of the family—even the children.

This had been my background. As a child I had training and discipline, but my father had insisted that I have freedom to make choices. He had come from Denmark and had been trained very rigidly and so I think he placed great importance on being a loving and *reasonable* father. He had a great deal of influence, of course, on my own thinking.

I believe the young women who made up PTA groups in the Depression years were searching for more modern ways to rear their children. I think they wanted to improve, and so I think my ideas of parenthood as a profession made an impression on them.

Two areas of education—district consolidation and kindergartens —were prime PTA goals in those years. It was my duty as state president to go all over Idaho and talk about these things. The PTA, like most organizations during the Depression, had no money, so I rode with the educators, the health division, or whoever else was going in my direction.

I would speak before groups of parents and teachers—presenting a case for consolidation and kindergarten. I was frankly more interested in kindergartens because of my early training in the Montessori method. At that time, only about one-third of the schools in the entire country had kindergartens and there were very few in Idaho.

Once I was in Moscow, Idaho, talking about kindergartens and laying out the reasons for them. After my lecture, a gentleman from the university came up to me and said, "If you don't stop this nonsense of kindergarten, we'll just knock out the PTA."

You see, he was just as determined to extend and enrich the high school program in the state, and he felt that I would detract from what he was doing.

That was the last public speech I made about kindergartens, simply because I was afraid that this gentleman from the university might make it very difficult for us in the PTA. Yes, I was intimidated because we had so many other problems. I thought I'd bide my time and little by little I could get my ideas over through my teaching of parents.

Idaho was even at that late date in time, a frontier state. For so many years the people who went on the Oregon Trail just crossed Idaho and didn't look back. That left Idaho in the state of pioneering longer, so some of the people, especially the men, had strange ideas of education. I even heard principals say they didn't want youngsters to get too much learning. They were afraid they'd leave the state for some other place, you see, if they got a good education.

"WOMEN HAD THE VOTE for a relatively short period of time by the 1930s," she said. "Yet my generation was aleady taking voting rights for granted.

"And yet, we young women of the Depression didn't take economic rights for granted. Take jobs. In our day, society said no girl whose father or husband could feed and clothe her should seek work.

"So for some of us who didn't work, the League of Women Voters was the only game in town."

Mary Ann Page Guyol lives in Washington, D.C., retired after twenty years as public relations director for the national league.

MARY ANN PAGE GUYOL'S STORY

Every time we got wind of an attempt to vote the city manager system of government out, the league would pack the council chambers. There I was, right in the middle of the action, and I simply adored it.

I majored in political science at Sweet Briar and at the University of Chicago, but when the Depression started to affect my family I quit and went home to Red Wing, Minnesota. I never did finish my degree work. And the league came along at that time—just when I needed it. It filled a tremendous void in my life.

August Andreson, the Republican congressman from Red Wing, actually brought the league there. He was a really liberal man for the time. He interested his niece Jan in the league and she, in turn, talked to me.

I was doing odd jobs—whatever I could get—a newspaper column on cooking about which I knew absolutely nothing, and I taught Shakespeare to kids in the park on Saturday morning—jobs like that. So when Jan invited me to go to Minneapolis with her to meet Margaret Wells, I went along eagerly. Margaret Wells was soon to become president of the national League of Women Voters, and I was very impressed by her. She had powerful ideas about government, and her whole notion of the league was that it was a training ground for women to learn about the function and structure of government so they could do something about it.

Afterwards Jan and I went back to Red Wing and organized a chapter. And I really did discover I could get things done. For example, at that time the visiting nurse in town was paid by a one-day annual fund drive that the women's clubs carried on. Some years her salary would be $800 and some years $1,500.

The league wanted to do something about this so we looked at the city charter, studied the state laws, and conferred with people. The city council had said they couldn't pay a visiting nurse since it was against the charter. But we discovered a way around this. At a meeting of the city council we presented our evidence and we won . The league got the visiting nurse on the public payroll.

I was really astonished to feel that I could research something, find out the facts, present them to the proper authorities, and get something done. Incredible!

About that time—in '34, I believe—one of our study projects was international trade. The first letter I ever wrote to a senator in Washington was two pages on international trade—and I got back two pages in reply. Well, I just got such a feeling of participation in government—one that I never lost.

Originally, the league was started in the early twenties to educate women on how to use their newly acquired vote. The founders thought this educational job could be done in a few years and then the league could disband. Now, of course, this didn't happen, because in the meantime young women like myself discovered that they had a great many things to do together; and so we embarked on an ambitious program to reform the world.

I got married in the mid-thirties and moved to Maumee, a suburb of Toledo, Ohio; my friends there were typical suburban housewives with children—darling people. They thought I was kind of a nut because every week I would go to a league meeting in Toledo.

I didn't have children and my husband was a salesman, away all week, so I had a great deal of freedom. Subsequently, I was asked to join the state board and then I became executive secretary of the Toledo league—for the grand sum of fifty dollars a month. Of course, that barely paid my expenses.

So every Monday there I was at the city council meeting, and I got very involved in saving the city manager form of government. The league had been instrumental in establishing this form of government, but there were enemies within and without who were trying to destroy it.

At that time we thought a city manager was so much better than one of the old-time bosses. We believed a business form of government was more responsive to people's needs.

Every time we got wind of an attempt to vote the system out, the league members would get on the telephone and pack the city council chambers—we would have the place absolutely jumping with women so that the council wouldn't dare take that kind of vote with all of us watching.

I was right in the middle of the action, and I simply adored it. It was very heady stuff, you know—like being a newspaper reporter —feeling "in the know."

Also during that time we worked a lot for women's laws—we advocated repeal of legislation that discriminated against allowing women guardianship of their children, property, and wages—that sort of thing.

And we also worked for minimum wage laws and a maximum hour ceiling. This protective legislation was badly needed because in those days an employer would hire a woman and just work her 'til she dropped.

One of the most important things the league accomplished in the thirties was that we women helped change the climate of opinion in this country from isolationism to internationalism. I think we did this more than anybody else. You see, there were these hundreds and thousands of women's study groups all over the country, and they were sending petitions and letters to their congressmen. They just sort of pounded and pounded on the concept of world trade agreements. It was not an emotional, breast-beating kind of thing—but just the whole business of opening up and developing countries and helping raise the standard of living for everyone. We thought more trade would just make a better life for all the world's peoples.

The league was truly democracy in action. We would receive a kit of study materials from Washington, discuss it, and write our opinions to the national headquarters. Then on the basis of those opinions the national league would decide its stand. In that way, we influenced food and drug laws, TVA, and dozens of other issues of the day.

The league was important to many women in the thirties. I remember one woman. She said that during the 1930s she was really tied to her home and to the view from her kitchen window. But after she joined the league, her world had opened. When she stood at her window washing dishes, she wasn't thinking about parties or dresses but about world issues and concerns.

You see, women rarely thought about going back to college or graduate school when the kids were gone. They couldn't afford it for one thing—and for another, it just wasn't done. So the league became our university, our graduate school—it was, well, just everything.

Although we always tried to get a cross section of members, I'm afraid we were never very successful; we were all mostly middle class. Our dues were just one dollar a year. But it takes time and money to be active in any organization—even though we held meetings at members' homes instead of in public places. I guess we probably weren't as sensitive to minorities and women in lower economic situations as we later became.

But I met wonderful women—they were so objective, so intelligent. Some were younger than I was, and others older. One I met—really a most marvelous woman—was my mother's age, and she was an absolute revelation for me.

Oh, my mother was a very good woman—she was on the hospital board, sewed for the poor, and gave baskets of stuff—she did the good work of her day; but the whole idea of causes was anathema to her and maybe just a little bit unfeminine.

One Christmas when both my sister and I were holding offices in the local league, I wanted a typewriter and my sister asked for a filing cabinet. Mother's only comment was: "What have I done to deserve daughters like these?"

"THEY HAD A REMARKABLE pioneer community spirit," she said. "It was as if I was living in an older time."

That's how Victoria Sudsbury remembers Murphy, Oregon—a small farming settlement on the Applegate River. "We were an Irish family—two bachelor uncles, my mother, aunt, and myself," she told me, sitting in the living room of her mobile home. "You know, in Irish families, if one or two stay single, lots of them will stay single and live together for the rest of their lives.

"I still don't understand how it happened, but we dropped in there like a pebble in a pond and didn't even make a ripple in the community. We understood them and they understood us."

VICTORIA SUDSBURY'S STORY

The Home Demonstration Unit was the club that became part of my life during the Depression years. Our agent showed us more about nutrition and homemaking than most teachers knew.

I joined two women's groups in the Murphy community when we moved there in 1932—the Dorcas Society and the Home Demonstration Unit.

The Dorcas Society met once a month in somebody's home—we took turns. The purpose of the Dorcas group was to make quilts for the old people and bachelors in the neighborhood. It was a charitable thing; we never sewed for ourselves there. At each meeting, we'd bring extra scraps and old coats beyond redemption. The society would buy the batting, and we all contributed five cents a month toward that.

Each month we'd work most of the day to finish a quilt—then give it away. We didn't meet the three months through the summer. As soon as the baby chicks came, the women were too busy.

But I guess the biggest club, and the one that became a part of my life during the Depression years was the Home Demonstration Unit. See, we were called units because each area had a different group. It was federally subsidized—the government paid for the agent as long as Josephine County provided the office and secretary.

Our agent was Sarah Wertz, and she came once a month to teach us. She came for years, until the women in Murphy knew as much about nutrition and homemaking as most teachers. The agent was a very special person in the community . . . she grew to know each of us well and we knew her . . . I guess we all depended on each other.

You know those Murphy women were ignorant in ways of education, but they were smart women and really very decent. I remember one woman especially, Ma Wilbur, was always full of beans about something. You see, every time the agent came she taught us something new; one time it was canning, the next home decoration, sewing, or landscaping, etc. Well, everybody got excited about the home decorating course this one year, and Ma Wilbur came to the meeting and announced she was going to paint her ceiling red. Now, the other ladies didn't think she should, but she said she had always wanted a red ceiling. They had a dreadful hassle over it.

For a time it looked like Ma had given up her idea, although I think she was a little bit provoked with the rest of us. But about a year later, I went to her house for something or other and there it was: she had painted her living room ceiling red.

We got unbelievable nutrition information from our agent. The different units would have contests to see who could prepare the best meals from food we found on the land. And everything we knew, we passed on to each other. If some woman figured out a way to make weeds into a good dish, she fixed it and took it to the next meeting.

And that's just what we did; weeds are delicious and one of the best foods available. One year, I quit raising pigs in this old pig pen, and the most beautiful mustard plants came up. I put them together in a salad with watercress from the stream and radish tops

—that's right, radish tops. My family swore by them . . . they were always our first spring greens.

Another time, I saw one of the men had a field of broccoli and had cut it and sold it, but he hadn't plowed it up before it started to sprout again. I came along and looked at it, and there were little bits of tops only as big as your little finger. I got a big pan full, put them in salads, and they were delicious. I took them to the unit meeting that spring, and everybody raved about them. My unit got extra points for that. You see, the units were always having a contest with each other.

Another time, I cooked radish greens with a strip of bacon and took them—the women just went crazy for radish greens.

I remember so many women with great character—one of them told the funniest stories when we were having meetings. She'd been married at twelve and had her first child at thirteen—she said she'd cry and the baby'd cry, and that's how they both grew up. She had kind of a dry wit. She told how one day she was sitting, her door slightly open with her gun poked out, trying to catch a chicken hawk in her sights. She was all primed and ready when this salesman came up and found this gun pointing at him. "Now, I tried to tell him it was all right," she said, "but you know, he left pretty quick. That's the only salesman I ever knowed that left that soon!"

There was this other woman—Mrs. Ellis was her name—who used to make us all laugh. We were having landscaping lessons at the unit meeting, and this woman grew flowers, roses, and all kinds of plants. The agent suggested to us that we make a master plan. Right in the middle of our work, Mrs. Ellis said, "Yes, this is exactly what I need. I've been diggin' up my plants and moving 'em around so much, I've got the roots all wored off of them."

Sometimes our unit would have psychology-type meetings . . . you know, how to get along with your kids and with your husband. I never knew any of those women to get a divorce during the Depression. They'd battle, some of them: get mad and fight like the dickens, but they didn't separate. They'd just hang together. They were farming families and they worked together. They *had* to settle arguments.

But in such a small town as Murphy—only 300 people—there weren't many secrets. I could never figure out how people knew, but they knew the ins and outs of everybody's private affairs. I don't think their gossip was malicious. They were basically good people.

I think part of the reason why they were good people was their competence. They were capable of meeting their lives and mastering them under any circumstances they had.

Remember, I told you about Sarah Wertz, our agent. Well, she was a very special person. She would look around and see the women needed things, and she would set about getting them done.

This one summer, she came up with the idea of a woman's camp. When she presented it to the unit, the women were wild about the idea. You see, those women just didn't ever get away from home. Farm people don't take vacations, and some of these women hadn't been any farther away than Grant's Pass in their lives.

Used to be a joke the women'd tell on themselves. One man would say to another, "I hear your wife went crazy." And the second man would say, "Yeah, ma went crazy. And if that don't beat all, too. I can't think how it happened. I knew there wasn't a thing that could cause it—she hasn't been off the place for twenty years."

So we went out on the Upqua River, just south of Roseburg, and made a woman's camp. Called it Camp Wywona. I don't remember what it meant—it was an Indian name.

And every summer after that in July, the women went camping by themselves—no men or kids allowed—for a whole week. And we had more fun together than I ever had before or since. There was a swimming hole in the river right below the camp and we'd swim in the hot afternoons. And we took wild flower walks. Sarah Wertz would teach us about the birds and wild animals we were to watch for on our walks.

We didn't have nice sleeping bags in those days, so most of the women just made bedrolls on the ground—some of them made tents. I remember we were always afraid we were going to get rained on.

But we had a gorgeous time. And believe me there were lots of high jinks. The camp was divided into two groups; each night one of the groups was responsible for the campfire entertainment. Well, this one year my group did a play called "Wild Nell, the Pet of the Plains."

The story goes that this beautiful young girl is out picking flowers and some Indian braves kidnap her and take her to their camp where the squaws all dance around her.

Well, you know, all those mothers and grannies up there dancing and whooping and acting like wild kids—well, it was the funniest thing you ever saw.

One year the men decided to play a trick on the women, so they got a piece of a log and hacked a face out of it, put some clothing on it, and sneaked in at night and put it out in the river.

Of course, the next day when the women went down to their swimming hole they found a dead man floating there. Oh, they were screaming and yelling. They ran several miles to the Forest Service Camp up the road. So the end was, that the coroner came in his ambulance all the way from town—which cost the county eleven dollars.

During the next election, there was a big hullabaloo about that expense, and this one judge voted to cut out funds for the county agent. You know, the women just seethed and bided their time, and the next election they dumped that judge out of office by a landslide.

HERE AND THERE IN HISTORIES of the 1930s the subject of pacifism is lightly treated as only a part of the isolationism of the period. It was much more than that to some. According to Mildred Scott Olmsted, director emeritus of the Women's International League for Peace and Freedom (WILPF), many thirties women were deeply committed to a peace movement that had begun even before World War I.

"Back in January of 1915, Jane Addams and Carrie Chapman Catt jointly called suffrage women together in Washington to set up the Women's Peace Party," she said, talking to me in her home near Media, Pennsylvania. "The WILPF later grew from that beginning."

When the war began in 1917, Mildred Scott, not yet a pacifist, was a Philadelphia social worker in her late twenties. "I got a leave of absence," she said, "and went to Camp Mead in Maryland to help set up recreation for the boys. It was there I met my first conscientious objectors. At that time, it was a new idea to me that anyone could resist the government.

"Later in 1917, I went overseas to Paris. It was a shocking experience. I began to see how these young men had been desensitized and corrupted by war and all that goes with it."

Young Mildred Scott was particularly concerned about the scores of ex-college men she met. "I felt the smashing of their ideals meant serious problems for the future of our country."

During 1918 and for months after the war was over, she interspersed the endless dances and lunches she organized with talks from visiting personalities. "I saw in the newspaper that Jane Addams, the noted social worker from Hull House, was in Paris," she recalled, "and I asked the boys if they would like to hear her.

"They seemed enthusiastic so I called her, and she came. She didn't argue for the cause of pacifism, but I remember she talked of the cruelty of war and the alternatives.

"Next, I invited a Princeton professor who was a specialist on the Far East, and he was a great success. The boys followed him down the stairs, asking him questions.

"After that—I think the very next day—I got a message from the Chinese delegation to the Versailles peace conference saying they'd like to send a speaker over.

"I thought all that interest was wonderful, and so did the soldiers. One of them told me, 'Maybe now, I'll find out what I was fighting about.'

"But before I could go further with this kind of entertainment, my boss got a message from Colonel House, President Wilson's special assistant. House thought what I was doing was endangering the peace conference. And I'll never forget the end of his note: 'Keep the boys dancing,' he said."

Mildred Scott, by this time, was personally disillusioned with the war she had believed would be the war to end wars. "When the American Friends Service Committee—the Quakers—offered me a job," she said, "I jumped at it.

"Within a few months, I landed in Munich with the Hoover Commission. I saw begging, starving children, women, and old people. I saw what the war had done to the Germans, and I came to realize that everybody connected with war is exploited. I made up my mind that I would never have anything to do with war again —and I decided to devote my life to trying to prevent it."

MILDRED SCOTT OLMSTED'S STORY

We American women working for peace were as worried about
our own rising militarism as we were about the fascist nations.

By the 1930s we knew that the Versailles Treaty, initially hailed
by so many people, had been just another treaty which would lead
to war. We saw the rise of Hitler as the logical aftermath of a
vindictive peace—such a peace always creates another war.

And we saw another thing happening. We saw the Allied powers
were secretly rearming Germany to maintain a buffer against the
Russians. So when Hitler came to power, we were not surprised
—he was just the result of that situation.

I think women were beginning to wake up during the 1930s.
When suffragettes said that women needed the vote because they
had a different viewpoint—that women would be more interested in
peace—I think they were naive. The new generation in the thirties
discovered that the vote wasn't enough—they'd have to be active in
politics, putting direct pressure on governments.

No, I don't remember how many women were members of the
WILPF . . . most of our branches were mainly old suffrage groups.
That was only natural because one of the arguments for suffrage,
as I pointed out, was that women would be peaceful—that we were
not natural fighters.

I'm not so sure about that after years of experience—I think
women fight, but they fight in a different way. They are more hu-
manely slanted than men, I think.

You see, women as a group are more concerned with the problems of children, the elderly, and education—the very things that
war most disrupts. Therefore, they naturally lean toward peace.

During the thirties the league was working on several problems—
we were against conscription and chemical warfare. And believe me
the army was afraid of our influence. We had our "CIA" in those
days, too. My executive office in Washington was right across the
street from the war department—and they would raid our offices
every weekend. That's right, the military would break in and go
through our files looking for evidence that we were Communists.
They were sure that only Communists would be against chemical
warfare.

Pacifism was misunderstood. I remember one community where I went to start a WILPF branch—it was a one-industry town. A woman later told me that her husband was called in by his boss who told him: "I hear your wife is lining up with this international organization of peace women. If you want to keep your job, you better get her out of it." The husband tried to reassure his boss that his wife was just playing bridge and talking about foreign policy and such things. But he said, "You keep your wife at home if you want to work."

Now, you can imagine what a powerful argument that was during the Depression.

Of course, at that time there was a lot of feeling about women being active out of the home at all. I think the WCTU and the Federation of Women's Clubs were the first steps in the emancipation of women. You know, all these national women's groups had committees somewhere down their lists dealing with foreign policy. Women *did* want to know what was going on in the rest of the world.

During the twenties and especially the thirties a curious thing was happening in our country. Remember, we had always been an antimilitarist country; our Constitution had provided for a civilian head of the army and navy.

This had worked all right until after World War I. It was after that that our military realized that the Germans had a better war machine than the U.S. did. Therefore they set out to copy it, and in order to do this, they had to change the atmosphere in this country —because military life really ran contrary to all American traditions.

At first, they started their free camps—Citizens' Military Training Camps for children. They offered vacations and recreation. They began putting stamps on letters—SEND YOUR BOYS TO CMTC.

We objected. Recreation camps for children are wonderful, we said, but why not put them under the Bureau of Education instead of the military? And, of course, later when they moved into the schools with their ROTC, we opposed them there—we felt they were slowly turning us into a military-minded nation. We could see this kind of atmosphere forming, and it worried us deeply.

At this point the military minds began their move to capture the veterans' organizations—and they did it, too. In France and

England, the ex-soldiers sided with the peace people, which is where they naturally belonged. But not in the United States.

As a result we women working for peace were as worried about our own rising militarism as we were about the fascist nations'.

And we had another worry as well. What was happening to our co-workers in Germany? After the peace convention in '34, WILPF sent me into Germany incognito to talk with our women members there. You see, after Hitler came into power they were afraid to make contact with us openly. Our organization was one that was on Hitler's list to wipe out . . . the president of the German peace women was on his list to be liquidated.

It had to be very hush-hush; I was warned not to take any papers with me into or out of Germany—over the border you know—but to memorize everything.

I went to Berlin, and I proceeded to a certain antique shop. I was to say to the shopkeeper that my friend so-and-so had told me she had the best antiques in all Germany. This was the way the woman would recognize me. She said: "Would you look around a little while?" Then when everyone was out of the shop she took me in the back and we talked.

I discovered that these women had worked very hard to persuade the government that they were only women, after all—that as women they hadn't really done very much, and therefore weren't dangerous. Hitler kept them under surveillance for about three years, then, apparently satisfied, took the guards off.

Women told me while I was there that they were still having small meetings in private, that they were spied on, and they always used the public telephone to communicate. Two women stood outside while we met.

They were very brave. And they asked me to take this message back: "You may never hear from us again, but know that we are standing firm in our beliefs, and we will move at the first opportunity."

The thirties were a busy and frustrating time for pacifists. It was a particularly difficult time for our Jewish members. One said to me in my office: "This is the only place I can really say what I think. Among my friends, I just have to keep quiet." Jewish pacifists were terribly torn between their pacifism and what they were learning about Hitler's Germany. And the same for our black members when the Italians invaded Ethiopia.

The WILPF was criticized by many people in the 1930s . . . "pie in the sky" they said . . . but actually peace was the only rational approach to world problems, as we found out.

Chapter Thirteen

WOMEN IN POLITICS

DOROTHY BUSH has been secretary of the Democratic National Committee and of every national convention since 1944. She had just returned from a party meeting in Washington the day I talked with her at her home in Columbus, Ohio.

"People ask me how I've survived," she said. "I always say that I've served the people; and I've been loyal to the party—not to any one person.

"I've worked with both men and women, and I've never been all out just for women. Don't get me wrong, I'm very much in favor of women having all the rights they're entitled to, but I'm not an activist."

I asked her: "Do you think if more women had been involved in the administration of politics, that such a thing as Watergate could have happened?"

"I don't know how to answer that," she admitted. "I think there are evil women as well as evil men. I do think if we had more women in top political jobs we would be better off, but I don't say there would be no evil or wrongdoing.

"To me the whole Watergate thing is just unbelievable. None of us thought it would go to the depths it did go."

DOROTHY McELROY VREDENBURGH BUSH'S STORY

As far as Roosevelt was concerned, my generation absolutely adored him. After all, he saved us. . . .

I got into the political picture mainly because at home in Mississippi we talked politics morning, noon, and night. Dad always voted —mother did from the time she could. It wasn't just local politics that interested our family, but the national scene.

My father had three daughters he wanted to educate—and we came along in the time when everything was rock bottom—nobody knew where the next meal was coming from. But the number one thing with my father was a college education for his daughters.

I graduated from Mississippi State College for Women at Columbus in '37, and moved to Birmingham, Alabama, where I became a secretary for U.S. Steel. At the same time I became fascinated with the Young Democrats.

As far as Roosevelt was concerned, my generation absolutely adored him. After all, he saved us; he was a "savior" to millions of people in my age bracket. I don't know what in the world would have happened to many of us. . . .

He helped women—remember the TVA? Reasonably priced electric power relieved many low-income women of the drudgery of standing over hot, wood stoves all day.

As a Young Democrat in Alabama, I worked in primaries—we supported various candidates, and a lot were women at the state level: secretary of state, state treasurer, and public service commission. Sybil Pool was a state legislator then and a wonderful woman . . . so we had women in top offices in Alabama long before most. Now, we had a law in Alabama that you could not succeed yourself in an office, but we had three women who did such an excellent job that they sort of revolved the jobs around; one would be auditor, and then secretary of state, and so on.

Of course, this provided me with an incentive. It didn't inspire me to run for an office myself; I have never had that desire. But it opened up the world of politics for me as a woman.

AN IDAHO REPUBLICAN

That Mrs. Roosevelt—she was a magnificent woman. I remember there was a lot of criticism of her, but it was due to jealousy. People were jealous because she stepped out to give the people encouragement. We never had a First Lady who ever stepped out like her.

She organized groups and got people interested in helping themselves. To me, she's one of the fantastic women of our country.

I was proud of her, but at the time I just thought she was helping her husband. You see, in those days I wasn't used to looking to a woman as great and powerful, with a lot of guts.

There was a feeling on the part of some people that she was taking advantage because she was the president's wife—but that wasn't it at all. It was just because she was a great woman.

AFTER SIXTEEN YEARS in local and state politics, ten years in Congress, and twenty-three years as a National Republican committeewoman, Cecil Harden is busier than ever now that she's retired. Plans for Daughters of the American Revolution and American Legion Auxiliary luncheons mingle with a stack of unanswered mail on her desk in Covington, Indiana.

"I never sought any of it," she told me. "I'd say, 'Don't nominate me,' but they did. And when I was elected, I thought it was my Christian and political duty to serve."

She had never dreamed of being a candidate for the House of Representatives. "There were fifteen men in the race for the Republican nomination in 1948," she said, "but when it came to the showdown, the men all withdrew and I was elected unanimously.

"I'd made so many speeches saying that I was in favor of qualified women doing things that I made every effort to establish a good record because I knew what I did affected women as a group.

"I couldn't have done what I did if I hadn't had the wonderful support of my husband. After giving the whole matter prayerful consideration, I asked him—he's passed on since—'What should I do?'

"He told me, 'I think you should run because I think you could be elected.' You see, neither of us wanted to lose a Republican seat in Congress that year, even though we both knew I would be gone a great deal.

"So I served the Indiana 6th Congressional District from 1948 to 1958. Some people thought I was a man because of my name.

After I was elected, my administrative assistant suggested I put my picture on my stationery. Even with that I received letters from people addressed to 'Dear Mr. Harden.' "

In 1952, Cecil Harden was a member of the Indiana delegation to the Republican National Convention in Chicago. "Eisenhower had been nominated," she recalled, "and Indiana was acting like a bunch of schoolboys—you see, the delegates from my state had been 99 percent for Bob Taft for president. They didn't take the Indiana banner and march around or anything like that.

"So when four gentlemen from different parts of the country asked me to second Dick Nixon's nomination for vice-president— 'We want a woman to do it,' they said—well, I agreed. I knew Dick and I thought if I did it, it might help get Indiana back on the right track.

"I took an envelope out of my handbag, jotted down some remarks, got up on the platform, and told Joe Martin that I was seconding Nixon. Now, at the same time I sent a note to the Indiana delegation, telling them what I was doing. My cards have always been on top of the table.

"I was really glad to have this honor. I'd served in the House with Dick Nixon, and when I asked him, he'd come to my district to speak—one Lincoln's Day Dinner he brought out 800 people.

"So I was happy to second his nomination. And I never did regret it."

CECIL HARDEN'S STORY

The responsibility rests on women. You have to have good women at the local level to make any election a success.

I started in politics during the '32 Hoover-Roosevelt campaign, working on the precinct level—seeing that everybody was registered and that women got to the polls on election day.

Now, I don't think too many women were vitally interested—nor as interested as they should have been—in local elections. But they were always very surprised when they woke up and found they had a Democratic mayor.

In 1938 I was elected county vice-chairman. Well, my county

had factional troubles as they do so many times. So when I went down to the meeting to elect the county chairman and vice-chairman, some of them came to me and said, "Cecil, I hear you're running for office," and I answered, "My dear, I'm not running for anything."

But right off somebody nominated me, then somebody moved the nominations be closed, and I was elected. I had to accept.

That was on Saturday—now the very next Tuesday the same thing happened at the district meeting—the 6th Congressional District had ten counties at that time. One man leaned over the back of my chair and said, "We're going to nominate you for vice-chairman." And I said, "Don't you do any such thing." My goodness, here I had the county vice-chairman position wished on me already. But I was nominated and elected, and I served as district vice-chairman for twelve years.

Now, that was a hard time—'course there had to be Republicans who voted for Roosevelt or he wouldn't have been elected—but I think for loyal, staunch Republicans, it was a terribly discouraging time.

I found a great deal of apathy—my first experience in the party organization was learning how hard it is to get Republican voters out when their county or precinct has always gone Republican. And that's stupid—especially when we were kind of swimming against the tide at that time.

Oh, Roosevelt's giveaway programs were popular—the WPA and all that—although some of the buildings fell down soon afterward, you know.

We had a lot of unemployment. Vermillion County adjoining us had more unemployment than any county in the U.S.

The party did everything it could. I don't think there was anybody starving—we wouldn't permit that. We sponsored gardens. We had rented vacant lots and donated some seed so people could grow their own food.

You know, we had to laugh because sometimes we went out to see how things were going, and we'd find cars parked there that were as good as the ones we were driving.

I remember there were a lot of free clothes distributed—people would go to the public library and stand in line to get them.

But precinct work was my primary concern in the thirties—I believed it was very important. After I was first elected county vice-chairman, I called in thirty-one precinct women for a luncheon, and I made this point: if they failed in their duty and responsibility to get Republican votes into the ballot box on election day, all the torchlight parades, dances, and rallies were for nothing.

The responsibility rests on the women. It always does; you've got to have good women supporting you at the local level to make any election a success.

A VIRGINIA DEMOCRAT

I would always go with my daddy at election time . . . I used to check off voters with him when I was just a child.

I would say that Eleanor Roosevelt carried a great deal of weight with young people then. That is, she was the first to become a human being instead of just a president's wife. And believe me, she was severely criticized by the press, but gradually she became more accepted. You know, it took years for the people of this country to accept a president's wife who gallivanted around instead of staying home pouring tea.

Always before, see, there had only been two places a president's wife was supposed to be: with her children or two paces behind him.

But Eleanor had opinions of her own, which she expressed. Yes, she was a person in her own right, the first in my lifetime. And I think this was a source of pride for us; at least, a little.

As for Franklin Roosevelt: well, he was considered very little below the Deity. And by some, above Him. 'Cause you know the Deity was there when the damned Depression started, but it took FDR to end it.

SHE MUST BE NEAR EIGHTY, but won't acknowledge it. "I never tell my age," she said, a bit angry with me for asking, "and I never ask anybody else theirs.

"When you tell other people how old you are, then they *see* you that age."

RUTH PROCTOR HUGHES'S STORY

. . . We women worked aggressively for our candidates. You
see, we didn't have politicians in those days—we had statesmen.

I helped elect John Bricker governor of Ohio three times. I was
a committeewoman then. For years I was a booth worker, but Roy
King—John Bricker's cousin and our third ward committeeman—
asked if I'd be a committeewoman.

I said "yes" hardly without thinking. Why did I take the job?
I like to get my information straight from the horse's mouth. And
as a committeewoman, I made the inner circle and got to talk to
visiting senators and congressmen.

I had twenty-one women captains under me. The committeeman,
you see, had men captains. All were good workers but men talk to
men better, and women talk to women better. At our general meetings we'd all mix together.

I remember in '36, I was just sick when Roosevelt won. It was a
landslide, of course, and we knew it would be—but we had such a
wonderful Republican vote in my ward: people got out and supported Landon.

My daughter Gwen said to me, "Mother, don't feel bad; you
had such a good showing. It wasn't your fault, you worked so hard.
It was just the handwriting on the wall."

Now, it wasn't women's lib, but we women worked aggressively
for our candidates. You see, we didn't have politicians in those days
—we had statesmen. They were there to do a good job for their
country. Bob Taft was certainly one of them.

Now, he was conservative in his manner, but his wife Martha
was a darling person. She came to our conventions—she went everywhere with him.

You know, Bob Taft was a man who stood for something—he
couldn't be wishy-washed around.

It's true though—it was a hard time to be a Republican. We had
to go along with what good Roosevelt did—that's for sure. He gave
America a toe-hold and a little hope . . . but like I said, it was a
hard time to be a Republican.

A BLACK WOMAN IN NEW YORK CITY

I became a Democrat at that time. My family had been Republicans since slavery, but I didn't feel the Republicans were doing
anything about our situation. I thought maybe we had some hope
going over to the other party.

Quite a few of my friends became Democrats in the thirties,
hoping for a change.

I remember thinking I'd picked the right party when Mrs.
Roosevelt stood up for Marian Anderson . . . you know, the singer
who had trouble with the DAR.

GLADYS TILLET has the cultured, sweet-cream smooth Southern
accent I could listen to all day. About the time I was convinced she's
an older version of Margaret Mitchell's Melanie, she told me she
heads North Carolina's drive for the Equal Rights Amendment,
standing eye to eye with that last flowering of Southern chivalry,
Senator Sam Ervin.

How old is she?

"I'm old enough," she said. "It's not how long you've lived, it's
what you've done with your time."

For Gladys Tillet, that's not an idle paraphrase of Thoreau. "I
was one of the early marchers for suffrage,'" she began. "I went to
the Women's College of North Carolina, and Harriet Elliot was
my political science professor. She was a great woman; she knew
Susan B. Anthony and some of the other leaders so she brought
women's rights to the classroom in a vivid, personal manner.

"After college, she encouraged me to become active in politics.
But then I didn't need a lot of encouragement. My father, A. C.
Avery, was a Supreme Court justice and I was raised in a family
that felt a great deal of public responsibility.

"I've spent fifty years working in the Democratic party—I don't
know if that's a record or not. The young people think so—they
asked if I would lead the ERA fight.

"I said 'yes,' and I've been at it since 1972. I've got a few cam-
paigns left in me. The young women, they say I can still outdo
them."

GLADYS AVERY TILLET'S STORY

A county chairman would sometimes appoint the wife of a politically active man—just a token—but we wanted women to run on their own and be real leaders.

After college I had the vote, but nobody invited me into the party. For a few years, I was active in the League of Women Voters—men didn't know what it was exactly but they respected us. Nonetheless, I wanted to get into Democratic party politics. But I didn't know how to proceed. I talked it over with my husband, and we decided the best thing for me to do was to go to see the county chairman.

And I did just that. I told him I was interested in the party and I thought it would be fine if he could appoint some women to the precinct committee. He said, "But Gladys, you couldn't be on a precinct committee; your father is on the Supreme Court." But I assured him I certainly could, and I knew about fifteen other women who were interested. So he made all of us registrars. You see, I pointed out to him that the more women he registered, the better the vote; and I suggested that his organization of men couldn't go knocking on a Southern lady's door—in those days if you were a woman, you were a lady. 'Course, he recognized that I was right.

We women proceeded to conduct such a good registration campaign among women in our precinct that we got a silver loving cup. We not only got women registered, but also we went into the polls to work. I'm sure that some of the men felt that was not altogether the place for us . . . but we went right in and worked anyway.

At the same time, we were working for laws that would help women legally. I had one woman in particular who was an expert on property rights.

I remember once I was talking about these problems when someone asked me if I had interested wives of prominent men. I said, "No, I'm using prominent women in that field."

So you see, women had a vital, personal stake in getting involved in the political process at that time—we had leadership and we had power. For example, we women were having trouble with garbage collections so a crowd of us went to the city council meeting; and there were spirited speeches made about having two collections a week instead of one.

You know, the men caught on rather quickly—after the meeting, one of them called me aside and said, "Mrs. Tillet, anything—just anything—you ladies want, you just come down here and tell us quietly. You don't have to appear before a public meeting."

The thirties was a great decade. Of course, North Carolina was a one-party state, and, as a matter of fact, the whole South was. There was a great deal of political activity. We were the first, I think, to write the rule requiring the chairman and vice-chairman of each party unit to be of the opposite sex.

In the past, whenever they had a good county chairman, he sometimes would appoint a woman who'd just had a baby, or sometimes the wife of a politically active man—but we wanted women to run on their own and be real leaders.

So we got rid of these token positions early in the thirties. The state chairman was very understanding—we all wanted to get along, you see—so he said, "We've got this passed through the executive committee, but we ought to have it passed at the state convention so nobody can dispute it." And he warned me, "There may be some people out there that will boo this, and if I'm presiding, they'll boo me—but they'll never boo a woman." And he was right. I presided and called for a voice vote. "The ayes have it," I said and slammed down my gavel. I learned the way to handle that kind of thing fast.

The thirties were a great time for women to become politically involved. It was in '34 that I met Molly Dewson—she was quite a power behind the scenes with Roosevelt—and she pulled me into the national scene. She got me to cover the state with what she called the Reporter Plan which was a way to let people know what the New Deal really meant. So I became state chairman of the Reporters and learned a lot from that remarkable woman—she attended our first regional conference, and often she would have us to Washington to talk about various things. It helped to see and hear women who were policymakers.

She came to speak, and Frances Perkins came. It was Molly who talked me into running the Women's Speaker's Bureau in the '36 campaign. Now, Roosevelt had a lot of faith in her because she had helped him win in '32—so when she asked me to join in the reelection effort, I was really honored.

But a national office—well, that was quite a decision in my family. I had my three children and husband vote on such things. But I have to admit, I learned to influence the vote—they always thought they would get to go places with me.

It was a big change for me. First day on the job we had a press conference and one woman asked, "Isn't it odd for the national party to go to the South for someone to run the Speaker's Bureau?" I was a little taken aback, but I thought I detected an accent, and I said, "Well, I don't know. It's not so much where you come from. Where are you from?" And she said, "Texas." Well, I felt I won that round.

I was asked back to run it again in the third campaign.

One of my great pleasures was meeting Mrs. Roosevelt. She had such a genuine quality. You know, she helped women, and we thought highly of her—she just gave all our efforts a lift.

She was so free of prejudice toward women, blacks or anyone— many black women adored her. And you know she always had a great deal of courage when she came to the South. She was always willing to take a stand, and there were stands to take about blacks and women.

You see, women were new in politics and had to struggle to establish themselves. It was the beginning of the women's movement because being in on the political picture helped women see what they could achieve.

Chapter Fourteen

WONDER WOMEN

"WOMEN HAVE BEEN FLYING since they started in balloons," said Jacqueline Cochran Odlum at her ranch in Indo, California. The night we talked she had just hired a cook who could make a caramel custard from scratch. "Women have been flying forever; we've tried everything men have tried.

"Now, I'm not a woman's libber you know. I even testified in the Congress against women going into military academies. Yes, ma'am, it's ridiculous for women to train for combat, and that's what the academies are for.

"Why drop a few hundred women down with 4,000 men to be a disruptive force? They can get training in some other institution just as easy and a lot cheaper. And besides I don't think it makes any damn sense. Told them so."

Jacqueline Cochran has been telling them so all her life. With sheer will and determination she has overcome every stumbling block life shoved in her way. Faced with the twin discriminations of poverty and sex, she flew over them to establish more international speed, distance, and altitude records than any other flyer, rich or poor, male or female.

As a feminist, I disagreed completely with her separatist philosophy, but as a woman, I celebrated the triumph of her life.

Orphaned, she lived in the "tobacco road" backwoods of Florida mill towns, finishing all formal education with the third grade. At eight, she was working a twelve-hour night shift in a cotton mill. "I bought my first pair of shoes there," she told me.

At a mature eleven, she became a shampoo girl and all-around helper in a beauty parlor. Three years later she'd learned enough to go into the business herself, a business she eventually turned into a multimillion dollar beauty products corporation.

The incredible chronicle of the young girl is recorded in her autobiography *Stars at Noon*.* The book traces her life through the 1930s; through her organization of the Women's Air Force Service Pilots (WASP) during World War II, and culminates in her record as the first woman to break the sonic barrier in a 1953 Sabre Jet. Since the book was published, she has added two pages (small type) to her official biography, setting her last world speed record in a Lockheed Starfighter during 1964.

"Oh, it's all in there," she said, sending her secretary, Mrs. White, for an updated biography sheet. "You've got one of those old ones. I've done Mach II since then."

I asked the sixtyish flyer-businesswoman, hall-of-famer the obvious question: "Do you still fly?"

She shakes her head: "No, three years ago last June was my first attack, and I've had heart surgery three times since then."

JACQUELINE COCHRAN ODLUM'S STORY

Any pilot is happy to win . . . man or woman . . . there's no difference. I don't think a woman feels any differently about winning than a man.

When I went to Roosevelt Field in 1932, I was the only woman taking lessons. Yeah, and I paid $495 for twenty hours of flying. In those days that was a lot of money—like paying $1,000 today.

I soloed within forty-eight hours. I had my first lesson Saturday and soloed Monday, and had a forced landing, too. I kept thinking, I just got to get this damn thing down.

When I first got my license there were probably 200 to 300 in the country who had one. Not as many flying professionally as for their own amusement. . . .

---

* *Stars at Noon*, Boston, Little Brown and Company, 1954.

Actually, I didn't start out to fly; it was sheer accident. I had started the cosmetic business and I had to fly to cover the territory, so in the beginning I thought of it purely as transportation and good publicity for the business and all.

That changed. Yeah. The way I got my commercial flying experience was that I used to get on an airline in Los Angeles. When I knew the weather was going to be bad, you see, I'd buy a ticket. They didn't have any hostesses in those days—nobody to take care of all the sick passengers, to serve them their trays if they could eat; but if it was rough as hell, they didn't want to eat. So I mopped up after them if I had to, and the pilots would let me fly. I'd wait until that group turned around to come back, and I'd fly back with them, and they'd let me fly. It was very, very valuable experience because there's nobody better than airline pilots.

I assume I was the first woman to ever get an instrument rating in the country. I don't know if that's true or not, but I think it is; and at that time only one-third of TWA pilots had instrument ratings. I'm talking 1934 now. They'd canceled the mail contracts so I hired one of TWA's pilots—one of the country's great instrument pilots—to teach me.

Hell, I was as good as anybody that could get in an airplane, but it took a lot of discipline and a lot of hard work. These things just don't come to you because they're handed on a silver platter. You work your heart out for them.

That year I was the only woman to enter the air race from London, England, to Melbourne, Australia. I was flying a Gee Bee. As a matter of fact, there were only three pilots that physically survived flying the Gee Bee, and I was the only person who survived who owned one. Anyway, I had to force land in Romania. It was kinda fun—landed with one flap up and one flap down. Then I took the Orient Express back.

I entered the Bendix in 1935. It was hard to persuade the officials to let me in because of the men pilots. I had to get the permission of every man pilot in the race.

Why? Well, it was for men only as far as I know, and the Bendix people didn't want to lose out on all those racing pilots— they were famous—people like . . . oh, hell, I can't remember their names now.

It was because I was a woman. But that didn't bother me; that's the only static I've ever had in my life. The man who was the chief pilot for United Airlines, Benny Howard, was a great pilot and a great airplane builder. He built a lot of planes in his "backyard"—I called it—racing planes like "Mike and Ike," "Mr. Mulligan" and all those silly names; but they were great airplanes. That was the kind of thing that made aviation great and brought it along as fast as it did.

Anyway, Benny got up before these men and he said, "This woman can out-fly practically everybody in this room. I don't know what the hell you men are bitchin' about." Now, I wasn't there. Benny told me later that somebody said, "What if the weather's bad?" And Benny said, "Well, you'll probably stay on the ground and she'll probably be up flying circles around you."

So they put up a special $2,500 prize for a woman, something the men couldn't win, but I could compete for both the men's and women's. . . .

In '38, I won the Bendix in eight hours and ten minutes. That year I went on to New York for a cross-continental record, and only two of us got to New York. Only four out of fourteen got to Cleveland. It was the worst weather I think pilots have ever flown in in the history of aviation up 'til that time. It was just unbelievable, it was so bad. I was on top of a cloudburst at 25,000 feet, and over Colorado I was knocked upside down. I was all over the sky. Didn't think I'd ever survive it, let alone win it.

As I said, I flew on from Cleveland to New York. I didn't know whether I'd won or not. Got to New York and landed, went from Floyd Bennett Field over to Newark, and took the airplane back to Cleveland and went to the ball that night.

I didn't really know I was the winner until I got back to Cleveland. I had a suspicion, but I didn't know it. I was very pleased. Any pilot is happy to win . . . man or woman . . . there's no difference. I don't think a woman feels any different about winning than a man.

Amelia Earhart was my friend. I remember her as a person whom I enjoyed and liked. She was a very intelligent, charming woman. When she let the plane get away from her and cracked up in Honolulu, she came straight to my ranch and stayed for three weeks to hide out. And Lord, she could; I've entertained presidents and nobody knew they were here.

I don't even talk to those people who say she's alive. One of them called me at two o'clock in the morning once. . . .

My husband Floyd was really responsible for persuading President Roosevelt to send a carrier out to search for her. They had to anchor a very long way from Howland Island because the waters had never been charted. The planes had to fly about 75 to 100 miles —a fairly good distance—and they had one hell of a time finding that island. They might have missed her by fifty miles.

It's hard to tell what went wrong. She had very poor navigational assistance, and Amelia was not very long on radio work. I used to plead with her to get a third-grade license for code—you know, where you use a key that sends a long, long way. She didn't even have one in her cockpit. She kept whistling into the mike. She never even held the button down long enough because she wasn't properly instructed on radio procedure. I don't mean this critically, but it's the truth. It cost her her life. Yes, I'm sure she's dead.

Never had a scratch on an airplane myself, except once, and somebody else was flying. I sat down on my fanny and knocked two vertebrae out. It was the only injury, and I've had pretty bad crackups: I had two bad fires in the air.

I don't know; I guess the Lord likes me and put a protective collar around me or something. He knows I've had plenty of opportunities to lose my life. I got shot at over the North Atlantic and I was in the Battle of Britain; I've even been shot out of bed at night. All those planes and all those races: well, I've been lucky. One time I jammed my little finger, or something, and sorta injured a joint. . . .

IN TODAY'S WOMEN'S MOVEMENT you often hear the term "foremothers." It is used to describe women of achievement who are unrecognized in male-oriented histories. I always associate foremothers with bloomer-wearing suffragettes—that is, I did until I met Genora Johnson Dollinger, an honest-to-goodness living foremother of heroic proportions.

I first heard of her from Barbara Wertheimer, director of Trade

Union Women's Studies at Cornell University: "Genora was head of the Women's Emergency Brigade during the Flint sit-down strikes* and has marvelous stories to tell."

Genora now lives in Los Angeles. Recently retired from work with the American Civil Liberties Union, she sculpts in her spare moments. "The University of Michigan just asked me to write about the roles of union women in those days," she told me. "You know, only a year ago, a Michigan student wrote her graduate thesis about the brigade. Her professor tried to discourage her. He said, 'Don't try to lay any women's liberation ideas on the women of '37 just because you young women today are up in arms.'

"But she wrote it anyway and became the first woman to win an award from the university's history department for a contribution to American history."

Genora Johnson Dollinger's parents received early warnings to keep an eye on their daughter. "I must have been a shocking child," she said, laughing, "because I tried to practice equal rights in the fifth grade. I wanted to take auto shop and naturally, I was refused. So I got four other girls and we came to school in dungarees —scandalous behavior then—with boy's names pinned on the back of our shirts. 'OK' I said, 'if we have to be boys to take auto shop, well, we'll just be boys.'

"When I speak to college students I usually tell them I have my Ph.D. in the theory and practice of male chauvinism. My first instructor was my father who honestly believed in the superiority of males, and practiced it."

Her exploits in the thirties with the valiant Women's Emergency Brigade didn't end her work for the United Auto Worker's Union or her willingness to put her life on the line for her beliefs. "Remember back in the 1940s," she asked, "when Walter Reuther and his brother Victor were shot by the Mafia? Well, these events were preceded by several vicious Mafia beatings within my UAW local 212 in Detroit. I was serving on the committee to find out about the beatings and harassments we'd been having, when one night I

---

* THE FLINT SIT-DOWN STRIKE: During the winter of 1936–37, a strike by auto workers paralyzed sixty General Motors plants in fourteen states, forcing the recognition of the United Automobile Workers Union as exclusive bargaining agent.

was awakened by two men breaking into my bedroom. One shined a flashlight in my eyes and held a gun on me while the other one went over me with a lead pipe. I was temporarily paralyzed on one side, suffered a brain concussion, broken bones, and couldn't walk unassisted for seven months.

"So when I say women played a role in the union movement, you can believe me."

Her voice quivered with anger, excitement, and pride as she reminisced about the Flint strikes almost four decades ago.

"I think I have the feeling of those women," I said, caught up in the contagion of barricade fervor.

"Oh, Jeane," she said, "Oh, my God! I can still see them now . . . those wonderful women . . . a vision of them, marching down Chevrolet Avenue."

GENORA JOHNSON DOLLINGER'S STORY

Don't volunteer for the brigade . . . I warned . . . unless you're prepared to stand in the front line against the onslaughts of the police.

I was raised in the city of Flint, Michigan. There are roads and streets in that city named for my family because they were among the early settlers there.

Actually, this was an advantage when the strike came. I could not successfully be labeled an outside union agitator brought in to cause trouble. My father was well-known and well-to-do—a portrait photographer who invested in real estate.

I was twenty-three years old on December 30, 1936, when the strike started. It lasted forty-four days, a very dramatic forty-four days, until February 11, 1937.

It was New Year's Eve when I realized women had to organize and join in the fight. I was on the picket lines when the men's wives came down. They didn't know why their husbands were sitting inside the plant. Living in a company town, you see, they got only company propaganda through the press and radio. So when they came down on New Year's Eve, many were threatening to divorce their striking husbands if they didn't quit and get back to work to bring home a paycheck.

I knew then that union women must organize on their own in order to talk with these wives.

At that time, I was a housewife myself with two sons, aged six and two. I had been exposed to socialist doctrine when I was very young . . . sixteen or seventeen, when I met my husband Kermit's father. He'd come from South Dakota bringing certain socialist ideas. So Carl Johnson, the father, and Kermit and I formed a socialist party branch in Flint. I knew what was going on within the AFL craft unions because our socialist party headquarters was in the Labor Temple where all their activities took place. Everybody knew me down there, and I had some pretty firm ideas about the responsibilities of industry to the factory worker.

So when the strike began, I already had many friends among the auto workers; and I was fairly well known by others in town, including the local newspaper, because of my father's position.

That's another matter: during the strike the bank threatened to shut off accounts on his photo business and land deals because I was renting an apartment in his building. They said until he got that daughter of his out of the premises they were going to freeze his credit; and they did.

Remember this was a company town: the bank directors were all stockholders in General Motors and were terrified of unionism.

So my father, who didn't approve of my activities either, ordered me to move out, kids and everything. He threatened to turn off the heat and the water, and I said: "If you do, I'll tell the ɔress you're doing this to your own grandchildren." So he didn't, of course. He was afraid of that kind of publicity.

Conditions were terrible in Flint. People were living in hovels . . . shacks constructed of packing boxes, some of them. Over 50 percent of the workers had migrated when the auto industry expanded, and in some working-class districts half the homes were without baths, indoor toilets, and running water.

In 1936, men were earning 42 cents an hour, and women working at A/C Sparkplug were earning 12½ cents an hour.

After the strike, the LaFollette investigating committee discovered what some women had to do to keep their jobs. This may shock you: in one department all the young women had VD traced to their foreman.

The situation was so bad that many girls would go right from school to the factory. Perhaps their father was laid off, and there was no other source of income to feed younger brothers and sisters. Now, you can imagine why they would do almost anything before they'd see their family starve. And at that time there were lots of fathers laid off—babies were dying of malnutrition at the county hospital and 40 percent of the hourly employees in those factories worked an average of only twenty-nine weeks out of the year.

And there was terrible cutthroat competition because of the Depression. Men in the plant who might even look like they were for unions—OUT! Management had lip readers—they had Pinkerton agents in there. If a worker mentioned the hated word "union," a foreman would fire him on the spot. His job was over. Men around him who were listening would be told, "Look out the window." Out on the lawn, every day, hundreds of men were waiting for a few hours work. It was a terrible threat hanging over their heads. Remember, there was no job protection—unemployment compensation, workman's compensation for injury, no sick or death insurance, no retirement benefits, and no welfare system.

You've heard of the speed up. Every last ounce of energy was drained from men and women. Young men eighteen to twenty years old came home and fell on the floor, their hands so swollen they couldn't hold a fork.

The plants would speed up production to an intense level; then they'd abruptly stop, and the men would be laid off. It was too much for some of them to take. Men went insane and were sent to the State Insane Asylum in Pontiac. That's the background of the organizational drive to build the UAW-CIO.

When the strike started, my mother—without my father's knowledge—agreed to take care of my two little boys, and other friends helped, as well. I was then relatively free, and immediately went to Roy Reuther and Robert Travis—those were the UAW organizers—and I volunteered to help. I was told to go to the kitchen and peel potatoes, but I said there were plenty of others who could do that, including some of the men. So they gave me a job setting up a press clipping bureau. I kept busy for a couple of days until I found out there was a person going over all the work I'd done. I decided anyone sitting with a pair of shears could handle that job, so I organized a sign painting department. We made signs and set up a children's picket line—and that's what the history books show. I remember one sign, my own little snow-suited two-year-old holding it high: "My daddy strikes for us little tykes." That picture went from one end of the nation to the other. Anyway, a professional sign painter friend of mine took that over, and that's when I got busy organizing the women.

Now remember, Chevrolet, A/C Sparkplug, and Buick were working—Fisher plants 1 and 2 were struck. On December 30, the police attempted to break the strike at Fisher 2. You see, the men were sitting-in on the second floor, and food was brought up to them by ladder—'cause the plant police had control of the bottom floor. On that night, the police decided to cut off the food, and the next thing we knew they started throwing tear gas at the plant to get the men out. That fight became famous as the Battle of Bull's Run and it went on into the long night. The street was barricaded on both sides by union men. The local GM-controlled radio was broadcasting that a riot—some people thought a revolution—had broken out in the city. People came to watch the police shooting us with rifle bullets, buckshot, and tear gas. We had nothing but rocks and car door hinges, but we picked up the tear gas bombs and heaved them back at the police before they exploded. Men were going down, and fourteen people were shot that night, one seriously. I saw blood flowing.

But before this happened union men had herded all the women to safety—all except me. I said, "I've got just as strong weapons as you've got. You've got no guns, neither have I. I can fight as well as you." I was the only woman too stubborn to leave, so I stayed down there. We were putting cold water on our faces in order to brave the sea of tear gas. Victor Reuther was in charge of the sound truck that night and the batteries were running down. They couldn't last but a few more minutes. Remember, the public had no other access to union information, so the sound car was a very valuable weapon for us. In this way we broadcast our message to the 3,000 people on both sides of the barricades, telling them why we were striking, the profit General Motors was making, and the unbearable conditions the men were working under. . . .

At this point Victor privately told some of us, "We may have lost this battle, but we're not losing the war." He seemed to be preparing us for defeat on this night. It was then I asked him: "Victor, can I speak to them?" And he replied, "We've got nothing to lose." He was a fine person, but still I could feel that he didn't think a woman could do much in this situation.

I got up on the sound car—I know it was an electrifying thing . . . a woman's voice calling to the people of Flint after so many hours of fighting . . . and I said, "I'm talking especially to you women out there. You didn't know that mothers"—I meant myself—"are being fired on by the police. The police are cowards enough to fire into the bellies of unarmed men. Aren't they also cowards to fire at mothers of little children? I'm asking you women out there behind the barricades to break through those police lines. Come down here and stand with your brothers, your sons, your sweethearts, your husbands and help us win this fight."

And so help me, I could hardly believe it—one woman started walking toward us. The police grabbed at her and she walked right out of her coat. She marched down, other women following her— the police didn't dare shoot all those women in the back. Then the union men broke through. The battle was over and the union had won.

The women had saved the day. It was then that I realized how much power women had, and I proceeded to organize the Women's Emergency Brigade.

This was an independent move. It was not under the direction of the union or its administrators—I just talked it over with a few women—the active ones—and told them this is what we had to do.

Women might, after all, be called upon to give their lives. That was exactly the appeal I made while we were forming the brigade —I told the women, "Don't sign up for this unless you are prepared. If you are prone to hysteria or anything like that you'd only be in our way." I told them they'd be linking arms and withstanding the onslaughts of the police and if one of our sisters went down shot in cold blood there'd be no time for hysteria.

Around 500 women answered that call. We bought red berets and made arm bands with the white letters "EB" for Emergency Brigade. It was a kind of military uniform, yes, but it was mainly identification. We wore them all the time so we'd know who to call on to give help in an emergency. I had five lieutenants—three were factory women. I chose them because they could be called out of bed at any hour, if necessary, or sleep on a cot at the union hall. Mothers with children couldn't answer calls like that—although they did sign up for the brigade. Even a few grandmothers became brigadiers and, I remember, one young girl only sixteen.

We had no communication system to speak of. Very few people had telephones so we had to call one woman who was responsible for getting the messages through to many others.

We organized a first aid station and child care center—the women who had small children to tend and couldn't join the EB took care of these jobs.

Listen, I met some of the finest women I have ever come across in my life. When the occasion demands it of a woman and once she understands that she's standing in defense of her family—well, God, *don't fool around with that woman then.*

The brigade developed in such a short period of time. Some of them we soon sent to Lansing, Pontiac, and other outlying automobile factory towns where the police were beating the heads of men attempting to organize a union. We went in carloads to give them courage. Women played important roles. . . .

I saw women stand up under circumstances where big men ran around the corner and hid under a car. I have seen them rise up when I would not have believed they could.

I'd get up in the men's meetings and say, "Bring your wives down here." I'd tell them, "Your wives should come out and join us so they will understand what their husbands are fighting for." I explained it would make for closer companionship within the family.

Finally, you know, everything just came to a head. With so many workers' homes without sufficient food and heat in the freezing January temperatures, and powerful General Motors benefiting from the unequal contest . . . well, it came time for a major decision. Plant 4, the largest plant in the Chevrolet division of ten plants, produced all the motors for Chevrolet throughout the country. That plant became our target. We knew if we could close it down, profits would be cut and that would bring General Motors to the bargaining table. We also knew that 4 was the plant they guarded the most vigilantly—so what historians have called the finest labor strategy of the twentieth century was devised.

We pretended to strike one of the other Chevrolet plants, Plant 9, which was far removed on the other side of the whole complex and had that action drawing all the company police, city police, and Pinkerton agents . . . a diversionary tactic, you see. The Women's Emergency Brigade was there and they broke the windows to allow air to get in to the tear-gassed union men. Women just played a fantastic role over there at Plant 9.

Now, my husband Kermit's assignment was to shut down Plant 4, the target plant. But I dared not let the brigade know about it because it had to be such a tight secret. The whole union movement had been infiltrated with company spies. After the Plant 9 action, I sent the brigade back to headquarters and with my five lieutenants, walked around the city streets that paralleled the big Chevrolet compound—very leisurely, very casually—so that no one would notice us too much. The rest of the brigade marched back to the headquarters so our absence wasn't noticed.

We strolled over to Plant 4 which the union men were attempting to shut down. I was very nervous because I knew it was a life and death matter for my husband and the other men inside. By the time we got over there there was a great deal of confusion. It was a huge place—imagine a plant with 8,000 workers. They had to seal doors that were as big as the sides of houses—gondolas of steel parts had to be brought up in order to barricade some doors, while others were welded shut. They were having a helluva time.

The plant foreman and his hired agents were giving them trouble. There were fist fights breaking out all over the place. The men yelled to us, "My God, we're having an awful time. Don't let anybody come in through the front gate on Chevrolet Avenue." Naturally, that was a big order, so I sent one of my lieutenants to call headquarters. "Tell the brigade to come at once," I told her. And the five of us left strung ourselves across the front gate.

When the city police got word what was happening they came, seventy-five of them, and found us women on the gate. We defied them . . . told them they would have to go in over our dead bodies.

And we used psychology on them. Eighty percent had relatives working under those horrible conditions in the plants. "Look," I said, "if you worked in this plant, and you were being driven crazy, and your health was broken down, wouldn't you expect your wife to come down here to see what she could do?"

It threw them off their guard and they began answering my arguments, just long enough. By the time they got provoked and said, "Well, we've got a job to do," and started pushing us, at that point the brigade came down Chevrolet Avenue. There came hundreds of those red berets bobbing up and down with the American flag at their head, singing "Solidarity Forever." The sound of it, from all those voices, just flooded the whole area.

They quickly set up an oval picket line in front of the main gate. This meant the police would have to club and shoot these women, and they had no stomach for that. Then the truck arrived filled with union men, and God, it dawned on me, *we'd saved the gate.*

The union had closed the huge and valuable Plant 4 with another sit-down strike. Soon after, Governor Frank Murphy declared martial law and ordered negotiations started. On February 11th, an agreement was reached recognizing unions in GM plants across the nation. That was a much greater victory than our small, inexperienced union ever expected to win.

After the settlement, I was sent on a public speaking tour of the major unions on the Eastern coast for at least a month, and when I returned to Flint, I collapsed completely and I had to go into a sanatorium. Did I mention that I had TB during this time?

The union raised money to send me to a sanatorium in the Adirondacks. But when I came back, I found erosion had taken place. The brigade had been disbanded with the victory. Maybe it's a good thing I wasn't around during this period because the husbands began saying, "Well, you women did a wonderful job, but now your duty is back there getting those kids in school, getting the wash done, and regular meals again. . . ."

Oh, the union had tremendous respect for us, but after the strike was over they said in effect, "Thank you, ladies, so much." And at the top level of the International Union they turned the women's group into a mockery that I couldn't even be a part of. They had courses in styling clothes, coiffure, and makeup—things which, of course, some women had an interest in—but that wasn't our whole interest nor did it represent our real concerns.

A few of the women tried to hang on, and they were meeting in homes and that sort of thing. But it was a phantom thing, and I decided I didn't want to carry on that way.

It's a measure of the strength of those women of the Red Berets that they could perform so courageously in an atmosphere that was often hostile to them. We organized on our own without the benefit of professional leadership, and yet, we played a role, second to none, in the birth of a union and in changing working families' lives forever.

EPILOGUE

ANAÏS NIN, THE WRITER, once observed, "We do not understand the psychology of women because women have not articulated their experience."

The same could be said for the *history* of women, as an earlier writer, William Shakespeare, unwittingly noted in *Twelfth Night*:

> DUKE: *And what's her history?*
> VIOLA: *A blank, my lord. . . .*

These lines, written in the sixteenth century, still hold true. The inescapable result of systematically omitting the female half of the human race has been to falsify history—or at the least, leave it half-told.

Making Do came about because, as a daughter of the Depression, I wanted answers to history's unasked questions—particularly concerning women of the 1930s: Who were they and why? How did they live? What did they think about their condition?

For a year I talked with women—in tiny apartments crowded with photos and mementos; in large family homes near-empty and echoing; in senior citizens' centers busy with the postponed hobbies of a lifetime—a year of poking into the places where we keep our elderly—America's "antique shops."

They were surprised for the most part that I was interested in their lives. "We have tried for a long time to tell our children what it was like," they said. "They just couldn't grasp it . . . had no idea what we were talking about."

I have sought in this book to put myself and other daughters of the Depression in touch with our foremothers—to build clear, simple, strong bridges of human experience between us. Their struggles and delights are different from ours in detail—not essence.

They had to create spaces for their personal integrity; they had to figure out what to do with their lives and which pitfalls to confront. They made compromises and dealt with failure and success.

It is no wonder that some Americans, after thirty years of frantic affluence and three wars, are looking back with longing to these women who achieved so much with so little. Despite Satchel Paige's advice: "Never look back, something might be gaining on you," some of us hope it might.

I do not agree that our absorption with the past is a repudiation of the present; but rather, a desire to better understand the day we deal with.

Barbara Tuchman, Pulitzer Prize winning historian, writes: "History is a great joker always likely to take an unexpected turn for which no one has planned. Its lessons cannot tell us what will happen next but only *how people tend to react.*" If she is right—and I think she is, based on my experience with make-do thirties women —we will react magnificently to whatever the future holds.

LIST OF WOMEN'S STORIES

PART THREE: WOMAN'S WORK

PART FOUR: WOMEN INFLUENCING THE
WORLD ABOUT THEM

INDEX